The Cutting Edge:
Current Theory and Practice
in Organization Development

The Cutting Edge: Current Theory and Practice in Organization Development

Edited by
W. Warner Burke
Clark University
Worcester, Massachusetts

 University Associates, Inc.
7596 Eads Avenue
La Jolla, California 92037

Contributors

John D. Adams, Ph.D.
Consultant
3202 23rd Street North
Arlington, Virginia 22201

Kenneth H. Blanchard, Ph.D.
Co-director
Center for Leadership Studies
Professor of Leadership and
    Organizational Behavior
California American University
230 West Third Avenue
Escondido, California 92025

Leland P. Bradford, Ph.D.
Consultant
Quail Hill
Box 548
Pinehurst, North Carolina 28374

W. Warner Burke, Ph.D.
Professor and Chairperson
Department of Management
Clark University
950 Main Street
Worcester, Massachusetts 01610

Philip B. Daniels, Ph.D.
Professor of Psychology
Department of Organization Behavior
Brigham Young University
Provo, Utah 84602

Stanley M. Davis, Ph.D.
Professor of Management
School of Management
Boston University
Boston, Massachusetts 02215

William G. Dyer, Ph.D.
Professor of Organizational Behavior
Department of Organization Behavior
Brigham Young University
Provo, Utah 84602

Gerard Egan, Ph.D.
Professor of Psychology
Loyola University
6525 North Sheridan Road
Chicago, Illinois 60626

Michael Fullan
Chairperson
Department of Sociology
The Ontario Institute for Studies in
    Education
252 Bloor Street West
Toronto, Ontario, Canada M5S 1V6

Jack R. Gibb, Ph.D.
President
TORI Associates
8475 La Jolla Scenic Drive, North
La Jolla, California 92037

Robert T. Golembiewski, Ph.D.
Research Professor
Department of Political Science
Baldwin Hall
University of Georgia
Athens, Georgia 30602

Leonard D. Goodstein, Ph.D.
Professor and Chairman
Department of Psychology
Arizona State University
Tempe, Arizona 85281

Ronald Hambleton, Ph.D.
Director of Research
Center for Leadership Studies
California American University
230 West Third Avenue
Escondido, California 92025

Paul Hersey, Ph.D.
Founder and Director
Center for Leadership Studies
Professor of Organizational Behavior
California American University
230 West Third Avenue
Escondido, California 92025

John W. Humphrey
Chairman and Chief Executive
The Forum Corporation
84 State Street
Boston, Massachusetts 02109

John E. Jones, Ph.D.
Vice President
University Associates, Inc.
7596 Eads Avenue
La Jolla, California 92037

Donald C. King, Ph.D.
Professor of Administrative Sciences
   and Management
Graduate School of Industrial
   Administration
Purdue University
Lafayette, Indiana 47907

George H. Litwin, Ph.D.
Vice President
Research and Communications
   Division
The Forum Corporation
84 State Street
Boston, Massachusetts 02109

Michael R. Manning
Ph.D. Candidate in Organization
   Behavior and Organization
   Development
Krannert Graduate School of
   Management
Purdue University
Lafayette, Indiana 47907

Newton Margulies, Ph.D.
Associate Professor
Graduate School of Administration
University of California, Irvine
Irvine, California 92717

Matthew B. Miles
Senior Research Associate
Center for Policy Research
475 Riverside Drive
New York, New York 10027

David A. Nadler, Ph.D.
Assistant Professor
Graduate School of Business
Uris Hall
Columbia University in the City of
   New York
New York, New York 10027

J. William Pfeiffer, Ph.D.
President
University Associates, Inc.
7596 Eads Avenue
La Jolla, California 92037

Edgar H. Schein, Ph.D.
Chairman
Organization Studies Group
Sloan School of Management
Massachusetts Institute of Technology
50 Memorial Drive
Cambridge, Massachusetts 02139

John J. Sherwood, Ph.D.
Chairman
Department of Administrative Sciences
Krannert Graduate School of
    Management
Purdue University
Lafayette, Indiana 47907

Noel Tichy, Ph.D.
Associate Professor
Graduate School of Business
Uris Hall
Columbia University in the City of
    New York
New York, New York 10027

Marvin R. Weisbord
Director
Organization Research and
    Development
Block Petrella Associates, Inc.
23 East Wynnewood Road
Wynnewood, Pennsylvania 19096

Thomas B. Wilson
Director
Organizational Development,
    Research, and Communications
    Division
The Forum Corporation
84 State Street
Boston, Massachusetts 02109

PREFACE

This book is the culmination of a significant conference devoted to organization development. The conference was "OD '78," and the presenters—most of whom are now the authors of these chapters—were many of the most prominent and active persons in the field. OD '78, although it produced some of the latest thinking and activity in OD and was indeed unique, was not the first conference of its kind. In fact, it was the fourth, the preceding three having been sponsored by the NTL Institute and also later published as books.[1] The last of these conferences had been held in February, 1974, when Bill Pfeiffer and I met in early 1977 and decided that it was time for another OD conference. This time, we decided, the conference, OD 78, would be sponsored by University Associates and its subsidiary organizations.

OD '78 was indeed timely from the standpoint of both those who attended (the conference was a "sellout") and those who made presentations. A group of approximately 150 OD practitioners and academicians in the field were invited to submit manuscripts, and the presenters were selected from an unprecedented and overwhelming sixty-five proposals, most of which were worthy. Thus, the reviewers had a heavy but pleasant task of selection. The persons who helped me as reviewers, and to whom I am most grateful, are Drs. Jerry B. Harvey, professor of management science, The George Washington University; Mark Plovnick, assistant professor of management, Clark University; and Leonard D. Goodstein, chairman and professor of psychology, Arizona State University.

Surprising was the fact that even though a number of those invited to submit manuscripts were women, not one woman made a proposal. This was disappointing for several reasons. First, women had been on the program in past OD conferences, and now we had none at a time when their absence was significantly noticeable. Second, organization development has been, and still is, an accessible and popular field for women, with a significant and growing number being practitioners. And, finally, since women are now having more impact in OD, they need to be heard from. This final factor partially may explain why no proposals were received from women; they may be busier these days than many of their male counterparts.

---

[1]Burke, W. W. (Ed.), *New Technologies in Organization Development: 1.* La Jolla, CA: University Associates, 1972; Adams, J. D. (Ed.), *New Technologies in Organization Development: 2.* La Jolla, CA: University Associates, 1974; Burke, W. W. (Ed.), *Current Issues and Strategies in Organization Development.* New York: Human Sciences Press, 1977.

Many women, however, attended the conference, and significant others were critical to the success of the conference and to the production of this book. For the latter, Marion Fusco and Arlette Ballew combined the unbeatable qualities of pleasant persistence and editorial competence. Invaluable and direct assistance was provided to me by Louise Janhunen, the secretary of the department of management at Clark University. In an informal but professional manner, she supervised all my administration of the production process, for both the conference and this book. And invaluable to her and to me was Joann Clark, who carried much of the typing load. On the home front, Bobbi, my supportive and indispensible companion, critiqued much of my planning and writing, even though our second child was born in the midst of it all.

I am very grateful to Bill Pfeiffer, John Jones, and Tim Boone. Bill was very helpful in the planning stages and a constant source of support. He seemed to know when to help and when not to. John was particularly valuable in planning and running the conference. Perhaps most responsible for the logistics and administrative conduct of the conference itself was Tim. Due to his efforts, OD '78 was probably the best conference of its kind yet conducted.

I have edited and co-edited a number of books, some better than others. I am particularly proud of this one. This pride and, I might add, deep gratitude are due to the splendid assembly of authors. They not only made a contribution but were highly cooperative in doing so. Since our field espouses collaboration and cooperation, it was a particular pleasure to see these qualities in action.

W. Warner Burke

Worcester, Massachusetts
September, 1978

CONTENTS

Organization Development: State of the Art

W. Warner Burke

Organization development—as a field, as a body of knowledge, as a relatively coherent approach to changing organizations—is about eighteen years old; still in its adolescence, as Friedlander (1976) has noted, but maturing rapidly. The chapters in this book attest to this state of maturation in that there is no discussion of whether OD is really a coherent body of knowledge, or whether OD has a future, or whether OD works. It is as if the authors have gone beyond the question of "Whither OD?" and have agreed implicitly to "get on with it."

But OD as a field has been criticized heavily in recent years (Bowers, 1976; Burke, 1972; Kahn, 1974; Strauss, 1973), if not maligned (Ross, 1971). Among other things, OD has been accused of being (a) just another fad (Mills, 1975; Strauss, 1973); (b) superficial and commercialistic (Bowers, 1976); (c) hard-sell and anti-intellectual (Strauss, 1973); (d) atheoretical (Levinson, 1972); (e) ambiguous (Herzberg, 1974); (f) a religious movement (Harvey, 1974); (g) nothing more than "a convenient label for a variety of activities" (Kahn, 1974, p. 491); and (h) a term that has reached obsolescence (Jones & Pfeiffer, 1977).

In spite of all this criticism—perhaps even because of it—OD is still alive and well. Even though OD may die in one organization, it is born and grows or becomes reincarnated in another; thus the OD-practitioner job market continues to be active. I still receive at least one contact per month from a practitioner who is in the market, an organization with an opening, or a search firm. And I am no longer as central to this activity as I was when I administered the OD Network.

OD is flourishing in academic circles. The proliferation of articles and books continues steadily. The OD division of the Academy of Management is now the fourth-largest division in membership among a total of fourteen. And the program for the 1978 National Convention of the Academy indicates that OD now is considered as legitimate as its more traditional parent (or older sibling), organizational behavior. In fact, the lines between these two areas are now more blurred than ever before.

Attendance at OD conferences, workshops, and related meetings is another index of the viability of the field. Attending these events costs money, and the costs are usually paid from organizational accounts, not from individuals' pockets. OD Network meetings, held nationally twice a year, have diversified programs and are well attended by the membership. The conference from which this book stems was a sellout and, perhaps more importantly, was swamped with proposals for sessions.

THE TRANSITIONS

A few years ago I considered OD over a period of ten or twelve years and described it as being in transition (Burke, 1976). Some of those transitions are still occurring. The current state of OD can be described in the same language as before—as changing *from* one stage *to* another—but some modifications must now be made. I described the transition as follows:

From a field limited almost exclusively to business/industrial organizations to a field affecting many different types of organizations. A clear indication of this transition is the fact that slightly more than 40 percent of the attendance at the OD '78 conference was from business/industrial organizations. Five years ago this percentage would have been at least 60—perhaps as high as 70—percent. At OD '78, almost a fourth of those attending were from government, with just under half (N=30) from the U.S. military. State and local government were represented, with a surprising number from cities and towns. Universities and colleges (9 percent) as well as public education (almost 7 percent) were significantly represented (compared with the past). And 19 percent were from other countries. Thus, the field of OD today is considerably more pervasive from the standpoint of both organizational type and international representation.

From advocating a specific managerial style to emphasizing a situational or contingency approach. Perhaps the strongest proponents of a situational approach are Hersey and Blanchard. Their chapter in Section III is a continuation of and a supplement to their advocacy. Moreover, according to Stan Davis (see his chapter in Section II), this transition already has occurred. But I am not sure. Participative management is still around (see, for example, Hebden & Shaw, 1977). And if a successful manager is defined as one who achieves a top-level position in an organization at an earlier age than most people, there is some impressive evidence in support of participative management (Hall, 1976) or the 9,9 style of the Managerial Grid® (Blake & Mouton, 1978).

From democracy as the primary value advocated to authenticity. The recent activities that come under the quality-of-work-life label have a strong flavor of the democratic ethic. Thus, what I identified earlier as a transition may be an addition rather than a replacement.

From a field based largely on the social technology of laboratory training and survey feedback to a field based on a broader range of social technology. This transition is still occurring. With the possible exception of the Dyer and Daniels chapter on consulting by tape (Section III), there is simply not that much that is new technology these days. There seems to be much more emphasis on using tried-and-true technology with new types of organizations (at least new for OD), for example, the U.S. Army.

From the consultant as a nondirective, purely process-oriented practitioner to the consultant as an authoritative specialist. The chapters by Golembiewski, Margulies, and Nadler address this transition. It is clear that process consultation (Schein, 1969) is a required skill for the OD practitioner, but it is not sufficient. As Nadler points out, there are times when the consultant needs to be directive. Although this transition is still in process, there seems to be no question about its validity.

From considering the OD practitioner as the change agent to thinking of the line manager/administrator as the change agent. As far as I can tell, there is no argument about this statement.

From the role of the practitioner as working almost exclusively with management to the role of the practitioner as working with both managers and other persons at all organizational levels. I stated (Burke, 1976), albeit somewhat tongue-in-cheek, that OD may be in the process of undergoing a name change, that is, to quality-of-work intervention or life. Although OD may yet have another name in the future, I do not think now that it is likely to be one of these. Be that as it may, the new kid on the block at the moment is "quality of work life." It has replaced "job enrichment" as the current emphasis. And QWL is primarily responsible for OD's movement downward in the organization hierarchy. So this transition is still very much in evidence.

But is quality-of-work life the same as organization development? Walton (1973) defines QWL just as broadly as, if not more so than, organization development. Although he makes no comparative statements, it appears that he sees QWL as parallel and a companion to OD—not one subsumed under the other. According to Walton (p. 12), QWL must include not only the values of earlier reform movements, e.g., child labor laws, the Fair Labor Standards Act, workmen's compensation laws, unionization, equal opportunity employment, etc., but "it also must include recently emphasized human needs and aspirations, such as the desire for a socially responsive employer." He then goes on to list and explain eight criteria of QWL that encompass essentially the same values as those underlying OD.

During the years since Walton wrote his definition, considerable amounts of money have been spent on a number of projects that may indeed have value (see the chapter by Nadler, Section IV). These projects are being closely watched and evaluated. Their value seems to be at least twofold: (a) improving the quality of work for the rank and file (not just management, where OD has predominantly focused), and (b) gradually adding to the knowledge of how to work more effectively with unions.

Quality-of-work-life projects, thus far at least, have almost exclusively directly involved the worker level and the most immediate strata of supervision, not middle management and higher. Thus it would seem that QWL will not encompass nor replace OD, but perhaps will be integrated within it as job enrichment has been in many instances. Walton may disagree with me, but as far as I am concerned, this integration would be all to the good, since OD could be improved with more use of QWL principles and practices. That is, OD would no longer be seen solely as a management tool but would become more of a total organizational process.

But Walton and others may not disagree, for it seems that there is little or no argument about what should be termed OD and what should be categorized as something else. OD practitioners have considerable license to roam around in organizations, in practically any "people area." This is an advantage. The disadvantage is that OD is still a jack-of-all trades and master of none or perhaps few. OD is all things to all people. So Kahn's (1974) criticism still holds: OD is only a convenient label for a bunch of activities.

From the OD function being merely a more glamorous name for training to a function that has organizational legitimacy in and of itself, with attendant power and official status. At the time I wrote that statement there was some evidence to support it. I now believe I was wrong in predicting this transition, at least from the standpoint of names, titles, or labels in organizations. I do see evidence that OD practitioners now have more power and status, but what they do is not called OD as much as it used to be. In other words, practitioners are just as active as ever, probably more so. They simply are not referring to themselves as OD consultants. Jones and Pfeiffer (1977) may be right: the label has outlived its usefulness. But saying it does not make it so. There is much activity, and even though the U.S. Army may call it OE—organizational effectiveness—the principles, the books read, and the sources used are the same.

THE CURRENT STATE

So where are we? Transitioned in some cases, not so in an instance or two, and still in the process for others. Overall, the following conclusions seem warranted:

1. There is less concern about defining OD. More people than ever are involved in the field, but comparatively fewer of them are calling what they do "organization development."

2. Academically, OD has more recognition than ever before. Two cases in point are (a) the growth and status of the OD division in the Academy of Management and (b) the fact that the two stalwart textbooks in the field, French and Bell (1973) and Huse (1975), are currently being revised. Their respective publishers have not been displeased with sales.

3. Although there is very little that is new, people in the field are moving organization development toward new domains (see Section IV) and into new types of organizations. This expansive occurrence is perhaps the greatest single cause of OD's continuing viability. Also, there appears to be greater emphasis on considering what works well under what conditions (see the chapters by Goodstein and Weisbord).

4. Even though there is need for a unifying theory (Burke, 1976), none yet exists. There are a number of theories on which OD is based, but no single theory provides coherence. OD remains a convenient label. We have not progressed beyond Lewin's theoretical steps of unfreezing, changing, and refreezing. Not that these plans are inadequate—far from it. Lewin's principles have stood the test of time. But more than thirty years have elapsed since he stated those principles. We must have learned some more

about change since then, especially since practice typically is far ahead of theory. It may be a matter of waiting for someone to write about it. Granted, there is no unifying theory; what have become more coherent and explicitly stated are the values on which OD is based. Golembiewski is a major spokesman for these values both in his present chapter (Chapter 3) and in his previous book (1972). Another recent and useful statement has been provided by Bowen (1977). From a value and ethical standpoint, then, we seem to be clearer about what we are doing or perhaps should be doing.

THE ORGANIZATION OF THIS BOOK

There are several types of edited books. One is the book of readings, in which the editor assembles articles—most if not all of which have been previously published—into categories he or she deems appropriate for the book's purpose. The recent book edited by French, Bell, and Zawacki (1978) is a good example of this type. Another category of edited book is one in which the editor commissions selected persons to write chapters specifically for the book he or she has in mind. These two types of books are relatively easy to organize as an integrated, relatively coherent package.

This book is a third type, one more difficult to organize. The final choice of chapters was based more on the quality of the manuscripts themselves and on whether the writer(s) demonstrated new thinking or work than on how well the paper fit a predetermined scheme for the book. In other words, the predetermination of this book was to reflect the current state of organization development regardless of its coherence or lack thereof. As it turns out, OD is now probably more coherent than it has ever been. The following chapters reflect a field that is more clarified, focused, and integrated than in previous years. The authors make their points more from an assumed common base and definition of OD than has been done in the past. Specifically, although Golembiewski and Weisbord do not agree completely, their chapters do help to articulate this common base.

Yet how one organizes these chapters is still a matter of choice and a fairly arbitrary one at that. I have attempted to categorize the chapters according to a theme or related group of concepts. The overview for each section is written both to explain this relationship and to summarize briefly each chapter. A simpler categorization would have been to follow some of the points made above; that is, which chapters help to articulate and integrate OD? This integration/clarification category would have included the chapters by Egan; Golembiewski; Goodstein; Litwin, Humphrey, and Wilson; King, Sherwood, and Manning; Fullan and Miles; and Weisbord. What is new in OD is demonstrated in the chapters by Adams; Bradford; Davis; Dyer and Daniels; Hersey, Blanchard, and Hambleton; Pfeiffer and Jones; Nadler; and Schein. Some new thinking is presented by Gibb. That leaves Margulies and Tichy. Their chapters can be labeled easily as "sobering" since they jolt our perception of the OD practitioner's role and future direction.

These categories represent one way this book could have been organized. But the way I have chosen is to organize the chapters into four sections that represent more clearly the current state of organization development. The first section deals with both OD as a field and the unique nature of the consultant's role. Section two pulls together some of the latest thinking and conceptualizing, and the final two sections respond to the "What's new?" question. Even though the published chapters were initially self-selected and then further selected by a small number of people, I believe they form a good representation and reflection of OD today.

REFERENCES

Blake, R. R., & Mouton, J. S. *The new managerial grid*. Houston: Gulf, 1978.

Bowen, D. D. Value dilemmas in organization development. *Journal of Applied Behavioral Science*, 1977, *13*, 543-556.

Bowers, D. G. Organizational development: Promises, performances, possibilities. *Organizational Dynamics*, 1976, *4*(4), 50-62.

Burke, W. W. Organization development in transition. *Journal of Applied Behavioral Science*, 1976, *12*, 22-43.

Burke, W. W. The demise of organization development. *Journal of Contemporary Business*, 1972, *1*(3), 57-63.

French, W. L., & Bell, C. H., Jr. *Organization development*. Englewood Cliffs, NJ: Prentice-Hall, 1973.

French, W. L., Bell, C. H., & Zawacki, R. A. (Eds.). *Organization development: Theory, practice, and research*. Dallas, TX: Business Publications, 1978.

Golembiewski, R. T. *Renewing organizations: The laboratory approach to planned change*. Itasca, IL: F. E. Peacock, 1972.

Hall, J. To achieve or not: The manager's choice. *California Management Review*, 1976, *18*(4).

Harvey, J. B. Organization development as a religious movement. *Training and Development Journal*, March 1974, *28*, 24-27.

Hebden, J. E., & Shaw, G. H. *Pathways to participation*. New York: Halsted Press, 1977.

Herzberg, F. The wise old Turk. *Harvard Business Review*, 1974, *52*(5), 70-80.

Huse, E. F. *Organization development and change*. St. Paul, MN: West, 1975.

Jones, J. E., & Pfeiffer, J. W. On the obsolescence of the term organization development. *Group & Organization Studies*, 1977, *2*(3), 263-264.

Kahn, R. L. Organizational development: Some problems and proposals. *Journal of Applied Behavioral Science*, 1974, *10*, 485-502.

Levinson, H. The clinical psychologist as organizational diagnostician. *Professional Psychology*, 1972, *3*, 34-40.

Mills, T. Human resources—why the new concern? *Harvard Business Review*, 1975, *53*(2), 120-134.

Ross, R. OD for whom? *Journal of Applied Behavioral Science*, 1971, *7*, 580-585.

Schein, E. H. *Process consultation*. Reading, MA: Addison-Wesley, 1969.

Strauss, G. Organizational development: Credits and debits. *Organizational Dynamics*, 1973, *1*(3), 2-19.

Walton, R. E. Quality of working life: What is it? *Sloan Management Review*, 1973, *15*(1), 11-22.

Section I:
ORGANIZATION DEVELOPMENT AND THE CONSULTANT'S ROLE

OVERVIEW

Just what is OD anyway? This is still an important question, and it continues to be asked after almost two decades. But the question is not as open ended as it used to be, and the responses, while perhaps not totally satisfactory, are more definitive. Leading off this section is Weisbord (Chapter 2), who does not merely define OD but does so in the context of when and why OD works—at least some of the time. Building on some of his previous writings, i.e., that OD is a process of redressing the balance between freedom and constraint in organizations, Weisbord goes on to discuss what OD consultants actually do. Most importantly, he sets forth criteria for a successful OD intervention, namely, when people experience (a) a reduction of unfocused anxiety and (b) enhanced self-esteem, derived from (c) a collaborative improvement of working conditions. (For a related discussion of Weisbord's first item, see the chapter by Adams.)

Weisbord's criteria are concerned with a *successful* OD intervention. Argyris (1970) has stated what he considers to be the three criteria for an *effective* intervention: valid information, freedom of choice, and commitment. Criteria developed by Hornstein and myself (Burke & Hornstein, 1972) differ from those of Argyris in the final point only. An intervention becomes OD when it responds to a felt need (valid information), involves the client in the planning and implementation (choice and commitment), *and* leads to change in the organization's culture. Although not incompatible with these latter two sets of criteria, which are more related to the nature of the intervention, Weisbord's three are perhaps more specific to individual behavior.

Weisbord thus takes the clarification of OD one step further. Moreover, he makes a strong case that OD's potential for success is significantly higher in an "output-focused" system, e.g., business, than it is in an "input-focused" system, e.g., government. Thus his point that OD works—sometimes.

This is the point at which Weisbord and Golembiewski (Chapter 3) part company. If the consultant manages reasonably well the tension between politics and OD principles and values, according to Golembiewski, there is no reason why OD cannot be as successful in a public agency as in a private one. Within the context of OD values and objectives, Golembiewski provides not three but *nineteen* guidelines for consulting "at the politics/administration interface." Based on his considerable experience as a consultant with both public and private

9

organizations, Golembiewski helps us to understand more about organizational politics, be they public or private. Most OD practitioners can use this understanding.

Perhaps most significantly, Golembiewski gives us one of the clearest definitions of the client. For him the client is always, from beginning to end, the total system—not the boss, not a subgroup, not the internal OD consultant, not management, not the union, not the board, but all of these subsystems as they form the totality of the given organization. For Golembiewski, OD is a process of total system change. His view is essentially the same as my own (Burke, 1971) and in stark contrast to those who are individually focused (e.g., Herman & Korenich, 1977).

Goodstein (Chapter 4) addresses even more directly the issue of consulting with public agencies. He is not as optimistic as Golembiewski. For those who consult with public organizations, Goodstein nevertheless provides pointed and clarifying help. Using Weisbord's (1976) six-box model of diagnosing an organization, not only does he show the differences between diagnosing—and therefore intervening in—a public organization versus a business, but he further provides assistance in consulting with a bureaucracy, whether it be public or private.

Weisbord, Golembiewski, and Goodstein all address, at some level, the role of the consultant. Golembiewski implies that the consultant must be above, "to the side of," not "caught up in," not a part of the system for whom he or she is consulting. In Chapter 5, Margulies discusses the role itself. He conceptualizes this consulting process in terms of "marginality." He maintains that effective consultation depends on one's ability to remain in a marginal or boundary role. This ability means that one can strike an effective balance between being personally involved with and vested in the people of the client system and not being involved. He goes on to state those conditions when "being in" is useful and when it is not.

In the final chapter of this section (Chapter 6), Tichy considers the consultant, but his treatment differs in that he is attempting to discern the future of OD by asking OD consultants about what they do and, even more importantly, about what they do not do. Thus, as he addresses both the consultant role and the state of OD as a field, his chapter is an appropriate one to end and, to some extent, culminate this section. Using interview data from both external and internal OD consultants, Tichy concludes that OD is in a phase of self-doubt, i.e., doubt that OD can survive with its emphasis on the people side of business when there is now, more than ever, a push for greater productivity. Somehow there still must be a belief, even among OD practitioners, that these two emphases are incompatible. Tichy's view is that OD practitioners are still "tinkering at the margins," working on projects that are far from the core of a given business or public enterprise. He recommends that OD become absorbed within the overall organizational function of human-resource management.

The first section, then, considers organization development as a field, how it is currently defined, how it works, what is considered successful, what the field's underlying values are, and its current state. It also examines the role of the OD practitioner and presents some guidelines and conditions for effective consultation.

REFERENCES

Argyris, C. *Intervention theory and method*. Reading, MA: Addison-Wesley, 1970.

Burke, W. W. A comparison of management development and organization development. *Journal of Applied Behavioral Science*, 1971, 7, 569-579.

Burke, W. W., & Hornstein, H. A. (Eds.). *The social technology of organization development*. La Jolla, CA: NTL/Learning Resources Corporation, 1972.

Herman, S. M., & Korenich, M. *Authentic management: A Gestalt orientation to organizations and their development*. Reading, MA: Addison-Wesley, 1977.

Weisbord, M. R. Organizational diagnosis: Six places to look for trouble with or without a theory. *Group & Organization Studies*, 1976, 1(4), 430-447.

2

Input- Versus Output-Focused Organizations: Notes on a Contingency Theory of Practice

Marvin R. Weisbord

OD works; why it works is less well-known and understood.

French and Bell, 1973

The other day I ran into a friend, a peripatetic OD consultant I'll call the Lone Ranger. He was charging down "G" concourse at O'Hare Field, having just arrived from California on his way to either Canada or Venezuela, I forget which.

"Hi, Ranger," I said, "How goes it? Changed any organizations lately?"

The Ranger smiled his most engaging and enigmatic smile, the one that time and again has melted resistant groups into compliance with the most bizarre instructions. "Hey," he said, "just came from a three-day teambuilding at ABC University. You should have seen the output: about one hundred analogies for the relationship between faculty and administration. And the drawings! I mean people who haven't touched a crayon since they were three! We even talked about male-female relationships. Of course," he added thoughtfully, "we're still in the unfreezing stage."

"Sounds great," I said, "but what about the goals? I mean, how do you know things are improving?"

"Well, for one thing, the evaluations—I mean everyone was at six on a seven-point scale, and you don't often see that in a college. Not only that, one guy who had never opened up before finally decided to start that hardware store in Florida he always wanted, and he was able to share it with the rest of the group! They're having me back for open-systems planning next fall—that is, if the chairman doesn't resign. They've still got a lot of problems: budgets, scheduling, tenure, stuff like that . . ."

"Fantastic," I agreed, "but . . ."

"See you around," he said, hugging me warmly. "Three cities, three clients, five days, four airplanes, got to run . . ."

And there I was, holding my bag, empty of tricks, containing just a shirt and change of underwear, and wondering what, besides them, I would be changing in the next few days.

Being something of a Lone Ranger, too, I appreciated his high feeling. Anytime a group stays until the end, you are way ahead. On the other hand, what, I found myself asking, did that little vignette have to do with organization development? *Toward what end was that university department developing itself? In what way was organization development relevant to the work lives of that faculty? Personal growth I could understand. Which of us cannot use more than we already have? But OD? What, I wanted to ask the Ranger, did* he *think he was doing?*

Organization development works. However, it does not work equally well everywhere. While hardly an organization exists that cannot use OD—in the sense that there is a better fit to be had between person and organization—relatively few organizations incorporate, at least initially, conditions that favor success. Something was working in that university department, but I would hesitate to call it OD.

If we are to experience OD's limitations, and therefore its strengths, we must come to grips with why it works when it does, and why it does not when it does not. Only then can we know what it is we are trying to do and whether we ought to try to do it. We might then know whether to call a particular intervention "organization development," when it might be better termed "personal growth," or "interpersonal encounter," or "systems analysis," or something else.

How one experiences OD's limitations, I think, depends very much on what one thinks about what OD is and what it does. In discussing each of these issues, I will explain why I think OD works—sometimes. I will hypothesize two major classes of organizations, "input-focused" and "output-focused," and speculate on why interventions that are most successful in one type are least likely to be successful in the other.

A DEFINITION OF ORGANIZATION DEVELOPMENT

I find "planned change" definitions to be very unsatisfactory. I understand OD's boundaries better when I view my practice as having: one "right" goal; one important practice theory; and a limited minimum contract, upon which the success of interventions—large or small—will depend.

In a recent issue of the *OD Practitioner* (Weisbord, 1977), I said that OD's "right" goal is to redress the imbalance between freedom and constraint in organizations. These polarities always create tension, which makes the dilemma essentially unresolvable. Thus, we help people to reduce or to create structure to insure the optimal social cohesion consistent with individual wishes for freedom, creativity, and so on. The reason OD works, when it does, is that it helps to redress this imbalance between freedom and constraint in a positive direction; i.e., OD works when it helps to reduce structures that are too tight and it works when it helps to create needed structure out of anarchy. Because there are no correct solutions, OD is by nature experimental, ad hoc, and oriented toward discovery.

I prefer the concept of action research, the systematic study of our own experiences in trying to improve work situations. I think we can *experiment* with trust, openness, shared influence, and mutual learning; it is impossible to prescribe the right mixture of these for somebody else. Moreover, I do not think that any of us knows whether an organization needs to change. That decision is best left to those who are most affected by the outcome.

Our one important practice theory has to do with the task/process relationship. It is the one element that OD—apart from other disciplines—brings to organizational life. Educators, management scientists, therapists, systems analysts, and other such professionals do not explicitly teach and demonstrate this concept to client systems as a central tenet of their practices. We in OD do use this theory to focus on the freedom/constraint dilemma, providing various insights about the way process issues block work. I define process issues as the nonrational and sometimes unproductive behaviors associated with strong feelings that are unrecognized or at least unexpressed. When their feelings about freedom and constraint are frustrated at work, people become more anxious, dissatisfied, irrational, and unproductive; their actions can be observed and categorized. The impact on tasks is obvious: people drift, meetings cease or go on interminably without action, machines stop, the union strikes. Somebody quits; others start looking. Everybody blames the government (in meetings) and each other (at lunch). In trade jargon, there is a growing gap between the way things are and the way they should be. Such issues traditionally have been identified as communication, decision making, control, influence, goal commitment, or leadership. It seems to me that *any* labels can be used as long as they are unified by some concept that deals with the open, systemic, interactive nature of organizations.

WHAT OD CONSULTANTS DO

OD consultants heighten awareness of the sources of dissatisfaction and anxiety. Sometimes we do it conceptually by feeding back data or by running through an ideal model that makes obvious the flaws in the model in use. Sometimes we do it in real time, catching people in the act of thwarting one another. In these ways we help our clients to consider whether they wish to achieve a more satisfying balance between freedom and constraint, since the process issues are symptoms of too much of one or the other. We help people to make choices about how best to preserve (or create) enough social structure so as to reduce alienation, but not so much as to wholly preempt free choice and creativity.

We provide alternative visions of what is possible. We support people in taking new steps, that is, in admitting the irrational and, in so doing, clearing their (emotional) decks for some rational problem solving. The core technologies—process consultation, team building, intergroup problem solving, group- and interpersonal-skills training, collaborative problem diagnosis, and the like—have certain features in common. These include the pooling of diverse information and viewpoints (data); the validation of conflicting wishes, ambivalence, and system dilemmas as legitimate, inevitable, and potentially useful; the mobilization of energy released; and so on. Technologies that produce these results can be characterized as structure-reducing. That is, they open up a system by temporarily removing (normative) constraints on thoughts, feelings, and behavior, making it legitimate to raise sticky questions about every part of the system, including the risk of raising sticky questions.

Sometimes we help people sharpen their skills: listening, supporting others' feelings, confronting conflict. It is the application by people of these skills, with each other, to solve joint, work-related problems that constitutes rational OD. This process, itself enhancing of self-esteem, often increases productivity too. When such productivity is visible to outsiders and not only to the producers, self-esteem goes even higher. People say, "We have a good organization."

Such are the bare bones of OD. A great many theories, values, and technologies can be hung on this skeleton: strategic planning, or sociotechnical redesign, or management by objectives, to name a few. In the end, all are reduced by the inevitable process blockages: the damnable tendency of perfect systems to elicit strong feelings and "inappropriate" behavior from imperfect people. I believe that *this* is primarily OD territory—where process issues block the accomplishment of work. If we, having fallen in love with a new technique or concept, become blinded to choice, commitment, authority, dependency, equity, responsibility, influence, or collaboration, few if any clients are likely to take the trouble to straighten us out.

In addition, as a scientist of sorts, I think there is persuasive evidence that the best way to work on the task/process relationship in a democratic society is with some version of democracy, participation leading to "ownership." Therefore, I think we are in the business of proposing, and showing people how to operate, democratic work structures: teams, task forces, committees, collateral organizations, and "transition structures" (Beckhard & Harris, 1977), including the impact of these structures on the rest of a system.

THE OD CONTRACT

I find Argyris' formulation of the goals of intervention—valid data, free choice, commitment to act (Argyris, 1970)—to be powerful. I see these as the legitimate minimum conditions for an OD contract. They should be equally binding on both parties. They do not constitute *all* that a consultant might commit to, but they certainly constitute the least. Without these contractual conditions, the consultant risks becoming part of the blockage, impeding rather than implementing self-governance, which is the basis for adequate productivity and satisfying work. By self-governance, I mean the ability to take responsibility for oneself and to share the risks and responsibilities for accomplishing tasks with others.

These conditions are what give OD its humanistic flavor. At their best, our interventions constitute the application of a psychology of self-governance. Moreover, concepts of shared influence, the responsible exercise of power, and task interdependence suggest that organizations have lives and social functions too; at the very least they have the potential for settings in which people talk and listen to each other, support one another's hopes, fears, tragedies, and celebrations, and provide relief from that ultimate anxiety we all face, which Ernest Becker has illuminated so poetically in *The Denial of Death* (1973). For this reason, I think OD fulfills important functions that once were the exclusive province of religion. Being mortal, being anxious about it, and—for most of us—being resigned to working with others for a living is the common fate to which most western religions have sought to reconcile us. Some religions promised relief in heaven. Some promised a lightened (psychic) load in return for faith now. There is a very fine line between defining work as a sacrament or a punishment for sin. Many jobs—including some in the professions—have a hellish quality more commonly attributed to the assembly line.

"Quality of working life," then, is a metaphor for living the good life here on earth. It is an especially important metaphor in an industrial society, in which machines make life easier on one hand and deprive us of a great many opportunities for mutual support and social interaction on the other. In this sense, I think OD—if you accept its goal as redressing the balance in the tension between freedom and constraint—functions as a secular religion. Thus, increased output is not the test of OD; rather, the test is increased output *in the presence of* important human factors.

EVALUATING SUCCESS

A great many evaluation models emphasize multiple, measurable factors. I think the complexity, rationality, and beauty of these models are what lead practitioners to admire them—like paintings in a museum—but not to imitate them in their work (Margulies, Wright, & Scholl, 1977).

OD, as I define it, is not so hard to evaluate. I believe that an OD intervention is working well when people experience: (a) reduction of unfocused anxiety and (b) enhanced self-esteem, derived from (c) collaborative improvement of working conditions. I find that these conditions most often result from successful, joint, rational problem solving, usually signified by increased productivity—what line managers call "results." Although I value productivity, I do not see OD mainly as a production technology. I think it is an integrating technology. It mediates between freedom and constraint by reducing structure when there is too much and by creating it when there is not enough—always toward the end of mutual influence and problem solving.

Getting people together is our stock in trade. Face-to-face problem solving and trust building are the building blocks of organizational change. Fortunately, there is no contradiction—and probably a positive correlation—between these processes and performance. There is not, however, a *necessary* correlation; goal focus and reward still determine an organization's output.

OD is not a panacea. You cannot do it indiscriminately, just because someone has managed to raise a crowd. *How* results are achieved makes a big difference. Feelings of competence and self-worth derive from what *you* have done, not from what someone else has coerced you to do or done for you.

Peter Vaill once brainstormed a list of forty-four hypotheses about what is going on in what he calls "high-performing systems." What is going on, Vaill wonders out loud, when the Boston Celtics' fast break is really clicking? Nearly all of his suppositions deal with processes symptomatic of little or no anxiety, enhanced competence, and mutually agreeable problem solving. Most include a close identity between people, their work, their technologies, the system itself, and others involved in the system (Vaill, 1975).

The paradox is that some organizations, tasks, occupations, and classes of problems lend themselves better to joint, rational problem solving than others. People require *incentives* for working together. An organizational score-keeping method is a strong incentive, for it shows whether one is winning or losing.

WHY OD WORKS—SOMETIMES

Consider OD as a psychology of self-governance. It is not surprising that of eleven leading hypotheses about successful change efforts, Dunn and Swierczek (1977) found, in their analysis of sixty-seven planned-change cases (both failures and successes) that only three stand up to close scrutiny. The authors cite: (a) *collaborative* interventions, (b) a *participative* change-agent orientation, and (c) "standardized strategies" involving "*high levels of participation*" as more successful than noncollaborative interventions, nonparticipative change-agent orientations, and low-participation strategies.

Does that sound at all familiar? How much of that is new? These propositions seem convincing, reassuring, and somehow incomplete. For they do not, by themselves, answer what is the most nagging question: Why, when an OD consultant has collaborated and involved large numbers of people in participating in change efforts, is persuasive evidence of improved working conditions not always seen?

In many places the "successful" strategies draw inordinate static, noncooperation, and outright sabotage, despite the efforts of influential people to bring about change. There are many examples:

1. The successful work-team experiment that evaporates overnight, leaving a residue of demoralization, when the new boss, despite accelerating productivity, declares, "It is not possible to manage without supervisors." (For him it is not.)

2. The government agency that invests several days of consultation and many staff people to design the objectives for a perfect evaluation system, covering inputs, outputs, throughputs, transfer of learning, and ongoing feedback to faculty, only to abandon the whole thing because participants and faculty in the training program are "too busy" to be interviewed. Indeed, they are so busy that the consultant is unable to reach any of them on the telephone to tell them that, without interviews, the OD effort cannot continue.

3. The medical-center retreat where two physicians walk out on a participative exercise in future planning, saying that it is a waste of their valuable time to discuss such matters with students and nurses.

4. An industrial OD department so bogged down in collaborative, long-range, strategic planning (walls and walls of schedules and flip sheets) that there is no time (willingness?) to consider the hypothesis that the strategic plans have little or nothing to do with line management's strategies—for the line managers have none, at least none on which they want help.

The common theme in these cases is that collaboration and participation produce *more* tension and irrationality, instead of reducing them. Expressing the resistance does not melt it; it makes it *real*. At the point of give-and-take, of institutional problem solving, of a commitment to *real* interdependence, which participation and collaboration imply, people back down. They back down because there is no penalty for holding on to the old and no discernible reward for embracing the new. They back down because if they go forward and the boss is wishy-washy or soon replaced, they find themselves on a limb half sawed through, with their former friends watching to see how far they will fall and how hard they will hit.

It is worth considering where the incentives lie for joint, rational problem solving. Interdependence is a psychologically risky business. Indeed, it can be downright inconvenient if the people you need are also the ones who disagree with you.

It takes some strong bonds (marriage is one) before people will admit or accept their responsibilities in a relationship. Where, in the world of work, do such bonds exist? What creates them? Under what conditions are people more likely to "own" their need for one another and therefore be more inclined to solve in civil ways the problems created when they struggle to fulfill themselves?

OD'S MAIN CONTINGENCY: AN OUTPUT FOCUS

OD works better in a cohesive organization—the kind in which people's lives, fortunes, sacred honor (call it self-esteem, if you like) are bound together. The less this is the case, the less successful OD will be. It is not enough that people have bad relationships and want better ones. There are four features that provide fertile soil for organizational improvement: (a) formal authority, (b) concrete goals, (c) task interdependence, and (d) performance measures. OD will be more acceptable and more accepted in organizations subject to the easy actualization of these four features, i.e., joint, rational problem solving.

I call these "output-focused" systems. They are organized around consumer requirements, which determine productivity for the organization as a whole. One person's customers are everybody's customers. A major feature of such systems is the recognition that some people have legitimate authority to hire and fire other people for whose performance they are accountable. Accountability is enforced through structure—a division of labor, policies, and procedures that are fairly well understood and assumed by people in authority to contribute to results.

If OD's goal is to mediate tension between freedom and constraint in organizations, then in output-focused systems the source of tension will usually be *too much structure* in the sense of overpowering authority (too little individual influence), too narrow a division of labor, unrealistic or too precise goals (no room for maneuver), too narrow measures, or too tight controls. Such systems risk becoming rigid and closed. These factors cause anxiety, loss of self-esteem, irrational feelings, and efforts—not always conscious—to subvert the system. The reason, I think, has to do with the close relationship between producers and consumers and the dependence of the organization, for survival, on consumer acceptance of its goods or services. Not only can production be measured, it is quickly evaluated, for consumer feedback is relatively swift and pointed. Output-focused organizations know *what* they have to do to survive. This leads to policy, procedure, close supervision, and so on, in an effort to insure the proper result. That the proper result does not always ensue more often is a flaw in the "how" than in the "what."

When systems become extremely rigid or closed, people feel impotent or out of control. Self-esteem deteriorates. People say, "The boss treats us like children, he won't give us any responsibility." The boss says, "My people behave just like children. They won't take any responsibility."

Enter the OD consultant. The OD contract, properly negotiated, symbolizes a change in the "how." Assuming that the contract is for team building and that it incorporates Argyris' three criteria—valid data, free choice, internal commitment—what is the intervention?

OD, in this case, functions to name the sources of constraint and anxiety and in the process to ventilate feelings (all valid data); to pose the issue of what should be on the agenda for problem solving (free choice); and to facilitate (with models, methods, procedures) the invention of new solutions (internal commitment to act).

This process always works *so long as* the consultant takes no steps without the client's informed consent. In this way, the flip sheets spin out; the issues are organized, categorized, and sifted; decisions are made; and during the event, the team is bound to examine its own work processes, for it is these that will help or hinder the solution of the problems selected. The consultant intervenes in these blockages, at whatever level of abstraction they occur. People together, confronted with a discrepancy, discuss it, confirm it, and if they so choose, do something about it. Sometimes the consultant suggests procedures by which the problem can be solved. In any case, the problem solving is undertaken jointly, by all or by a representative group of people in the client system. Having gone through the process together, people are much more committed to making the solutions work. This is self-governance in action in the work place.

OD provides ways to actualize such self-governance. Why does OD work in this situation? It works because there is some common understanding of organizational goals, some agreed-upon performance and evaluation measures, some rough correlation between performance and rewards. There is a ball park to play in, a set of agreed-upon parameters that most of the participants can link to desirable outcomes. Of course, over time, a good deal of irrationality and anxiety have built up around some or all of these factors.

OD works because it:

1. Reduces or contains anxiety, helping to focus it on common purposes;
2. Surfaces/legitimizes expressions of irrationality and conflict;
3. Helps people to use the energy thus released to set up a *new* balance between goals, authority, measures, and interdependence (and *not* to eliminate any of these features); and
4. Enhances self-esteem as a result of joint achievements.

In an output-focused system, self-esteem, to a remarkable degree, derives from performance. Managers feel good when "the numbers" improve. I find this point made repeatedly by industrial clients. "I feel very fortunate that most of my goals are measurable—quantitatives," one manufacturing director told me recently. "I have a chance to win. I know whether I did it or not." While managers embrace OD for a wide range of personal (and often surprisingly humanistic) reasons, what makes OD salable in output-focused systems is the strong possibility that output will improve.

INPUT-FOCUSED SYSTEMS

What happens, though, in systems where there are multiple goals or unclear goals? Where measurement of results is difficult or impossible? Where evaluation is a personal and highly controversial matter? Where administrative action (constructive use of authority) is seen as capricious, irrelevant, or worse—an illegitimate interference with the organization's main purposes? What happens when there is no obvious correlation between working together and getting the job done?

Organizations that share these characteristics are what I call "input-focused" systems. The critical characteristic of such systems (a university is a prime example) is that the main producers (professors for instance) derive major rewards, and therefore self-esteem, from sources external to the organization itself. Usually, these people practice a form of expertise that can be applied in toto *without* the assistance of others. Collaboration is possible, but not essential, for tasks such as teaching, research, consultation, design, therapy, and the like.

In professional systems, each producer tends to have customers who are not easily transferable to colleagues, unless the colleague has a different expertise. Consumers are loyal to individuals much more than to the organization as a whole. Doctors, for instance, tend to keep their patients no matter what group they belong to or what hospital they practice in.

Therefore, there is little to collaborate on in terms of service to any particular customer. In a typical output-focused system, delivering just one jar of aspirin to a single consumer requires the close cooperation of dozens, if not hundreds, of people doing a variety of tasks. By contrast, the most brilliant university teaching, intellectually complex and capable of stimulating thousands, may be the tour de force of a single unique professor. That is input.

One way to think about the central contingency in input-focused systems is that the incentives towards joint, rational problem solving are low. Each professor, lawyer, social worker, accountant, physician, scientist, or OD consultant can explicate the personal goals, ways of measuring, evaluation criteria, and actions that he or she would take as a result. Few or none can articulate such matters in ways that would bind the organizations in which they work.

Input-focused systems do their main systematic, clearly understood, highly proceduralized evaluations at the input end. They evaluate admission to the system through various governing boards. Once a person is admitted, uniting with others to create an institutional output is a very low priority. The output focus in such systems moves to the individual professional level. Organizational goal setting, evaluation, and action are seen as restrictive, punitive, and undermining of innovation. Moreover, they are *experienced* that way, for there is little or no organizational reward for participating in joint exercises with others to negotiate such value-laden matters when concrete goals do not exist. There is even less motivation when the person in authority lacks the formal clout to compel such problem solving. There are a great many things that a talented consultant might do with groups in such organizations. Rational, deliberate, planned changes in the organization's culture are not among them.

The *organizational* problems of low goal clarity and commitment and low recognition of authority are very difficult, if not impossible, to solve through participative and collaborative strategies involving large numbers of people. Such strategies themselves are viewed as part of the problem. When you go to a meeting feeling constrained, put upon, and undervalued, when you think your time is being wasted and you ought to be back in your office solving "real problems," that is a loss of self-worth.

In another context I have suggested why this happens in academic medical centers (Weisbord, 1976). Briefly, the sources of physician identity are *external* to given institutions. Thus, management—the coordination of work toward certain outcomes—undercuts instead of supports such identity; it deprives physicians of the right absolutely to decide everything of consequence to the care of their patients. Yet their training (and society's expectations) have socialized them to do just that.

I think such conditions may pertain in *all* professional organizations where individuals see themselves as creators and entrepreneurs rather than as employees.

Demand on the input system is insatiable and infinite. It cannot be satisfied, for there will never be enough knowledge, health, or education. The problem is not a marketing problem (to create a demand); it is a limitation problem: deciding on constraints to live within and then learning how to live within them. Output systems manage output. Input systems must learn to manage input.

While it is relatively easy to help managers in such systems diagnose their situations, it is much harder to find legitimate ways to encourage professionals to enter the dialogue. Professionals wish to be left alone. At best, they wish to be critics. Few show enthusiasm for sharing the risks and responsibilities inherent in making policies that constrain their own behavior, even when such constraints are based on rational analysis. This stance becomes increasingly risky as consumers demand more voice in evaluating the quality and quantity of the professional services they receive.

To the extent that input-focused systems must take consumer pressures seriously, they become better candidates for OD intervention. Nevertheless, a different kind of OD is called for: one focused more on creating *legitimate structures* for change than on interpersonal and group processes. The latter will become appropriate only when the new structures are valued.

Where, then, is traditional OD most likely to succeed? The most obvious answer is in industry—in companies that make and sell something tangible. Line organizations in production industries constitute, in my opinion, the optimum possibility for more humane organizational arrangements using OD models. If you want to humanize the performance of work, do not look to social-work agencies, mental health centers, or university departments of the humanities; instead, think "cardboard-box factories"; think "chemical businesses"; think "pet-food plants." These are the settings in which people have maximum incentive to engage in participative problem solving, to confront each other face-to-face, to stand or fail together in the daily performance of their tasks.

This is not to argue that auto assembly plants are humane environments or that executives who drive themselves fourteen hours a day, six days a week, are living the good life, or that rapacious profits and polluted air are essential concomitants of humane industrial settings. I am merely saying that people whose livelihoods depend on joint efforts are more susceptible to collaboration and participation than those who can earn their livings working alone.

Dunn and Swierczek (1977) find no strong relationship between economic organizations and successful change efforts. This suggests to me that making profits is not the issue so much as incentives to collaborate toward some concrete goals. OD is not, by and large, for artists, scientists, professors, rugged individualists, or mad geniuses. The world needs all of us, but not all of us have a use for organization development. For that matter, OD is not of much practical use to OD consultants, except on such time-bound tasks as joint design of a program or a workshop. Indeed, none of us need OD unless we have an organization that we wish to develop. If so, we will have to work with others on tasks with finite ends that can be judged by the organization and by each person involved as having been done well or badly. In short, we need an output system to engage in development.

It is too bad that we cannot all use OD; after all, it is such beneficent stuff. But then, given a choice, how many of us would like to live the way our clients do? Persistent interdependence is fertile soil for more humane organizations, but it also means a persistent struggle to establish and maintain identity and to live within constraints.

Therefore, OD is for factory workers and industrial management teams and sales forces. Given top management's commitment, there is no reason why it should not succeed with police, fire fighters, and sports teams. I am not sure whether OD is appropriate for civil servants, diplomats, politicians, physicians, lawyers, or university professors. I go very slowly in such settings. Where, I ask, is the output focus? Commitment can be high when it looks as though fast, easy solutions are forthcoming. It may deteriorate rapidly when the solutions begin to merge into rough, emotionally demanding interpersonal encounters over values, goals, beliefs, ethics, and morality, especially when these are the only available measures of output. This is especially true among people who have been evaluated at the input end, found worthy to enter their profession, and now have individual output goals of their own.

Management scientists will tell you that the job is to make the input-focused people more output conscious. They would do this by forcing the system to set concrete goals and performance measures. These provide an illusion of structure which, like beauty, is only skin deep. Such procedures and protocols may make things worse for the professionals and may cause whatever informal control systems there are—joint administrator/professional problem-solving mechanisms—to deteriorate.

Suppose that input-focused systems cannot be rationalized that way. Suppose that the professionals are right—that the cost of coordination is alienation, demoralization, reduced creativity, and less commitment. I think that the right stance for administrators in such straits is to help professionals do their work better, to help them solve the problems they want solved. In return, perhaps professionals can help to define and defend institutional goals consistent with resources and social demands. I am not sure how to facilitate this, although I welcome good opportunities.

The theory I have found most helpful in working with input-focused systems is Lawrence and Lorsch's (1967) concept of differentiation and integration. There are a great many subtle possibilities for using this concept; it has such face validity that people who hear it for the first time can, after a short exposure, make applications not envisioned by the authors, e.g., as a team-building model, for managing conflict between administrators and professionals, for understanding the different orientations required to wear multiple hats (such as teaching and research). Indeed, there is even an intrapsychic analogy: Gestalt therapy, which seeks integration in the full experiencing of polarities (differentiation).

The theory conceived by Lawrence and Lorsch is an organizational variation on a common biological concept: that organs—heart and brain, for instance—require unique structural differences for each to function well. However, while these differences are necessary, they are not sufficient to insure a healthy organism. Integrating systems also are required to tie together the special parts into a coherent body/mind.

So it is with organizations. Sales, production, and research units require certain ways of seeing and being in the world to work well. These necessary differences include goals, time horizons, degree of interpersonal contact, and required structure. To the extent that units maintain required differences, they keep their integrity and they function well. Such differences also increase the probability of conflict. Thus, for optimal results, organizations must also find ways to integrate, or manage, conflict caused by (necessary) differences.

Lawrence and Lorsch's theory—like all management concepts—derived from and was tested in industrial settings, that is, output-focused systems. There, Lawrence and Lorsch could show higher output in plants that achieved higher integration without artificially reducing required differences among functions.

What happens in input-focused systems? One obvious use of the theory is to consider which tasks can be done autonomously by professionals and administrators working alone and which tasks require joint work. For example, professors in an academic department or lawyers in a law firm or OD consultants with a common employer may do most of their professional work alone or in ad hoc groups, in ways solely determined by themselves. However, matters of policy, scheduling of time, compensation and benefits, minimum standards of (individual) productivity, budgets available, and other matters affecting everyone might, from time to time, require joint problem solving, if not by all individuals, then by legitimate representatives to achieve lasting, credible solutions. Deciding which tasks can be done alone and which are best done in concert with others might be a legitimate OD intervention.

Sometimes, an input-focused organization gets into such straits that all sorts of people are motivated to want to save it. My introduction to academic medical centers came when I was consultant to an ad hoc task force on planning that included physicians, nurses, administrators, and scientists. Their charge was not to plan anything, but simply to come up with a "plan for planning" that would be responsive to the needs of a fast changing environment. It was a task in which all had considerable interest and the meetings were lively, the output useful. The process they created led to important changes in mission, structure, and budgeting procedures, all of which were designed by joint committees of faculty, students, administrators, and trustees. In this case a superordinate goal—an overall planning process in which all would have influence—provided an integrating focus for otherwise extremely diverse groups that were not used to close collaboration.

When an institution is not in crisis, it is much easier to explore a widget-building relationship (toward a joint result) than it is to invest in an exploration of differences in deeply held values when joint decisions are at stake. The latter is especially difficult if there is no measurable flow of widgets by which one can calibrate the significance of one's differences with others. This, it seems to me, constitutes the practical as well as the theoretical limits of OD. What is to be done in the name of OD in widget-free situations? My best answers at this point are:

1. Find the incentives for rational, joint problem solving.
2. Find the superordinate goals that create incentives for people to work together, e.g., good laboratory practices in research and development labs, cost containment in hospitals. External threat is a dependable incentive.
3. Help people to make choices about *whether* they wish to collaborate and toward which ends. Help them examine how real such commitments are and what the incentives are for working together.
4. Help people in authority to assert and test the limits of their mandates to articulate goals for their institutions and to measure, evaluate, and reward or punish for performance.
5. Facilitate management training, personal-growth workshops, and individual experiences that "empower" people.

Where does that leave OD with all its potential new interventions? The intervention tool kit in both output- and input-focused systems seems infinitely expandable. The major incentives for *doing* OD, however, remain few in number:

1. Sanction—a person in authority wants OD for his or her benefit;
2. Goals/measures—people know what they are trying to do and are not doing it;
3. Interdependence—people cannot do the task without each other, and they are not working together very well;
4. External threat—the government, or someone else, is exerting a lot of pressure that is hard to respond to and even harder to ignore. Pocketbooks are pinched.

These, in my experience, are the main reasons why people are willing to democratize the work place, using OD methodologies. Most of us will not share risks unless we have to. Such incentives are more often found in output-focused systems. When this is the case, and the consultant—mindful of what makes a strong contract—employs collaborative diagnoses and democratizing change structures, then anything is possible.

How long will OD changes last? Continuity of OD, e.g., long-term efforts in a particular system, is governed by a different law, that of *stability*. Stability means that the person in authority remains on the job or is succeeded by someone who is intimately involved in the change effort. Nearly every OD contract I have had was terminated or began to degenerate when the person who initially brought me in moved on. Normative changes seem as ephemeral as snowflakes in July in the absence of high-influence people to insist on "the way we do things around here."

I feel optimistic about what is possible for OD, with the right contingencies and extremely tentative (and open-minded, I hope) where they do not exist. If we cannot find some, perhaps most, of the conditions listed above, then we should seek (collaborative/participative) ways of initiating such conditions. If people invest in this initiation, I think OD has a chance to succeed. If they will not, then maybe it is a job for management science, Batman, or Wonder Woman. Perhaps the Lone Ranger has a hole in his June calendar. I know I do not, anymore, because what I wish to practice is OD—the way I have defined it here. Such practice requires, first of all, a cohesive organization to practice on. Without it, what is left is just a big fat D—a set of very fancy solutions in search of a problem.

REFERENCES

Argyris, C. *Intervention theory and method*. Reading, MA: Addison-Wesley, 1970.

Becker, E. *The denial of death*. New York: The Free Press, 1973.

Beckhard, R., & Harris, R. T. *Organizational transitions: Managing complex change*. Reading, MA: Addison-Wesley, 1977.

Dunn, W. N., & Swierczek, F. W. Planned organizational change: Toward grounded theory. *Journal of Applied Behavioral Science*, 1977, *13*(2), 135-157.

French, W. L., & Bell, C. H., Jr. *Organization development: Behavioral science interventions for organization improvement*. Englewood Cliffs, NJ: Prentice-Hall, 1973.

Lawrence, P., & Lorsch, J. *Organization and environment*. Boston, MA: Division of Research, Graduate School of Business Administration, Harvard University Press, 1967.

Margulies, N., Wright, P. L., & Scholl, R. W. Organization development techniques: Their impact on change. *Group & Organization Studies*, 1977, *2*(4), 428-448.

Vaill, P. B. Reflections on technology. *Social Change*, 1975, *5*(4), 3-7.

Weisbord, M. R. Why organization development hasn't worked (so far) in medical centers. *Health Care Management Review*, April 1976, pp. 17-28.

Weisbord, M. R. How do you know it works if you don't know what it is? *OD Practitioner*, October 1977, *9*(3).

3

Managing the Tension Between OD Principles and Political Dynamics

Robert T. Golembiewski

Despite its boundary-spanning tendencies, organization development (OD) literature has only tentatively attended to one critical and ubiquitous interface: the one between politics and administration, at or near the top of public agencies. Such an interface exists at the federal level between legislators, senior administrators who are political appointees, and the top levels of the career service. These boundaries are defined by constitutions, laws, and traditions in ways that inhibit spanning.

This paper describes experience at the politics/administration interface and focuses on cases that (a) involve a moderate-to-high-technology mission, (b) are characterized by active and intense oversight of the managerial mission by legislative or political officials, and (c) involve an OD consultant working both sides of the politics/administration interface. The analysis also applies—sometimes quite directly, at other times in various degrees—to the political aspects of all organizations.

Two points must be noted. Although the following guidelines reflect the delicacy of the matter, successful interventions at the interface and in public agencies are possible (Golembiewski & Eddy, 1978). Moreover, the thrust of OD as a professional activity well suits major developmental needs in the discipline of public administration (Golembiewski, 1977). Consequently, this paper often contrasts with some of Marvin Weisbord's theories (see Chapter 2 in this volume). Similarly, if for different reasons, this paper also takes a different stance from approaches that focus on development at the individual level, which do not suit interventions at the interface.

GUIDELINES FOR INTERVENING AT THE INTERFACE

Nineteen guidelines derived from experience at the politics/administration interface provide both direction and counsel within the context of typical OD values and goals (Golembiewski, 1972, pp. 1-202).

Guideline 1

The OD consultant's basic concern should be with the system as contrasted with specific units or individuals. Intervenors will work with and for individuals or groups; yet essential guidance includes translating a sense of the possible into a concept of the ideal at a systemic level that transcends individuals and groups. The same overall approach characterizes much private-sector consultation.

Two derivative needs are paramount. The intervenor must help groups and individuals to develop a sensitivity to systemic needs, i.e., they often will be encouraged to take perspectives and positions contrary to their own apparent individual or group interests. Operationally, moreover, the OD intervenor at the interface needs a well-developed system of values, a philosophy for action that he can make substantially clear to others and that can be applied to many sets of operating conditions, as well as a model of how major desired effects can be attained in organizations.

Specifically, the OD intervenor at the interface often will have to go far beyond emphasizing process/task interaction, which Weisbord sees as the "one important practice theory" in OD. Persons at the interface typically will demand to know "what" is happening more than "how." Given the importance of "healthy processes," those persons will be even more interested in alternative structural relationships, job designs, and so on that are more—rather than less—appropriate to specified conditions. Those at the interface obtain little comfort from assurances that these crucial outcomes will be "emergent" or "organic." Even if there is no one best model for organizing, we know much about the costs/benefits of alternative models under relatively specified conditions (Golembiewski, 1977, Vol. 2, pp. 31-40).

Operating at a systemic level in the public sector also raises two greater challenges—one emotional, the other associated with the pervasive multiple levels of OD consultation at the interface. The first challenge is to develop *hope* that things can be different; the second requires *competence* involving skills and theory about how to make a difference at so many levels, often simultaneously, when so many forces oppose any lasting impact.

Prevailing Emotional Tone. The modal emotional attitude about their "system" among those at the interface ranges from despair that it is unredemptively bigger than all of us, at the worst, to the resigned humor reflected in the public bureaucrat's pencil—the one with erasers on both ends. Political persons, whether appointed or elected, tend to sputter and fume about the unresponsive bureaucracy; and career officials tend to despair about passing political fads and personalities. But agreement exists on one point: attempted change at the interface often is like punching warm Jello: if you hit it hard and often enough, you can splatter some of it, but it soon takes the form of the bowl as it cools and then congeals. The associated emotional tone takes many forms, some aggressive but most tending toward withdrawal or resignation (Alsop, 1966, p. 14).

Pervasive Multi-Levels. Life at the interface is complicated, with everything being so subtly related to everything else. The impact of these multiple levels on OD interventions at the interface may be compared to the pressures of a geologic fault line, the point of contact of all the massive and conflicting forces that bear on multiple-issue areas. This results in two basic considerations.

First, most intervenors specialize in either interpersonal *or* rational/technical models. This bias need not be troublesome at many levels of organization; indeed, it often will simplify the consulting contract. The politics/administration interface seldom permits that simplification, however, and failure to be sensitive to multi-level issues can be serious. Reddin (1977, p. 38) describes one case of his own myopia in applying interaction-centered designs at the private-sector interface. He concludes: "The company had really needed a cost accountant rather than a change agent." Reddin illustrates better than he prescribes, in this case. The choice should not have been between change agent or accountant. The situation called for a change agent whose diagnosis would take the system's reward and punishment practices into account.

Second, at the politics/administration interface, the OD intervenor is working between *professional* and *political* people. By "professional," I do not simply mean engineers, chemists, behavioral scientists, and the like; nor by "political" do I refer only to elected officials. Rather, I prefer to focus on two generalized roles, following Mosher (1968, pp. 103-109):

1. The professional role emphasizes "specialized knowledge, science, and rationality."
2. The political role "focuses on negotiation, elections, votes, compromise."

This distinction implies two opposed orientations for testing truth-value: one seeks truth in empirical regularities, in theory, or in technology; the other seeks truth in volatile constituency building.

The public interface has several distinguishing features. Primarily, the political role often overwhelms the professional role. In addition, many practices and traditions in this country reinforce the role specialization of politicals and professionals at the interface. Popularly elected legislators seldom have administrative roles, for example, except in some "commission" forms of government; and constitutional and institutional provisions generally separate legislative and executive/administrative branches, each of whom have different constituencies. This specialization exacerbates the "built-in aversion between the professional and politics" (Mosher, 1968, p. 109). Finally, politicians exist in the private sector, but not in the profusion nor with the many independent power bases that are characteristic of the public sector. And private-sector analogs of political institutions (e.g., the board of directors) tend to be weak replicas of popularly elected legislatures, despite contemporary efforts to politicize those institutions by stockholder protests and so on.

Although the twain seldom meet, the interface can be characterized by a mutual humility. Professionals recognize that technology cannot make value choices, that only humans can—often by utilizing processes that may be broadly characterized as "political." Politicians recognize that no amount of negotiation or exchange can change some realities; and both seek to define with growing precision in diverse issue areas what is "political" from what is inseparable from its processes.

Costs/Benefits of Systemic Bias. Taking the systemic view at the interface is not easy and the greatest difficulty is in determining just what that is. This is not intended as a rationale for whatever an intervenor prefers. Along with liberal portions of realistic humility and a passion for testing, the organizationally relevant literatures provide major perspectives for seeing the forest as well as the trees. For example, the huge literature on behavioral and attitudinal consequences of alternative structural arrangements can provide invaluable guidance, even though that literature is far from complete. Moreover, on a case-by-case basis, one can distinguish the more-systemic from the less-systemic perspective. This paper contains several such examples.

The virtues of the first guideline are numerous, nonetheless. First, and most important, an identification with the system rather than the parts reinforces the intervenor's interstitial role and also should signal that he intends to rise above office politics. This does not prescribe an above-it-all attitude; rather the prescription is to better and more credibly engage in systemic politics. For example:

A chief executive told an OD consultant that he had decided on a major appointment. The proposed appointee was saleable for various reasons, but (it soon became clear) had the basic attraction of being no threat to the chief executive. In fact, the executive was bypassing an individual with better credentials for the job, but who also posed a greater threat to him.

The appointment might be good ward politics, the consultant agreed, but its systemic implications were serious. To illustrate, the executive had, over time, importuned several subordinates to develop strong backups for all the usual public reasons but also to make it easier for the chief executive to reassign and terminate employees. The executive encouraged others to "put it on the line," but when he had his chance he—like they—was motivated to take the easy way out. Few would be fooled, the OD consultant said.

The chief executive reconsidered his choice, and the discussion soon shifted to the topic of highlighting how he had "bitten the bullet to set an example for one and all." This would be "good medicine for the system." Besides, he concluded, the odds were better than even that the new appointee soon would "dig his own grave with his mouth."

When informed that the OD consultant thought it would be wise for him to spend some time with the new appointee, the executive first balked, but finally agreed, in terms that were realistic although lacking in charity. "If you can help him, that will help me, if I play it with any finesse. And if you mess him up, or can't help, that also will help me."

Prescribing a systemic orientation may increase the consultant's vulnerability, and it clashes with the reasonable advice that the change agent needs a client, first and foremost. But there is a very high probability of one of three outcomes in cases of interstitial consultancy: (a) either the consultant inherits a "balance of power" that initially demonstrates recognition of the value of an external person playing an interstitial role, or (b) the consultant quite quickly encourages such a balance of power, or (c) the consultant is very unlikely to become effective in trading back and forth across the politics/administration interface.

In the third outcome, the consultant likely will either come to be—or come to be seen as—identified too closely with one subsystem to perform a credible interstitial role. Moreover, appropriate balances of power at the interface typically are temporary. This implies a disciplined boldness at times, a reticence at others.

Finally, attaching oneself to one or a few people near the interface can be foolhardy. Political appointments are vulnerable or at least short-lived, and changes there typically result in a great deal of turnover among both patronage and career employees. Since OD programs typically must have long lead times, establishing a tie with a system rather than a specific regime is not only difficult, it may be necessary (Warwick, 1975).

In addition, an intervenor's focus on the system can be valuable, since few others at the interface may be motivated to understand and evaluate systemic issues. Thus, politicians may be very active in developing the kind of agreements we call "policy," and they later may become involved in episodic case work for individual constituents, but beyond that, their attention is likely to be spotty. The usual preoccupation among politicians—even among those in executive or managerial roles—is to get re-elected or reappointed, not to manage some system. Their focus is likely to be segmented and superficial, that is, centered around those interests that can be bundled into a *sufficient constituency*. The OD intervenor can be useful in reminding these people about systemic facts that they are so likely to forget.

Professionals also may need systemic help if they specialize in one function. This may constitute a trained incapacity—its effects are clear, for example, in the budget process. Each functional specialist tends to fight for his or her own programs. Moreover, politicians may reinforce these pervasive, fragmenting tendencies. Powerful members of Congress, for example, may use such an approach for dual purposes: to help control the presidency or political appointees, and to facilitate agency response to interests important to legislators.

Guideline 2

Public-sector interventions often will involve features that are unique or that at least differ in noteworthy degree from those in private-sector practice. The associated argumentation is complex, but three perspectives can provide some clarity.

First, in many public agencies, conditions exist that do not permit unqualified acceptance of Shepard's (1976) usually appropriate counsel that OD interventions should build strength and build on strength. There are some systems that cannot lose for winning, and there seem to be others that cannot win for losing. The latter do not permit building strength and building on strength. Rather, the orientation may be to inspire some hope—even by risking dependence of the client on the consultant—while building on acknowledged and pervasive weakness, if not perversity.

Many approaches can be used to distinguish such conditions or stages (Golembiewski, 1972, pp. 30-39). For example, the same input of data via the same OD design could have profoundly different effects in the two types of systems. In the public sector, the approach may have to be "I know that is what is wrong, but there is just no way to change that around here. It will always be that way, or at least for so long that I will never see it change."

Second, the prime implication is that OD interventions appropriate to one organizational condition or stage might be inappropriate to another, perhaps even seriously counterproductive. To illustrate, at the interface, I tend to deal far more with single individuals, personally and as a go-between, with all parties mutually aware of my role, and especially so when a new issue is being worked. Individualized designs such as third-party interventions and role negotiation exercises also can prove very useful. This approach reduces the risk for principals and permits face-saving should things not work out. In contrast, public or group designs might only confirm what everyone at the interface already knows: that openness, owning, and trust are so low (and risk is so high) that candidness about the system permits only the conclusion that conditions will not likely be changed by anyone, even given herculean effort and uncommon good fortune.

Third, a key issue—perhaps *the* issue—then becomes how the *hope* of remedial change can be nurtured in spite of massive squelchers of that hope. Somehow, that hope might be kindled by itself; or a determined politician in high office may come along who seems seriously bent on renewing the state administrative system and who can successfully avoid charges of empire building. Short of these unhappy circumstances, the OD intervenor consciously can try some things in a degenerative system that might be ill-advised in a regenerative one.

Without prescribing them for any other OD intervenor, let me sketch a brief catalog of things that have worked for me. Basically, I have found that more personal risk taking by the intervenor seems appropriate in degenerative systems. Instead of being personally "up front" to develop the point by contrast, the usual prescription for the OD intervenor-as-facilitator sagely encourages getting clients to "own" attitudes and behavior, to express themselves openly, etc. To this, many public-sector clients will respond: "That is easy for you to say, but it is much harder for us to do." And so it is. One way to generate some hope that regenerative features can be built into an organization is for the OD intervenor to be the "point man," relying on infantry jargon, typically with respect to some power figure, such as chief executive officer or other executive with a reputation for staunchness if not insensitive autocracy. If we can do this, subordinates may feel a glimmer of hope. Whether we make it or not, however, the signals can be very revealing to others.

The role of OD intervenor as point man can go several ways, of course. It may encourage dependence, and it clearly builds on the "weakness" of suspicion, mistrust, and so on. But having a point man is often part of the culture of degenerative systems, and beginning from where the system *is* typically constitutes sound practice. Moreover, the risks for the OD intervenor are far less substantial than for system members, and some associated modeling may be useful to all concerned.

When the system is alleged to be the inhibitor, an OD intervenor should test aggressively. In some cases, the essential cause may lie in an unapproachable, unalterable, and unavoidable source. The intervenor may then resort to worst-case analysis: "What would be the worst possible outcome if you (or your agency) did X?" Sometimes the worst turns out to be pretty mild stuff, or various ways of blunting the effects of "the worst" may be revealed. It might even be possible to work toward changing the system.

But cases clearly exist in which the worst consequence of evasion is very wicked, while playing the game is both unavoidable and costly for participants.

Here the intervenor faces a dilemma: whether to be content with band-aid interventions, as in "cooling-out" designs for disaffected participants, or whether to push, probably quixotically, for preventive interventions that reduce or eliminate the source of disaffection. There are no general answers; sometimes it ends up being a little bit of both. Appropriate design elements can help guarantee that the result is not all alleviation with no prevention.

I am certain of one thing in cases of the system as inhibitor. I think little of the OD intervenor who says, "Look how easy it is for me to thumb my nose at the system. Why don't you try it? It is fun." This consultant can precipitate clients into harmful situations whose effect the consultant might experience in only attenuated degree or escape altogether.

Guideline 3

The public-sector "production function" is very complex, especially because the weighting of its numerous components may be highly volatile over time, and because its heavily weighted components have little to do with effectiveness or efficiency, as they are conventionally understood. The point is not so much that a production function is impossible in the public sector, as some have argued. Rather, the public-sector production function fixates on keeping the polity sufficiently together, rather than on producing specific goods and services. The underlying criterion of effectiveness is a very broad one, and considerations of efficiency are far less central or even irrelevant. Consider the role of "spoils politics." History shows it to have been wildly inefficient, but major claims can be made (Van Riper, 1958, pp. 43-56) for its fundamental effectiveness at certain stages in the development of viable and relatively popular regimes in Great Britain and the United States, particularly through the nurturing of political parties, which, in turn, are significant in representative political systems.

There are two exceptions to this view. Keeping the polity together may eventually depend on providing radically more efficient services, in which case the minimal criteria jump to a new level. This has happened several times in our history, and may be happening now. There also will be periods, e.g., of reform movements or popular wars, when the public-sector production function takes on substantial clarity and stability. But even then that definition is likely to have no relation to efficiency as it is normally defined, and it typically will be "politics as usual" before very long.

The term "politics as usual" can be defined more specifically by three points. Each of these points applies to both private and public sectors, albeit in variable degree. The degree of overlap merely testifies to the fact that all organizations have political aspects, but that some have more of them, more commonly, and more intensely than others.

Gaining/Retaining Power Is Primary. A priority in all organizations is in building appropriate constituencies to gain and maintain power. For good and ill, our characteristic political institutions and traditions encourage much constituency building, which has the effect of complicating the provision of goods and services and often is more or less irrelevant to their effective or efficient provision. Most party platforms provide ample evidence of this tendency, their goal being to attract a constituency that is big enough for the purpose at hand rather than to guarantee delivery of goods or services. Similarly, the specialization of the legislative role can induce painful tension between energetic narcissists who promise everything to everybody and those administrative hewers of wood and carriers of water who have to deliver the services. At their best, legislators can help to check corrupting tendencies in the executive, as well as reflect a sense of collective purpose in public agreements.

The gaining/retaining of political power in the public sector possibly could be equated with some definite production function, but that probability is not high. Since the available subconstituencies have compound and confounded interests, the gaining/retaining of power goes on in many arenas, involving subconstituencies that overlap in wondrous ways, with interests that vary both within as well as between subconstituencies, and emphasizing elites that are variously (but, on the whole, not much) constrained by their several mass memberships.

Goal/Performance Incongruities. Public-sector goal setting is often complex and conflicting far beyond private-sector experience, both in the number of interests and in the range and diversity of conflicting goals. Moreover, the measurement of performance in the public sector often is not only difficult, but may require the passage of long periods of time before any reasonable assessment of performance can be even attempted. Consequently, many public-sector organizations—and especially at the interface—are not likely to have meaningful real-time feedback relevant to their production function, even if they want it.

The point can be made another way. Public-sector organizations are likely to be in close touch with the elites who represent their constituency base (Kaufman, 1973). Indeed, too much of such feedback may be their basic problem, as when the components of the production function salient to elites representing agency and client differ radically (as they often do) from the interests of agency service providers and service recipients. A common complaint below the interface is (a) we know what is wrong, (b) we know how to improve our performance and satisfy clients, but (c) we cannot act because of high-level agreements made by superiors.

Timing Is Everything/The Mood Is All. Severely complicating these issues related to the public-sector production function are the instabilities—even vagaries—of its major components. Politics is the art of the possible, and "the possible" resembles quicksilver more than commandments carved in stone. The possible is the product of enormously complicated dynamics, including substantial admixtures of misinformation, puffery, and plain deceit. But that combination can take on solidity, and often does. Consequently, people at the interface will emphasize that "it is all timing," and the talent required of the intervenor is the ability to act quickly to fit the prevailing mood.

What intervention will work, therefore, is difficult to say. The intervenor who is skillful and lucky enough to take advantage of appropriate timing is more likely to be successful. In addition, since people at the interface tend to give reasons why it is not possible to initiate change "now," it may be wise to proceed immediately in order to obtain a tactical advantage over those whose modus operandi is to procrastinate.

These features of politics cannot be wished away. And they provide numerous opportunities for OD interventions, limited though they might be. (See Guidelines 15 and 16.) In general, Weisbord's problems with public-sector OD applications are often really opportunities.

Guideline 4

Public-sector organizations characteristically pose great difficulties in drawing boundaries for OD interventions at all levels, but especially at the interface. The literature contains numerous examples (Klein, Thomas, & Bellis, 1971) of this point, which reflects one of the costs of a relatively open and representative system. "Leaks," for example, are a common tactic in the complex maneuvering that goes on more or less continuously. This may dampen individual willingness to be open and to "own" ideas and feelings, for a half-truth may seem far safer when one contemplates the various and well-entrenched enemies that any public agency or program is likely to have. Problems are greatest with public designs such as group confrontations or mirroring efforts, for obvious reasons.

Guideline 5

OD consultants at the interface unavoidably find themselves actors in the network of power; they are spokesmen for the allocation of values within the system, even though they often will play other strictly facilitative or helpful roles. OD intervenors may strive for a politically neutral role, they may plead that they only advise certain clients within the system, or they may more justifiably say the goal is maximum ownership by all involved of any changes or choices. These common restrictions often make sense at other levels, but not at the interface. For there, by definition, any significant intervention is politically charged. Hence, the usual arguments that restrict the intervenor's role are beside the point at the interface, and they seldom will convince anyone who counts of the typical reality or perception of the OD intervenor's role.

Effective OD ideology and designs applied at the politics/administration interface will impart directly on organizations whose structure, policies, and procedures derive in large part from some multiple, extra-organizational authority (complex legislative constitutencies, for example) that may be difficult or impossible to reach, and that has the capability of disciplining subunits perceived to be out of line. The weight of previous political agreements can also be great. Consequently, interventions may be momentous, especially if they work, and OD efforts can have serious political implications in the way they affect constituencies, legislative access, and so on.

The fact that public agencies are imbedded in a broad and pervasive legal/institutional context puts them in a class by themselves, compared to even the largest and most centralized of private-sector organizations. Their common ethos may be described as one of "legal rational formality [which] creates an organizational climate that is conservative and careful, where conflict-avoidance is a way of life, whose employees have little ability to influence their reward system by their productive or collaborative behavior, and where win-lose dynamics characterize the nature of relationships within and among organizations" (Heimovics, 1977).

What Virginia Schein (1977) calls the "politics of implementation" will be significant in efforts toward systemic change in all organizations. But no situation rivals the politics/administration interface for providing aid and comfort to enemies of a change effort—enemies that may not only be numerous, but who have independent power bases and more often than not answer to no common discipline or authority.

The OD intervenor at the interface in the public sector really has no great range of operational choices. Following Schein (1977, pp. 46-47), and again referring only to the unavoidable politics of implementing OD efforts:

1. The OD intervenor can conceptually "play down the politics of implementation and deny the pervasiveness of political behaviors in organizations," thus avoiding any direct confrontation with prevailing OD values as to openness and trust. The price may be ineffectiveness or failure, as the intervenor's ideology provides inadequate real-world guidance, especially with respect to systemic change.

2. The OD intervenor can conceptually acknowledge the potential conflict of OD values and the politics of implementation and consciously restrict him- or herself to interventions in which the conflict is least likely. This may be reasonable, but it patently forfeits most opportunities for systemic change, and it may relegate the intervenor to "band-aid" or "cooling out" activities, which may be important but are self-limiting in crucial senses.

3. The OD intervenor can acknowledge the potential conflict of OD values and the politics of implementation in order to consciously face the trade-offs that often will be required for effective implementation.

There should be little question about the bias advocated here. The OD consultant at the interface must resolutely help to induce an *alternative system of power*. Here, I like Weisbord's contention that the basic OD preoccupation is with shifting the balance of freedom/coercion. That makes the OD intervenor an advocate, of course, and probably a target for those with an interest in what already exists. But little is lost thereby, because at the interface any significant intervention is by definition "in politics," and no virtue inheres in trying to ignore that fact.

Guideline 6

Whatever the point of entry, the consultant should, from the start, reveal an intent to work toward multiple access. Multiple access permits more synergistic and systemic interventions, and it may even mean greater consultant freedom. But it is not likely to come easily. Specific clients may wish to restrict their relationship, and clients must agree that they gain more than they lose when the consultant gains multiple access. Bold signals, both at early and later stages, can be used to make the point. For example, the consultant may tell a chief executive with whom he has established a confidential relationship, "You say this business with X is not troublesome for you now. But I believe that it can be a source of difficulty for the whole system and, in the long run, for you as well. Unless you object very strongly, therefore, I propose to. . . ."

Guideline 7

The consultant should operate to expand the "range of credible discretion" for individuals and groups. For a chief executive, the ideal organization is one containing representatives of a diverse range of opinion. Diversity can maximize the range of available information and policy alternatives. Moreover, should the executive have to make the final decision when major disagreement exists, his ability to be both credible and yet consider a range of positions probably will be greater in direct proportion to the diversity of opinions and perspectives introduced.

Working toward an expanded range of credible discretion at the interface represents the orthodox view, of course (Argyris, 1974, pp. 269-288), but it has some interesting implications at the politics/administration interface. For example, one executive eventually accepted regular performance appraisal of his subordinates because—despite his demands—he got more out of it than he put into it. But he was troubled initially when his governing body wished to apply the same technique to him. Fortunately, he had been urged to wrestle with the issue before proceeding with subordinates. The OD intervenor should continue to emphasize, early and late, the implications for self of what is done unto others.

In addition, many major decision makers at the interface simply do not want an expanded range of discretion. Most are confident, if not opinionated; habitually, they tend to seek converging support for a position they somehow already favor, in contrast to diverging data that expands the range of credible decisions. They often want to build corrals rather than to expand horizons. And when they are not building corrals for others, they often find themselves trying to avoid being corralled by others.

Lastly, when an issue is politically hot, a standard approach proliferates sources of data: multiple committees, commissions, study groups, and so on. Typically, this buys time while a bargain is struck among the central actors. Intervenors can be asked to play this game in the mistaken belief that it seems consistent with their preferences. It is not. A certain cunning about not being used in such elemental ways can go a long way toward earning credibility for the intervenor at the interface.

Guideline 8

The intervenor from the beginning should announce his intent to work toward multiple public channels of information and evaluation. This is an orthodox OD precept that seeks to increase the probability of reliable and valid information. It applies more broadly at the interface than in most OD formulations.

Multiple Channels Within a System. The OD intervenor at the interface should strive to develop and maintain multiple channels of information and evaluation within a *system*. This parallels efforts in the private sector, of course, although with a unique twist or two. The politics/administration interface is infested with numerous "insiders" who have information of very diverse quality. Moreover, these insiders at the interface have independent power bases that insulate them from retribution or discipline, whatever the quality of their information. Moreover, the development and maintenance of that power base often will require (or encourage) them to present different views of reality (if not patent falsifications) as the overt reflections of basic differences in policy preferences or in supporting constituencies. In addition—and this may be hard for some to get used to—many persons in this situation will have a genuine acceptance of "doing what has to be done," by themselves or others, no matter how discrepant the action may be from their perceptions of the situation or their preferences.

Multiple Channels Between Systems. The OD intervenor at the interface will find the richest opportunities for helping to develop channels of information and evaluation between large *systems*, and especially between those that are antagonistic. Major increments in cooperation may result. Moreover, given the delicacy of the effort, it may also be possible to induce competitive forces to alleviate the critical productivity crisis in government (Rosenbloom, 1973). Antitrust laws often preclude similar intersystemic efforts in the private sector.

Guideline 9

The consultant will earn most approval for ameliorative successes, but both professional and systemic considerations urge substantial and growing attention to preventive efforts. This is not simply a way of encouraging consultant suicide, for risking that unhappy outcome can be a very good thing at the interface.

These considerations can be put in some kind of balance. OD interventions are best applied when the hurt is obvious to the client, who can ask for help, participate in diagnosis and prescription, feel the relief of any successful interventions, and experience the increments in self-esteem associated with psychological success in these regards. Consultants seldom will succeed if they raise havoc with an authority system by seeking to remedy evils and rectify wrongs that have priority only (or largely) within their own framework for interpreting reality and in terms of their own values. Moreover, patient helpers on the sidelines can be significant resources when an organization becomes polarized by conflict.

Equally weighty considerations encourage a strong emphasis on preventive work, however, on the general principle that avoiding a mess is often preferable to merely tidying up afterward. Purely ameliorative effort also can imply a small role for the intervenor, and it can pose ethical dilemmas relevant to cooling-out those disadvantaged by organization processes, by professionals acting with full knowledge that those processes will not be changed. As our knowledge of organizations and behavior increases, so also will it be ethically and professionally more difficult to "stand by."

In summary, the OD intervenor would do well to give attention to preventive interventions, perhaps especially at the politics/administration interface. This is the case even though preventive efforts:

1. may not induce great managerial enthusiasm, especially when they impact on the authority system or imply changes in standard procedures and policies;
2. have effects that are difficult to ascertain, especially in the sense that only vulnerable arguments support the position that some specific stimulus X inhibited some outcome Y, which never occurred;
3. present consultants with substantial opportunities for self-delusion about what needs doing and about the impact of their interventions; and
4. often constitute no-win situations in that consultants not only are rightly criticized for ameliorative interventions that fail, but even their successful interventions can be dismissed as mere proof that no intervention was necessary.

Guideline 10

When in doubt, despite the danger, the intervenor should work toward OD values and emphasize systemic and preventive interventions. This does not seek to provide encouragement for the power hungry, or for those desperate to make an impact. There usually will be numerous proponents of other perspectives on narrow or limited issues. Few participants will have either the motivation or the relative safety to take a systemic and preventive perspective. Typically, there is little reason to fear that the OD intervenor at the interface can make things happen and so should let them happen lest he compromise voluntarism, owning, and so on.

Guideline 11

When in doubt, the OD intervenor should work toward OD values, emphasizing individual and systemic development, as contrasted with political or power considerations. Again, numerous others are very likely to espouse other perspectives, so this encourages an active role by the OD intervenor. Since the prescription requires that the intervenor take major risks, having substantial "money in the bank" with the client seems a prerequisite for attempting what needs to be done.

The conflict between personal development and political leverage is common. In one case, a female executive secretary had the opportunity to take on managerial responsibilities but also was attracted to a secretarial position in another office, in which she could be of great aid to her present boss because he had continuing difficulties with that office. She also envisioned returning to her present job when relationships improved with that other office.

Clearly, the woman's boss (also my direct employer) strongly preferred that she take the secretarial position. She felt such strong loyalty to him that she applied for that position, despite her attraction to the managerial job.

On my initiative, and with her present boss's unenthusiastic sufferance, she and I held several career-planning sessions to clarify needs, payoffs, etc. She was willing at first, but became obdurate as the choice-point grew near.

She finally decided to take the new secretarial job, after some major struggles between her needs and her loyalty. "It would have been easier," she observed, "if you had just let me alone. I knew what I had to do."

My relationship with her has cooled somewhat, although her boss is more ambivalent. "I know you really had to do it," he said, "so I didn't tell you to buzz off. I ended up respecting you for doing a dumb thing, from my perspective. That's what it all comes down to."

Guideline 12

Value congruence between intervenor and persons at the interface is not a necessity in OD efforts, but clarity about values always is. Value differences at the interface often will be great, but they need not be consequential. The intervenor and others at the interface need not always read from the same text of preferred behavior, as in the example about systemic politics in the discussion of Guideline 1. But the intervenor should try never to forget, or to allow others to forget, that the intervenor leans toward greater systemic freedom and away from coercion. And value differences must be kept in mind, for they might later become consequential.

Guideline 13

An OD intervenor's effectiveness at the politics/administration interface will be determined by his management of an inevitable tension between those high versus those low on status, influence, and so on. The OD intervenor often will be seen as encouraging or even permitting influence by the deviant or by some minority. This occurs in many process interventions, in team building, and in similar designs.

The interface provides a particularly inhospitable home for such OD interventions. Public officials at the interface tend to maintain short chains of command, encouraging or forcing decisions to be made at their own level. The primary motives are likely to be caution, fear, insecurity, and perceived vulnerability to powerful and adverse forces. These common adaptations result from common features of the interface: the need for procedural caution, the short tenure of political appointees, the consequent lack of trust of career personnel deriving from lack of common experience, the need for swift and sudden response to hostile legislators, the media, or other interests (Golembiewski, 1969).

The effective OD intervenor should have ambitions far beyond being careful about acting as someone's hit man, as in checking for any "walking dead" prior to a team-development effort. Basically, top officials must come to see that—within wide limits—a viable minority can expand its range of credible discretion as well as add potentially vital inputs of information and values. This lesson definitely goes against the grain of most of those with whom I have worked at the politics/administration interface. Their operating rule is more likely to be that the best way to treat minorities is to make certain that they never exert any influence.

The intervenor also will be likely to experience difficulty in the public sector because the intervenor is another someone who may exert influence. Consequently, the intervenor's treatment may be different in the public sector from what one can expect in the private sector. One reaction has been experienced in the same form a number of times at the public interface, but never in a private-sector intervention.

The typical setting is the post-intervention euphoria, where all sides agree that major progress has been made and where plans are being made for another meeting. "How does that date fit your schedule?," someone may ask the consultant. I have learned to delay an answer at the interface because quite often a colleague's message to that person is "What's the matter? Are you afraid you can't do it without him?"

This question suggests important aspects of the common culture at the politics/administration interface. The *machismo* is dominant but is suffused with caution about adding a potential new competitor or an additional resource for an old competitor. Also prominent is the quick ownership of something that *has worked*. Should the original intervention have failed or still be in doubt, the follow-up meeting would certainly involve the consultant in a leading role.

The OD intervenor at the interface is more likely than his private-sector counterpart to experience reactions to himself. I am impressed with how much more often the consultant is encouraged to become a silent servant, reporting only what the client already knows and merely wants reinforced by an external. Often the consultant must work through a severe adversary stage with the client. Both reactions suggest a delicate equilibrium at the interface. A silent servant does not disturb that equilibrium. An intervenor who will not play that role threatens that delicate balance, and hence is likely to generate adversary relationships with those having special interests in the status quo who do not wish to risk change or with those who just feel that their comfort level has been lowered by the interloper.

Guideline 14

OD interventions at the politics/administration interface almost invariably will generate mixed reactions when they affect a special kind of minority: the "rogue" or the "renegade." The rogue is basically uncontrollable and thus is a fearsome beast at the interface. Few rogues exist in the private sector. This may be because executives in the private sector are less likely to have an independent power base, except through such uncommon means as the ownership of large blocks of stock. Roguishness no doubt derives in part from deep psychological wellsprings; but an independent power base certainly helps. An example is the congressman who can run on a long leash because the good folks back home will return him to office, almost no matter what.

The rogue can be a triumphantly principled figure, but far more often than not he is a gutter fighter, a person careless with the truth, often two-faced, ambitious without discipline by even casual principle, a tattle-tale in his own interests, and so on. But he has a power base.

OD designs typically have the effect of disciplining the rogue. Indeed, virtually any sharing of valid information probably will reduce the rogue's ability to have an impact. The rogue tends to be most influential when his peers do not "have their act together," for example, when two relatively equal factions stand in opposition to one another, are mutually suspicious, and refuse to share information. The rogue then can take the expedient side of the issue, or even all sides, given sufficient ingenuity and—ah—flexibility.

The disciplining of rogues is clearly not always good, for substantial reasons. First, rogues often are sinners, but they also might be saints. The engines of group forces could stamp out the one as well as the other. So the OD intervenor faces serious ethical issues in such cases—issues that are only superficially dealt with by pleading that one plays the role of "neutral group facilitator." Second, the disciplined rogue may become a resourceful enemy, even if he can be a grudgingly respectful one. Third, peers of the rogue tend to have bittersweet reaction to this disciplining aspect of many OD designs. "Next time it may be me." Fourth, the word gets around quickly at the interface, and this raises ethical issues for the intervenor. I have long since stopped counting the times when, in a burst of intense openness, someone at the interface wished me well in general and then noted specifically how pleasant it would be "to pull Joe's fangs" through some team-building design. Of course, one can refuse to participate in an effort that is obviously a punitive expedition. But one can be fooled, for there are masters of deception aplenty at the interface.

Guideline 15

The OD intervenor at the interface is safest when setting realistically pessimistic aspirations for the pace and extent of change. The institutional and historical character of the interface tends to have profound effects far down the hierarchy: effects which can be summarized briefly and with basic accuracy. Except for occasional "conversions," of which I am generally suspicious, most officials at the politics/administration interface behave in ways sharply at odds with OD values.

Especially for those at the interface, but extending far down the hierarchy as well, the primary behavioral systems emphasize suspicion rather than trust, protectiveness rather than openness, a basic preoccupation with winning and losing rather than with giving and sharing. Their behavior focuses dominantly around power rather than affect, around aggregations of capital far more than around human needs, around top-dog status or at least survival rather than around sharing influence. On the latter point, indeed, most of those at the politics/administration interface seem interested in only one kind of sharing: sharing blame, and then only when they cannot avoid it altogether. As for success, so many claims are likely to be put forward that the real motivators can go unnoticed, especially if they are modest or truthful.

These conclusions describe a tendency for behavior that does not necessarily call for despair about making progress. First, the discussion has been about central tendencies in *behavior*; those at the politics/administration interface generally have *values* consistent with OD. "It's a shame," goes a typical refrain, "that the world isn't a different kind of place. But I have to deal with it as it is." OD interventions can build on such normative preferences for a different world, if slowly and carefully.

Second, this tension between value and behavior—unlike the tension in the formulation of Argyris and Schon (1974)—is likely to be conscious. The politics/administration interface simply can be treacherous. As one public official told me, "When you have been harpooned as many times as I have, and then have had the wounds salted, peppered, and sandpapered, you tend to grow a thick, protective skin." This consciousness constitutes both an opportunity for, as well as a challenge to, OD interventions.

Third, however—and this is a crucial however—selective and sometimes dramatic progress can be made in decreasing the value/behavior gap as well as in overcoming harsh past experiences. Witness the success with team building among elected public officials (Le Baron, 1977). Using designs common in the laboratory approach to OD, resource persons at the University of Southern California have been able to design learning environments in which officials tend to come to a significant conclusion: that important payoffs *to them* can derive from reducing the behavior/value gap. As Le Baron explains (1977, pp. 3-4):

. . . local officials live within a dichotomy of power and trust; they are more familiar with—and therefore, more capable of handling—power than trust. Power is inevitable to someone elected to local office and its appearance cannot be avoided. Politics is the struggle for power. . . .

[This emphasis on power bases for individuals can be seriously dysfunctional when elected officials must act together, as on a board or council.] Power, in a group situation, often blocks as much process as it creates. It also tends to prevent council/board members from seeing their own humanness, and blinds them from the human qualities in others. We have found that council/board members recognize, once their attention is diverted from a strict power orientation, that trust is the cosmic glue which holds a relationship together. The foundation may be power, but the support structure is trust.

The movement from power to trust is accomplished through communications. Particularly, communications which release some of the unnecessary unknowns in the relationships of council/board members.

While one can expect a low congruence between OD values and the behavior of officials at the politics/administration interface, greater congruence is possible, especially as experience demonstrates that useful bottom-line effects can be achieved.

Although the orientation here could encourage avoidance, the discussion above implies that the OD intervenor should usually expect progress to come in bits and pieces, although great leaps forward may occasionally occur. Anecdotal evidence suggests that many intervenors with mostly private-sector experience find it difficult to cope with different standards in the public sector.

Fourth, I have come to expect an up-and-down effect at the interface, far more so than in the private sector. There are many indications that regression at the interface seems more likely after real progress has been made. So OD intervenors can profit from a certain elasticity of spirit, as well as from a sense of the related ebbings and flowings of the political tides.

One can interpret this effect in several ways. One interpretation argues that OD interventions at the interface can temporarily reduce symptoms but do not have much effect on their institutional causes. I have no problems about such pressure-relieving interventions, given mutual knowledge and my belief that the pressure results from "something out there that is bigger than all of us." Periodic ventilation can, indeed, be recommended. So intervenors may be succeeding realistically even as they seem to fail essentially.

Guideline 16

Public-sector OD interventions often will be used to test mutual intent, or degree of resolve, relevant to a specific issue by participants who have no interest in getting together in any sense and who have no desire to talk about the issues, let alone to seek to reduce differences. Frequently, in fact, an OD intervention might prove very effective in terms of such a limited and important outcome, even though the parties involved have a real fear or even abhorrence of getting together. Since polarization may be the key to retaining their power bases, the parties choose not to threaten them by attempting to reduce the conflicts. Some black/white issues become framed in just such terms (Klein, Thomas, & Bellis, 1971).

I have no objection to such bounded OD interventions, although lack of clarity about goals can lead to disillusionment or worse. Politically, moreover, the most that we probably can agree to is to disagree within certain limits and institutions. Perhaps there would be no politics if there were no opposed interests.

Guideline 17

A relaxed or flexible approach to confidentiality with members of the client system is useful. Rather than admonishing people to "keep this to yourself," the general contract can be: "If you tell me something, you will have to rely on my discretion as to whether and when I will mention it to others or allude to it." Generally, it is a good idea to get the involved people talking about the issues, and complete confidentiality does not help. Other ways of saying this are: "When an absolute confidence is required, which should be necessary only rarely, an explicit agreement should be made," or "What goes for me goes for you too, of course."

There are many norms about confidentiality. I believe that Drucker observed that "I never talk about my clients." For him, that no doubt works.

My experience at the politics/administration interface is contrary to this, however, for several reasons. First, "leaking" is a basic mode of political life. Contacts at the interface tend to regard substantial confidentiality with amused incredulity, and evidence of complete confidentiality is met with the awe reserved for those ascetics who shun strong drink, crude talk, fast women, big money, and (above all) power over others. Second, those at the politics/administration interface have been known to use confidentiality to control others. Third, substantial confidentiality can forfeit major opportunities to make a difference, particularly when systemic matters are at issue. Confidentiality is a simpler matter in other cases, such as when one acts as an adviser to a senior executive or when one acts as a sounding board against whom someone can toss his or her ideas or concerns for a disinterested reaction. Fourth, the OD intervenor need not devote much attention to fostering secrecy, distrust, or suspicion, which overuse of confidentiality can breed. Those will no doubt have been well attended to by masters at the craft.

In summary, both benefit and cost are inherent in a relaxed concept of confidentiality. Taking advantage of systemic opportunities strongly encourages running the inevitable risks.

Guideline 18

The media have all the trump cards at the interface, which massively distinguishes public-sector OD applications from counterparts in business. I know of no similar media firestorm in business, for example, like that induced by the OD application in the U.S. Department of State. I refer to dominantly useful features in our institutions and practices that may bedevil public OD applications. Although one cannot proclaim that the media may be harmful to the health of public-sector OD projects, it may well be true.

First, the media tend to condense and simplify in ways that separate action from context and focus on the dramatic moment in often tedious lines of development. At its best, this saves the time of media users and may dramatize some essential truth. At its worst, this tendency may distort reality and make grotesque what was benign or even beneficial.

Second, the OD intervenor typically will be limited in what seems reasonable to share with media personnel. One can always direct inquiring newspersons to responsible agency officials for responses to such questions as: "So what did you do to earn your fee that was so great?" On questions about OD techniques and philosophy, one can expound eloquently, but this makes boring copy and is rarely used.

Third, the media can serve as agents of rogues, for good or ill. The advantage is definitely with the rogue, who is often a source of "good copy." Some preposterous things have been written about several public programs because whatever X says is news, independent of its truth value.

Fourth, even though discretion by the overwhelming bulk of media personnel can be counted on, useful background or off-the-record exchanges often are impeded by concerns over what a small minority might do with information that could be shared but often is not. Since there is no way to exclude the latter newspersons, the former tend to be deprived as well. One public executive touched on an aspect of this issue in distinguishing media stars and nonstars (Bower, 1977, p. 136): ". . . a star is interested in . . . looking very good. The way that he's going to look good is, usually, to make you look bad. . . . Other reporters, probably the vast majority, really seem to be interested in what is going on."

Fifth, newspersons may have various personal and philosophical issues with OD at the interface, centering around the efficacy of zesty conflict in connection with public matters, although successful OD interventions may reduce the gross amount of overt conflict as individuals or groups order their priorities, reduce the interpersonal garbage in their interactions and begin to cooperate. The elimination of conflict per se is not a particular goal of the kind of OD interventions I prescribe at the politics/administration interface, however. Indeed, it is ironic that, especially in the early stages, an OD intervenor frequently will be accused of "creating conflict where none existed."

Guideline 19

Finally, and perhaps paramountly, intervenors should try to focus on what they accomplish rather than on how long it takes. This is usually good advice although it can be hard to take for many reasons: lack of knowledge, lack of courage, need for fees, etc. But nowhere is the advice more appropriate than in the public sector. Opportunities may come quickly, but they can also disappear mercurially. Few public officials can give a clear go-ahead on anything, but numerous veto-centers exist.

REFERENCES

Alsop, S. Let the poor old foreign service alone. *Saturday Evening Post*, June 1966, p. 14.

Argyris, C. *Behind the front page*. San Francisco: Jossey-Bass, 1974.

Argyris, C., & Schon, D. A. *Theory in practice*. San Francisco: Jossey-Bass, 1974.

Bower, J. L. Effective public management. *Harvard Business Review*, March 1977, 55, 131-140.

Golembiewski, R. T. Organization development in public agencies. *Public Administrative Review*, July 1969, 29, 367-377.

Golembiewski, R. T. *Renewing organizations*. Itasca, IL: F. E. Peacock, 1972.

Golembiewski, R. T. *Public administration as a developing discipline*. (Vols. I & II). New York: Dekker, 1977.

Golembiewski, R. T., & Eddy, W. *Organization development in public administration*. (Vols. I and II). New York: Dekker, 1978.

Heimovics, D. Personal communication, 1977.

Kaufman, H. *Administrative feedback*. Washington, DC: The Brookings Institution, 1973.

Klein, E. B., Thomas, C. S., & Bellis, E. C. When warring groups meet: The use of a group approach in police-black community relations. *Social Psychiatry*, 1971, 6(2), 93-99.

Le Baron, M. New perspectives toward more effective local elected councils and boards. Unpublished, 1977.

Mosher, F. *Democracy and the public service*. New York: Oxford University Press, 1968.

Reddin, W. J. Confessions of an organizational change agent. *Group & Organization Studies*, March 1977, 2(1), 33-41.

Rosenbloom, R. S. The *real* productivity crisis in government. *Harvard Business Review*, September 1973, 51, 156-164.

Schein, V. E. Political strategies for implementing organizational change. *Group & Organization Studies*, March 1977, 2(1), 42-48.

Shepard, H. Rules of thumb for change agents. *OD Practitioner*, November 1975, 1, 1-5.

Van Riper, P. P. *History of the United States Civil Service*. New York: Harper & Row, 1958.

Warwick, D. P. *A theory of public bureaucracy*. Cambridge, MA: Harvard University Press, 1975.

4

Organization Development in Bureaucracies: Some Caveats and Cautions

Leonard D. Goodstein

Bureaucracy is the most rapidly growing industry in the United States. Innumerable statistics support such a conclusion. For instance, from 1961 to 1975, the increase in the number of federal, state, and local government employees in the United States was more than double that in the private sector—70 percent compared to 27 percent. During that same period of time, the population of the country increased by 16 percent. While in 1961 there was one government worker for every twenty-one inhabitants, this had increased to one for every fourteen by 1975. There were a total of 8,750,704 government workers in 1961; that number had grown to 14,850,448 by 1975. Clearly government is a "growth industry."

While one's interpretation of this trend will depend to some extent on one's politics, there is no question that this burgeoning bureaucracy is seen as a fertile field for organization development, which is itself another growth industry. It is not surprising that organization development (OD) practitioners often regard this most rapidly increasing segment of the potential market as a reasonable arena in which to promote themselves and their profession.

But there appear to be some other reasons for this promotion of OD wares. No one seems to love either bureaucracy or bureaucrats, both of which are under continual attack, even by those who see the increase of government as both necessary and inevitable. Consequently, government agencies are interested in obtaining help to change both their images and their impact, and OD practitioners are eager to provide such help. So, while the coming together of these two expanding industries may be seen as inevitable, it is not a relationship made in Heaven.

There are a number of reports, both published and unpublished, of failures of OD interventions in the public sector (Glaser, 1977; Goodstein & Boyer, 1972; Marrow, 1974). While it is probably not possible to extract any generalizations about why these interventions failed, one may conclude that there are important systemic differences between private and public organizations—differences that are not well understood but that have critically important consequences for any interventions into these systems. At the beginning, one can note that most OD practitioners are trained in graduate schools of business and most of their early exposure is in the profit-making segment of our economy. Thus, most OD consultants begin to work with government agencies with no understanding of the substantial differences between the public and private sectors. The major focus of this paper is on the differences between the private and public sectors and the implications of these differences for OD consultants.

Although there have been several other attempts to address this issue (Eddy & Saunders, 1972; Golembiewski, 1969; Thompson, 1967; Warrick, 1976), most of these comparisons have been "laundry lists" of the perceived differences between the public and private sectors. The implications of these differences for OD practice have not been adequately spelled out. This is not surprising, however, since the intended audience of most of these published reports is public administrators rather than OD practitioners. This presentation is intended to be both more theoretical and more practical than any of the earlier attempts.

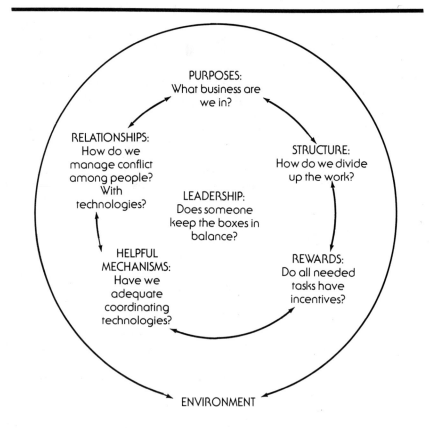

Figure 1. Weisbord's Six-Box Model

[1]Reproduced by permission of Marvin R. Weisbord and Organization Research and Development.

THE SIX-BOX MODEL

The Six-Box Model of organizational diagnosis developed by Weisbord (1976) provides a systematic analysis of the organizational differences between the public and private sectors. Weisbord's model identifies six interrelated processes that are inherent in all organizations. As can be seen in Figure 1, organizations exist in environments, and the interactions between any organization and its environment—particularly the management of the boundary conditions—need to be understood. In each of the six boxes two aspects require attention: the formal and the informal systems that operate within each. When we examine an organization's *purposes*, we must be concerned with both the formal goal clarity and the informal commitment to those goals. When we study *structure*, we need to be aware of the formal organizational chart and the informal ways in which work is actually accomplished (or not accomplished). The formal aspects of *relationships* involve who deals with whom on what issues, while the informal aspects involve the quality of those relationships. In examining an organization's *rewards* or incentive system, we must consider both the explicit system of salaries, wages, bonuses, and the like, and the more implicit rewards of how members of the organization emotionally respond to successful task accomplishment and how much support for achievement there is in the system. In the area of *leadership* we need to note both what the management responsibilities of the leaders are and how effectively they carry out these responsibilities. Finally, the formal aspects of *helpful mechanisms* involve the management information, budgeting, and planning functions of the organization while the informal aspects involve how well, if at all, these mechanisms are used. This Six-Box Model provides a useful overview of the critical components of organizational life. It is appropriate to examine each of these components on both the formal and informal levels in order to clarify the critical differences between organizations in the public and private sectors and how these differences can affect potential OD interventions.

Purposes

Making a profit is clearly the major purpose of private-sector organizations, and serving the public or "doing good works" is the less measurable goal of public-sector organizations. Because business and industrial organizations have serious problems with implementing and realizing their goals (e.g., short-term versus long-term marketing strategies, product quality versus marketing demands, environmental impact versus the need to use natural resources, etc.), the preoccupation of managers in the private sector with the "bottom line" reflects an absolute necessity. Accountability does exist, and failure to meet the criteria of profitability has obvious negative consequences.

On the other hand, there are no clear-cut criteria for "doing good works," and few, if any, public service organizations go bankrupt. Another critical difference is that public service organizations have built-in clientele and are thus excluded from considerations of marketplace competition. People use the local fire and police departments, send their children to the local school, and receive their mail from the local post office, or do without these services. Although there are a few exceptions to this rule, it is safe to conclude that not only do public service organizations have rather ambiguous goals but that these organizations do not have to deal with competition.

In public service organizations, the absence of clear goals is often obscured. While virtually all such organizations do have catch phrases that are presented as goals—quality education, modern health care, protecting public safety, and so on—when we attempt to operationalize these lofty ideals we learn that there is little or no agreement on whether "quality education" means teaching educational fundamentals or life adjustment or whether "modern health care" means treating illnesses and returning patients to the disease-producing environment or treating both the patient and the environment. Thus, there is little other than superficial agreement on goals or purposes in the public sector.

In one university medical-school faculty, there was a high degree of goal confusion with little consensus on how the goals of teaching medical students, meeting patient needs for treatment, and conducting research should be prioritized. Not only was there little agreement, but there was no forum through which these differences could be explored. Even more importantly, there was strong resistance on the part of this client system to open up this kind of dialogue.

As was suggested earlier, there are similar dilemmas in the private sector, as these organizations strive to clarify how profits can be made within a value framework. But one of the major differences between the public and private sectors is how these dilemmas are resolved. In the private sector there is vigorous confrontation between proponents of different positions and, more often than not, a genuine attempt to reach some agreement, even if it is only temporary. In the public sector, however, differences are rarely discussed, and whatever differences occasionally surface are quickly smothered "for the good of the organization." This illustrates the impossibility of any commitment, at least on a behavioral level, to the ambiguous and ill-defined norms that are typically found in the public sector.

There are at least two clear implications for OD in the public sector: first, that OD consultants will almost always need to help the client system to examine its goals carefully, both for clarity and commitment; and second, that the norms of most client systems will strongly interfere with such an examination. The OD consultant can expect recriminations for surfacing strong, apparently irreconcilable differences among members of the organization and for creating disharmony.

Another important difference in purpose between public- and private-sector organizations involves their *raison d'être:* the providing of human services rather than the creation of tangible products. While there are some service providers in the private sector, e.g., lawyers, physicians, and a few proprietary educational institutions, the public/private dichotomy closely fits the service/product one. This public-sector focus on human-services delivery produces some further differences.

First, there is a higher percentage of professional personnel involved with human-service delivery than with product production. Human services require a high proportion of such professionals. These professionals (teachers, lawyers, social workers, law-enforcement officers, and the like) maintain a dual loyalty— to their direct employers and to their professions, usually diluting the commitment to their employers. Further, professionals are bound by their specialized training, their codes of ethics, their guilds and associations. This often means that professionals are less dependent on the support of the employing organization and are less threatened by the sanctions that can be used by that organization. Their professional identification shields them against intrusions on their autonomy. All of this, of course, limits the commitment of professional personnel to the organization and its purpose. Similar organizational difficulties are experienced by private-sector organizations in which professionals deliver human services: group practice of medicine, private law firms, and so on. Many of these organizations have the same type of problems as public-sector organizations, even when there is clear agreement on the common goal of profitability. All of these examples indicate that the professional is *in* the organization, but not *of* it.

Second, producing a product requires a high degree of interdependence. It is not possible, ordinarily, for step four to be attempted before step three is completed. The paint cannot be applied until the surface is cleaned and primed. The production of practically any product requires such a "serial interdependence" (Thompson, 1967, p. 15). In contrast, there is much less interdependence in the public sector (in the provision of human services). The welfare client can receive medical care independently of food stamps; the college student can take English before or after taking psychology. This means that the people who provide human services can separate their functions, can feel that each has done a competent and effective job without worrying about what anyone else in the system is doing. Indeed, since many, if not most, of the others are equally well-trained and autonomous professionals, it would *not* be appropriate to inquire about their activities.

This professional autonomy and lack of functional interdependence in the public sector requires special consideration by OD practitioners. Such practitioners ordinarily expect more organizational commitment than they will find (or can produce), and they tend to see work as more interdependent than it is in the public sector. The OD consultant needs to know when the need for interdependence really exists—in setting a school curriculum, in setting work or performance standards, in establishing organizational objectives—but must not expect it in the day-to-day performance of tasks.

We noted earlier that organizations operate in a social environment and that the interface of the organization and the environment is particularly important. Nowhere is this more important than in human-service delivery systems, and the failure to have clearly articulated goals creates a lack of confidence by the public in these institutions. If there is a lack of clarity in what a welfare agency is supposed to accomplish, it is difficult for the public to trust or value such an agency. The failure of human-service organizations such as schools, hospitals and clinics, child care institutions, and so on to be clear about their purposes—both in their formal policy statements and in the way they actually provide service—erodes public confidence and precludes strong public support. The lack of any need to compete for clientele can make such organizations blind to their alienation from the public they are supposed to serve. Such organizations rarely solicit and process feedback from their consumers. One aspect of a consultant's task in working with such organizations, therefore, is to focus on the need for such feedback in order to help the organization focus on its need for greater clarity of purpose, especially on a behavioral level.

Structure

In all organizations tasks are differentiated in order to facilitate their accomplishment. Regardless of whether structures are based on a function, a project, or some combination of function and task, there needs to be some integration of the structure in order to accomplish the work of the organization. Here again, the lack of intrinsic interdependence of the tasks to be accomplished in the delivery of human services makes such integration difficult to accomplish.

Attempts to produce greater interaction or interdependence in the public sector will be further impeded by the heavily bureaucratic nature of these organizations. Bureaucracy was initially established to improve organizational effectiveness through the creation of a rational and impersonal system managed by permanent, professional, competent officials selected according to their merits. However, abuses of the system have made "bureaucracy" and "bureaucrats" invidious words. From an intended basis of efficiency, rationality, pyramidal authority, the separation of functional units on the basis of mission, and a system of rule and procedures to control and direct the behavior of the organization (Eddy & Saunders, 1972; Weber, 1947), bureaucracy has come to represent waste and inefficiency. The structures have become so codified that they are very difficult to change. The nature of the task to be performed in the public sector has dramatically changed from routine clerical and administrative chores to the delivery of sophisticated and complex services. The task environment is now often chaotic, and the need is for warmth, compassion, flexibility, tolerance, and risk taking, not for the old virtues of rationality and impersonality.

As organizations in the public sector become more and more involved in human-service delivery of a modern sort, especially as the tasks involved become less routine, there will be greater public dissatisfaction with these organizations. Indeed, as these changes occur, members of these organizations will themselves become increasingly dissatisfied with their organization and how it operates. Unfortunately, however, the most likely response to such dissatisfaction, from either external or internal sources, is to propose to modify the structure—to reorganize. The most useful thing that an OD consultant can do under these circumstances is to attempt to focus the attention of members of the organization on the systemic issues—on the lack of clarity of purpose, on the bureaucratic norms that regard the way things are done as more important than the consequences of what is done, on reducing the negative sanctions for risk taking, and so on—rather than on reorganization.

This is not to suggest that restructuring the organization may not be an important step in making it more effective, but to be effective, reorganization must include solution of the issues that lie at the root of the organizational difficulties. Yet a strong norm exists in bureaucratic organizations to reorganize rather than to confront difficult issues (reorganization provides a convenient excuse for the organization's difficulties). Further, since there often are limits on what changes public-sector organizations can undergo, OD consultants working with such organizations need considerable patience and understanding, especially if they are used to the greater flexibility of the private sector.

For example, in one mental-health agency, there was much uncertainty about the role of the agency: whether it should be concerned with direct treatment, with consulting to the schools, with training of paraprofessionals, and so on. The executive director was clearly an incompetent manager and spent most of his time away from the agency. The sixty-member board of directors had little or no idea that there were any real problems confronting the agency, since a clique of mental-health professionals on the board controlled the information flow. In a three-year period, the agency had been drastically reorganized seven times. This resulted in role confusion and a serious morale problem among the staff members. Obviously, reorganization had not solved the real problems that were affecting the agency.

There is at least one other important difference in structure between organizations in the private and public sectors. In the private sector, different functional activities (e.g., manufacturing, research and development, the assembly of various subunits) are assigned to different units that were created for the accomplishment of that purpose. When it appears that the task assigned to a particular organizational component is too complex or involves too many different functions or responsibilities, the organizational unit involved is reorganized or restructured in order to provide greater role clarity and, hopefully, greater goal commitment. In the public sector, however, such clear task differentiation is rare.

There are several reasons why public-sector organizations cannot organize themselves quite so neatly into task-differentiated units. The first and perhaps the most important reason is that the human services that such organizations provide are not neatly distinguishable, as are the tasks involved in the creation of tangible products. Also, since there is little interdependence in the delivery of human services, there is a temptation for each of the organizational subunits in human-service agencies to attempt to "own" the client and not to put the client in touch with other parts of the system. In human-service delivery systems—particularly those that are highly professional—there are a number of functions that are deemed necessary to the structure, some of which are overlapping and some of which are in conflict. For example, university academic departments are supposed both to teach and to conduct research. Teaching at both the graduate and undergraduate levels is carried out by the same department, even though these functions are often in conflict. Most human-service systems that are run by professionals such as physicians, lawyers, social workers, and teachers have several different purposes, and individual members of the organization are expected to accomplish these multiple purposes in a single organizational structure. Again, in this instance, we note the interactive nature of organizational structure and purpose. The OD consultant needs to be aware of these structural confusions, since they are very much a part of the organizational philosophy of public service organizations and do not appear to be readily alterable.

Relationships

There are three kinds of *relationships* that can be examined in the third of Weisbord's six boxes: (a) interpersonal, between the various members of the organization; (b) intergroup, between the various subgroups of the organization; and (c) interactive, between the workers and the technology or between the people and the system or the equipment. In bureaucracies there tends to be little in the way of equipment; thus, interactive relationships usually are more important in production-oriented organizations in the private sector.

In the human-service systems that predominate in the public sector, there is a strong norm that conflict is "bad" and that professional people ought to be able to "get along." In practice, this means that differences between people and between groups rarely surface, and conflict is managed by denial and compromise rather than by confrontation or the acceptance and working out of differences.

One of the most important reasons that this style of managing differences is not more damaging than it is stems from the low interdependence of human-service organizations. What appears to happen is that those organizational issues that require real collaboration—such as long-term planning—are either poorly done or not even attempted. Sweeping differences "under the rug" seems to have little impact on the day-to-day effectiveness of these public-sector agencies.

Perhaps the most serious consequence for the OD consultant of this style of conflict management is when a team-building intervention is attempted, particularly when a low-structure T-group is used. In such cases, much interpersonal anger can be surfaced. It is usually interpreted as having little to do with organizational issues, and the raw wounds created by such a process heal slowly, with a net decrease in organizational effectiveness. The OD consultant in these cases is usually judged to be less than helpful, and there is great wariness about future consultation.

Instead, as is suggested by Beckhard (1972), the focus of such team-building activities should be (a) on the clarification of the organization's purpose and priorities, (b) on the way that work is accomplished in the organization, and (c) on the processes used by the group in setting norms, making decisions, and so on. The examination of the interpersonal relationships among members of the organization should be given very low priority in the design of the team-building process.

Interpersonal processes may be of low priority in *any* team-building intervention, but these processes are of *least* concern in the public-sector bureaucracies, given the low interdependence of their organizational teams. In these bureaucracies there is, however, a great need for organization members to voice their differences about what the organization is and should be, in some fairly concrete terms. Clearly, the nature of team work is an important difference between the public and private sectors and is one that has not been addressed adequately in the OD literature.

Rewards

How the organization rewards its members, both on the formal structural level and on the informal personal level, is the concern of the fourth of the six boxes in Figure 1. In a recent newspaper article, W. Michael Blumenthal, the Secretary of the Treasury, comments: "The personnel policies and practices could not be more different. . . . In the corporate world of today, managers are judged by how well they make use of the resources which they have been given. . . . But in government, success is too often measured by how many resources are at one's disposal, instead of how well they are managed" (*Arizona Republic*, September 25, 1977, p. A6). To paraphrase the Secretary's major argument, rewards come to those managers in the public sector who can build major empires without too much regard for how well the empire is managed, while the smaller, better managed empire is well rewarded in the private sector.

Although this point can be overstated, many civil-service regulations require major supervisory responsibility for the attainment of most of the senior grade levels. The number of people whom one supervises determines one's grade level and salary, not the quality of one's supervision. Bureaucracy is not even consistent in this respect, however. At several universities with which I am familiar, departmental secretaries are lower in status, grade, and salary than are college secretaries, even when the college is smaller than the department. Thus, the secretary of the College of Pharmacy (with a faculty of fourteen) can have the title of Administrative Assistant II while the secretary of the Department of Psychology, with thirty-seven faculty members, can be classed only as a Secretary II, with a salary difference of almost $2,000 per year. The bureaucratic model followed rather slavishly in the public sector rewards scope of responsibility rather than quality of work, seniority rather than innovation, conflict avoidance rather than confrontation, low-profile compliance rather than risk-taking, and the putting in of time rather than task accomplishment. While these norms have some similarity to the norms of the industrial sector—particularly on the assembly line—they are not formally articulated in the rules and regulations of that system.

These structural controls are supported by the informal norms of the public sector. One must be at one's desk by 8:00 a.m., so one is there. But the first order of business is reading the daily paper and drinking a second (or third) cup of coffee. The horse can be brought to the water but cannot be made to work. These informal norms are well known in the adult world, and one wonders about the people who voluntarily choose an old-line public agency, with such coercive norms, as their place of employment. There clearly must be some initial match between person and organization, even if we grant substantial influence to the socialization process that occurs during the beginning phase of working in an institution.

The implications of these differences in reward systems are quite important for organization development. Any change will come slowly, the norms will interfere with risk taking, work sessions that involve unusual time periods—weekends, evenings, or whatever—will be resisted, and the consultant needs to recognize and understand these issues if he or she is to achieve effective entry and effective impact on this system. Again, the watchword seems to be patience.

Leadership

The task of leadership, the fifth of the six boxes in Figure 1, is to monitor the operations of the other five boxes and to keep these other functions in harmonious balance. Successful leaders are aware of failures or potential failure in each of the other five boxes, on both the formal and informal levels, and they attempt to solve such problems as soon as they become apparent. However, organizational norms in the public sector conspire against effective leadership behavior.

Golembiewski (1969) has identified several such norms. One is the tendency of managers in the public sector to fail to delegate but rather to maximize information and control at the top levels. This produces an overload of both information and decision making that precludes any monitoring of the agency for organizational effectiveness. Further, there is a layering of multiple levels of managerial review, which tends to centralize power in public agencies and to prevent innovation and self-direction. At the level of middle management, innovation is not part of the job description, and at the top, the managers are simply too overwhelmed by day-to-day issues.

Another important element is that more specific rules and regulations surround appropriate and inappropriate work behavior in the public sector. The roles are more carefully spelled out, and there is less possibility that these can be changed by a manager, even a dynamic and well-intentioned one.

The interface between civil-service career employees and politically appointed or elected public officials constitutes another difference that is of major importance. In almost all public agencies the top layer of management—the mayors, the commissioners, the departmental secretaries in the federal departments, and so on—are elected or appointed, frequently on platforms of reducing or controlling the entrenched bureaucracy. As soon as these officials take office, they find that they must interact with career public employees—the "faceless bureaucrats" they promised to control. These career people are the only ones who know the system, who understand what needs to be done, and they serve to initiate the politicians into the system. Although a politician's entry into the system may be made with reformer zeal, the grizzled veterans of the bureaucracy know that they have both the keys to the executive washroom *and* the staying power to last out this latest intrusion. Indeed, many of these career veterans see their primary task as buffering the organization from the succeeding waves of elected or appointed reformers, i.e., not participating in any change. The net impact of this buffering on leadership, especially on leadership for change, is hardly ever positive.

Still another problem involves the several different constituencies to which leaders in the public sector must respond. Managers in the public area must respond to elected officials—presidents, governors, mayors, and the like—who regard themselves as responsible for public agencies in some overall sense. These managers are also responsible to the legislative branch, the Congress, and state and local legislatures that fund the agency and pass enabling legislation. Similarly, they are responsible to the judiciary branch, which reviews and monitors the actions taken by the agency. In addition to these there are also special interest groups, such as professional associations of teachers, physicians, and the like, that attempt to influence agency policies. There are the lobbyists for manufacturers, consumers, and so on, who attempt to make certain that the interests of their clients are protected. Finally, the news media monitors the work of public agencies much more carefully than those of private organizations, and they are usually determined to point out bureaucratic waste and inefficiency.

The implications of such surveillance on public agencies is clear. Extreme caution and a strong norm to protect oneself quickly become necessary defenses to such multiple pressures. For any consultant who might enter such a system, it means doing business in a fishbowl. The account by Alfred Marrow (1974) of efforts to work with the United States Department of State is but one illustration of how these pressures affect consultants and their efforts.

Helpful Mechanisms

The last of Weisbord's six boxes depicts those formal and informal devices that facilitate intraorganizational understanding and serve to bind the organization together. On the formal level the helpful mechanisms are planning, budgeting, control, and measurement. These rarely exist in a meaningful fashion in the public sector, especially on the operating level. While public organizations may attempt to plan, budget, control, and measure, such functions are ordinarily politically, rather than rationally, determined. Most managers, certainly at the middle levels of public agencies, rarely take such tasks seriously, since they have learned long ago that their plans, budgets, and forecasts have little impact on what actually happens. While one can write elaborate justifications for new programs, for budget modifications, or whatever, the public-sector budget typically is based on that for the last year, with a modest increase for inflation.

On the informal level, the helpful mechanisms include staff meetings, report and memo distribution, and informal get-togethers. In the public sector, there are a plethora of such mechanisms, but there is usually little sense of cohesive organization. Rather, there appears to be a blizzard of paper, a surfeit of staff meetings, and mandatory and highly structured interactions. There is little in these activities to give the participants a sense of really sharing in the shaping of the organization. Thus, neither the operating managers nor the workers really feel involved in the work of planning the direction of the agency, and there is little sense of clarity or commitment to the organization and its goals. At this point, we have returned to the first of the six boxes.

From this discussion there seem to be clear implications for the organizational consultant. What is needed is not attention to improving or adding helpful mechanisms; rather, the critical need is to sharpen the focus on organizational goals and to determine the degree to which some planning is possible, usually within sharply circumscribed limits. The question that needs to be asked is what we can do with what we have, rather than what we could do with greater resources.

SUMMARY AND CONCLUSIONS

The increase in bureaucracy, together with the clear need to increase the organizational effectiveness of the agencies that affect all our lives, make the public sector appear to be an attractive area in which OD consultants can ply their trade. There are, however, some critically important differences between organizations in the public and private sectors—differences that are all too often not clear to OD consultants (particularly to those whose work has been primarily in business and industry) and that doom to failure the kind of interventions that are typically attempted in the private sector.

In describing Weisbord's Six-Box Model for understanding organizations, we have pointed out that public-sector organizations have far less clarity of purpose and much less commitment to organizational goals. The structure of public agencies tends to be more compartmentalized, hierarchical, and rigid than that in profit-making organizations. But because there is less task interdependence, the nature of these structures tends to interfere less with task accomplishment. The relationships among both individuals and subunits are more remote and structured; conflict is managed primarily by avoidance, smothering, or compromise; rewards are given for compliance rather than for accomplishment; and there is little risk taking. Leadership is more authoritarian, with built-in issues at the interface between political and career managers. There is little use of helpful mechanisms at both the formal and informal levels.

These facts raise several implications for OD consultants. Goal clarification and organizational commitment need to be the focus of team-building activities, rather than the traditional examination of interpersonal and intergroup issues. The relationships between the political and professional managers are important but highly volatile problems to explore. Working with public agencies requires greater patience on the part of the consultant because of the reluctance both of individuals to be open and of the system to change. Working with public agencies exposes the consultant to the harsh light of public scrutiny and attack. But the OD consultant who can demonstrate his or her understanding of the public sector, who can be both determined and patient, and who can tackle manageable issues without attempting to change the entire system can be extremely helpful to agencies and other organizations in the public sector.

REFERENCES

Beckhard, R. Optimizing team-building efforts. *Journal of Contemporary Business*, 1972, *1*, 23-32.

Eddy, W. B., & Saunders, R. J. Applied behavioral science in urban administrative/political systems. *Public Administration Review*, 1972, *32*, 11-16.

Glaser, E. M. Facilitation of knowledge utilization by institutions for child development. *Journal of Applied Behavioral Science*, 1977, *13*, 89-109.

Golembiewski, R. T. Organizational development in public agencies: Perspectives on theory and practice. *Public Administration Review*, 1969, *29*, 367-378.

Goodstein, L. D., & Boyer, R. K. Crisis intervention in a municipal agency: A conceptual case history. *Journal of Applied Behavioral Science*, 1972, 8, 318-340.

Marrow, A. J. *Making waves in Foggy Bottom*. Washington, DC: NTL Institute for Applied Behavioral Science, 1974.

Thompson, J. D. *Organizations in action*. New York: McGraw-Hill, 1967.

Warrick, D. D. Applying OD to the public sector. *Public Personnel Management*, 1976, 5, 186-190.

Weber, M. [*The theory of social and economic organization*] (A. M. Henderson & T. Parsons, trans.). New York: Oxford University Press, 1947.

Weisbord, M. R. Organizational diagnosis: Six places to look for trouble with or without a theory. *Group & Organization Studies*, 1976, 1, 430-447.

5

Perspectives on the Marginality
of the Consultant's Role

Newton Margulies

Attempts have been made over the past several years to develop guidelines and sets of behavioral criteria to improve both the practice of consultation and its conceptual models. For the most part, these guidelines and criteria represent various polarized views of the consultative process and of the consulting role. This paper presents a conceptual approach to consultation that may help consulting practice to move away from the polar positions now common.

TRADITIONS IN CONSULTING PRACTICE

Ornstein (1972) developed the idea of a two-sided person—*rational* and *intuitive*. The rational side encompasses analytical, verbal, problem-solving, linear thinking, reflected in much of our scientific and industrial development and, indeed, in the learning processes that dominate many of our educational institutions. The other, more intuitive side emphasizes the nonverbal, emotional, more esoteric, and even mystical approaches to learning, knowing, and being. There is a growing awareness that each person has both major modes of consciousness available—one rational, analytical, and linear and one irrational, emotional, and intuitive. One current line of study attempts to achieve a balance between these two different but complementary modes. The literature in organizational behavior abounds with pleas for integration, connection, and mutual development, but theoretical models of many behavioral phenomena (e.g., leadership, managing, communicating) still reflect the coexistence of the poles and the maintenance of the poles as they are. Consultative models using the dichotomy suggested by Ornstein are also often presented.

Organizational consulting was developed from two primary traditions (Jacques, 1947; Margulies & Raia, 1968). The major objective of the first was to provide a *technical* service to the client system. The consultant using the technical consulting model is primarily concerned with bringing expertise to bear on a

---

An earlier version of this article, "Notes on the Marginality of the Consultant's Role," appeared in *Social Change*, Volume 7, November 4, 1977.

problem experienced by the client. The consultant's relationship with the client is viewed as incidental to the problem-solving process, and generally the client is reasonable for formulating a plan for the implementation of the proposed solutions.

The second approach, process consultation, is aimed at facilitating an organizational diagnosis of the internal and sometimes external processes that affect the organization's behavior and subsequent performance. This approach is closely linked to the field of organization development and is the central consulting mode employed by OD practitioners (Margulies, 1971).

The key to process consultation lies in the ability of the consultant to create an empathic and symbiotic relationship with the client. In fact, to some extent, the effectiveness of and/or satisfaction with the consulting projects undertaken is often attributed to the degree to which such a working relationship has been developed between client and consultant. Briefly, the best client-consultant relationship might be described as one in which there is considerable openness between client and consultant, mutuality of interest, shared responsibility for direction and outcomes of consulting projects, and ongoing feedback about activities and behaviors relevant to the consultant project.

Characteristics of Technical Consulting Model

The technical consulting model in some ways is similar to Ornstein's (1972) description of the functions of the left hemisphere of the brain, which connects to the right side of the body and is predominately involved with the analytical, logical, thinking processes. The left side operates in linear fashion, sequentially dealing with data and sequentially following the problem-solving process. This mode may be thought of as the essence of the scientific process, in which order and logic prevail. The technical consulting model may be identified by the following characteristics: (a) focus on a specific organizational problem; (b) sequential data collection and analysis; (c) utilization of a problem-solving process that incorporates a series of sequential steps; (d) establishment of logical cause-and-effect relationships; and (e) emphasis on planning and future orientation.

These characteristics are remarkably similar to those described by Ornstein as the prevailing dimensions of the left brain hemisphere.

Characteristics of Process Consulting Model

The right brain hemisphere, which controls the left part of the body, is generally involved with processes that are described as feeling or emotion oriented, spatially rather than time oriented, and holistic and Gestalt oriented rather than sequentially oriented. Process-oriented consultation also is quite similar to Ornstein's analysis. The process model involves the following: (a) focus on the processes of the organization; (b) more orientation toward the human dimensions of organizational life; (c) present orientation; (d) focus on "helping" rather than specific technical expertise; and (e) more appreciation for the intuitive and little emphasis on logical or analytical approaches.

Interestingly enough, organization development, from which the consulting model has emerged, began as a holistic, basically intuitive process with major emphasis on the emotional, perceptual dimensions of organizational life. The approach was much needed in organizations in which the emphasis was much more on the analytical, logical, problem-solving processes. It has been suggested that because society values the latter dimensions more than the holistic, emotional dimensions, they are most cultivated and rewarded by the educational institutions and thus by most other organizations. The inception and popularity of organization development is not surprising. Organization development seemed to fill an important need or replace a missing ingredient. Organizations, being predominately task oriented, linear, and analytical, were aware of an imbalance in their organizational and managerial processes deriving from the lack of emphasis on right-hemisphere functions, an emphasis supplied by the organization development approach of the 1960s.

Because of a preoccupation with respectability and acceptance, however, OD practitioners have tended to emphasize the analytical, logical, linear aspects of the field and to neglect the intuitive, holistic aspects. Hence, even process consultation has developed its own technology, its own logical frameworks, its own sequential data gathering and processing, and its own logical problem-solving methodology. This causes the method to appeal both to the academic community and also to many managers who find their own methods to be more compatible with the left-hemisphere approach.

The role of the consultant is much more tenuous, much more *marginal*, and much more peripheral than is suggested by the process model; it is not nearly as distant, uninvolved, and task oriented as the technical model.

MARGINALITY AS A CHARACTERISTIC OF CONSULTANCY

The sociological concept of marginality (Gardner, 1945) refers to a person who is required to function in two or more groups for which norms, values, and goals differ. Sometimes the differences are not significant, and sometimes the differences are considerable and result in stressful situations for the individuals and the groups involved. Marginal roles are inherently stressful and anxiety producing (Lewin, 1951; Ziller et al., 1969).

Conceptually, the notion of marginality is not unlike what some social scientists have referred to as *boundary roles*. A person in a boundary role is related to one particular work unit but also belongs to another unit within the same organization or to another organization entirely. The importance of the boundary role is associated with the amount of time the boundary person spends with each unit as well as the *significance* of the contact between the boundary person and the organizational units.

Boundary roles are important both organizationally and psychologically. The consultant, although connected to the organization by his consulting role, is not a part of the organization. (This is obviously true only for external consultants; the boundary role is very complex in the case of internal consultants.) Psychologically, feelings, reactions, and ultimately behaviors utilized to cope with the difficulties of the boundary position can affect the performance of the consultant.

The contract-building phase of the consulting process involves more than establishing activities and conditions on which the consultant and the client agree. This phase establishes the boundary, which must be firm enough and clear enough that the integrity and the separateness of those operating at the boundary position are maintained. The boundary must, of course, also be permeable enough to permit transactions, inputs, and changes to occur between the consultant and the client system.

Boundary Functions

The Activities Boundary. Only one clearly specified set of activities can be called consultative, but the client may confuse these with other activities. The client may ask the consultant to perform certain activities that should be done by the client or that at least are not within the consultant's realm. For example, in a case in which "homework" is required of the team members prior to a team-building session, the manager may want the consultant to inform the team members of the importance of the homework and of the necessity to complete it prior to the team meeting. This is usually not the consultant's responsibility.

Membership Boundary. The external consultant is not an organization member; even an internal consultant must maintain a membership boundary, although the boundary is much more vague for internal people because they depend on salaries or rewards. In either case, the psychological distance between client and consultant is very important.

Model Boundary. Resorting to either the technical or the process model removes the consultant from the boundary. If he or she maintains a position on the boundary between the two, the consultant may utilize appropriate functions from each model. However, boundary positions, because of their inherent marginality, tend to generate considerable stress, tension, and personal conflict. These phenomena are of particular interest for consultants because the strategies used to resolve stress and tension can have a major impact on how effective the consultant is.

The consultant is continually faced with stress and ambiguity (Cotton, 1977). For the most part, these conditions have been attributed to the complexity and difficulty of the consultant's *job* as a change agent. However, although it is true that the problems of change often are compounded by the complexities of relationships, technologies, management processes, etc., the consultant's stress experience per se does not result from the situation or the processes of change but is inherent in the consultant's role because of the boundary position of the consultant, which by its nature is ambiguous, stressful, and tense. Traditionally, OD consultants have tended to overlook this reality and have focused on the nature of the consultant's skill, the inherent uncertainty of the change situation, or the complex situational variables—all basically external to the consultant. The stress and tension of the consultant's role are derived from the boundary position, and the suggested "principles of good consultation" try to alleviate the stress and tension by resolving the essential and existential dilemmas experienced at the boundary. The difficulty is, of course, that these dilemmas cannot be resolved through the application of models or principles but must be faced existentially by the person occupying the boundary position.

I feel that effective consultation is related to the consultant's ability to build marginal relationships and to stay on the fringe, rather than the consultant's ability to build close, sensitive, empathic relationships with clients or the consultant's ability to utilize his or her technical expertise. The behavioral dilemma for the consultant is first to find the fringe area for each of several dimensions and then to maintain the boundary relationship with the client rather than to assume any extreme or polar position. The use of polar positions (either process or technical models) is a way of avoiding or resolving personal dilemmas experienced in consulting. Although resorting to one pole or the other resolves the conflict, important characteristics represented by the other position may be ignored.

Existential Dilemmas of the Boundary

Both the process and the technical consultation models ignore the boundary notion and work toward resolution of the existential personal dilemmas by identifying and suggesting extreme behaviors for the consultant.

Consultants who are acutely aware of their personal experiences in the consultant's role face a number of dilemmas (personal conflicts) that must be resolved continually as consultant work progresses. An existential approach to these dilemmas would encourage the consultant to ask, "What dilemmas (or conflicts) do I experience now, and what might be an appropriate resolution so that I can behave effectively in my boundary role?" By using this approach, a consultant might learn to live with the dilemmas effectively rather than to avoid them.

The Involvement Dilemma. The technical OD model implies that the consultant takes the client's statement of the problem at face value and provides the client with a technical solution. There is little need for or emphasis on building client-consultant relationships; the consultant simply provides the best technical solution for the problem facing the client. The consultant remains detached. In the OD process model, on the other hand, the consultant works toward building an effective working relationship with a client, which is characterized by openness, confrontation, and involvement. The client and the consultant work together to promote solutions to problems and organizational growth.

Each model represents a different view of reality. The dangers in both are evident. Using a technical model, the consultant can become so detached from the client system that sensitivity to the client is lost. The client system's ability to use proposed solutions and to muster resources to solve identified problems, or even whether the consultant is working on the "right" problems, may not be addressed. Using a process model, on the other hand, may cause the consultant to be overly responsive to the client and more a part of the client system than not. The consultant's usefulness may diminish as he or she becomes enmeshed in the organization. If the consultant is seen more as an advocate than as a consultant, the consultant's role is additionally diminished. What neither of these models incorporates is the marginal role of the consultant, who is neither attached to nor a part of the system but in a boundary position.

The Responsibility Dilemma. Using the technical consulting model, the consultant develops a strategy to resolve the client's problem and generally leaves the implementation of such solutions to the client. The consultant who uses the process model stresses the importance of joint action between client and consultant; however, the consultant devotes a good deal of attention to creating client ownership of the change process as well as of the implementation phase. Each model provides an opposite view of required consultant behavior in relation to the ownership of problems and problem solutions. The consultant in a boundary position neither owns nor disowns the process and the project. The consultant assumes responsibility for certain aspects and insists that the client bear the major responsibility for others. The issue of ownership of the project is dealt with as the need arises, is examined, and is decided in light of particular steps, phases, or activities that must be accomplished. The consultant determines responsibility for specific change activities and for change in the client system. The most effective response is probably on the fringe—certain aspects of the responsibility fall into the client's realm and others fall into the consultant's. Because conflict is at the boundary between system and consultant, it must be faced and resolved there.

The Acceptance Dilemma. Another issue for a consultant on the boundary is personal acceptance. The consulting role can be lonely, especially at the boundary, where the consultant is neither in nor out. Two ways to resolve the dilemma are (a) to work for acceptance by the client system or (b) to assume a consultation stance with minimal contact on no personal relationship with the client so that the issue does not have to be faced. To stay on the boundary at a point at which acceptance is never totally achieved nor ever totally denied is a real challenge. The consultant is seen as an "outsider" who is becoming "one of the family."

The Problem with Contingency Approaches

Polar models are simply abstractions of reality, useful for descriptive purposes, but rather narrow from the point of view of practice. Basically, contingency theories have incorporated the fact that situational variables, to a large extent, determine the appropriateness of the model employed. In some cases, contingency approaches also take into account the fact that the characteristics and skills of the individual manager or leader will in part determine the particular behavioral model that is apt to be most effective. In essence, contingency models are *alternating* models; as the situational variables change, the individual simply employs the appropriate model. This approach is used in the areas of leadership, management, and organization, as well as consulting.

The steps in the contingency approach are as follows:

1. Identify the models that encompass the behavioral phenomenon (e.g., leadership, consulting). Presumably these models are inclusive and cover all situations and the subsequent behavior.

2. Identify the factors that influence the choice of a particular model.
3. Assess these factors and choose the appropriate model for the appropriate situation.

Because contingency approaches emphasize alternating styles or behaviors, depending on situational factors, these approaches tend to stress extreme examples of the desired behavior. Another dimension of the contingency approach could be a decision about whether or not to adopt a marginal role, but because any other role is not optimally effective, the decision must be to adopt one. Some approaches, most notably the Tannenbaum and Schmidt Leadership Model (1958), emphasize variations of the general contingency approach by suggesting possible mixtures of the polar situations, but the result, once again, is the development of several models, distinct in nature, to be employed under certain conditions. What is often ignored is the *simultaneous existence* or *complementarity* of the polar positions and the need to integrate them at the boundary.

Staying at the Boundary: Toward Simultaneous Complementarity

Effective behavior in a marginal or boundary role is difficult for two reasons. First, there is the tendency to develop and use polar models to relieve the consultant from the dilemmas of the boundary position. This tendency may be analogous to the physiological reality of the left and right brain hemispheres, but, nevertheless, the preference for one mode over the other detracts from each situation and from effective creative consulting.

Second, it is difficult to recognize the *complementary functions* of the technical and process models and to develop an integrative rather than an alternating approach to them. How to stay on the boundary and how to develop a simultaneous-complementarity approach are difficult questions with no clear-cut answers. Some suggestions for consultants who wish to remain on the boundary follow.

Cultivate the Poles. The technical and process models imply certain sets of skills: rational, analytical, and theoretical on the one hand, and intuitive, emotional, and holistic on the other. Most consultants prefer one set of skills to the other and rely on those that are most familiar and comfortable. Being on the boundary requires a consultant to use and integrate both sets of skills.

Considerable theory has been developed, primarily in Gestalt therapy, that deals with polar opposites and the process of integration. Perls (1951) used the term "creative pre-commitment" to describe the situation in which an individual is poised *at* the "indifference point" of a continuum—aware of the situation but not yet committed to action on either side. Creative precommitment is not a state of indecisiveness but rather "a phase of orienting to diverse possibilities" and choosing the required characteristics of each polar position. Some consultants may experience difficulty and discomfort in situations that demand unfamiliar behavior. More creative consultation can surely emerge if consultants integrate aspects of the polar positions rather than retain a commitment to one particular consulting approach representing only one polar model.

Recognize and Appreciate the Polarity. Most consultants are committed to their own approaches and tend to be critical of other approaches. They may overuse theoretical skills to the point at which a strength becomes a weakness. Most training and educational programs for consultants emphasize the need for consultants to operate from their own frames of reference and to do what "feels right" from their own points of view. The fallacy is that consultants are likely to neglect other possibilities. Training that is integrative and that develops skills related to both models is necessary.

Be Aware of Complementarity. The consultant periodically must reassess his or her own strategy and approach to be sure that complementary features of the polar models are being employed. The most common error is to think that either the technical model or the process model is complete in itself. It is difficult but possible for a consultant to incorporate both models at one time.

Avoid Polarities as a Way to Solve Existential Dilemmas. The existential dilemmas of the consultant's role come with the job and must be faced and resolved again and again. Escaping the stress and conflict of the boundary role by resorting to a polar model may seem the easy way, but a consultant must continually reappraise strategies and approaches that are to be used, thus avoiding taking a polar position.

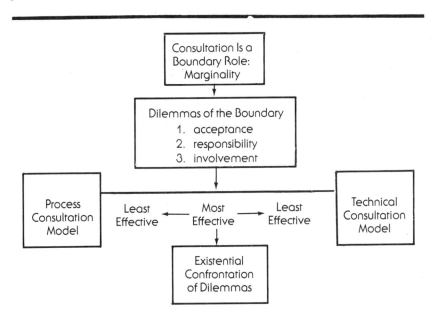

Creative Precommitment

Figure 1. Marginality and Consultant Effectiveness

SUMMARY

To summarize, the consultant's role (particularly that of the external consultant) is marginal, and the effective consultant operates at the boundary. When key consulting issues such as involvement, responsibility, and acceptance are resolved in ways that do not allow the consultant to operate on the boundary, the effectiveness of the consultant's role is diminished. Consultants must learn the personal and professional skills to resolve these consulting issues in ways that reinforce the boundary position.

Perhaps the traditional methods for developing the consultant's personal awareness and sensitivity are not enough. Gestalt therapy does offer a way to approach and integrate polarities, but Ornstein (1972) suggested even more radical approaches to personal education.

Individual development of "emotional muscle" to cope with the stresses, tensions, and conflicts of the boundary role is vitally important because, in a sense, the consultant at the boundary will always experience those *existential dilemmas* related to the role. Effective consulting is related to the consultant's ability to confront and resolve these dilemmas as they arise in each situation. Resolving these conflicts by adopting behavior that is exclusively at one pole or the other undermines the boundary role and creates a consulting mode that may be a distortion of the real demands of the situation.

The first step in the development of consulting behavior, which takes the need for both the technical and process aspects of consultation into account, is understanding the two polar positions thoroughly. This approach is different from the "usual" contingency model, which suggests that process and technical behaviors can be utilized alternately. A conceptual approach to consultation and the consulting role can be developed that views these behaviors as complementary. The result can be a more effective consultation process, a more flexible consulting style, and, perhaps most important, a consultant who is less apt to resort to only one style and is more apt to be responsive to needs of the client and demands of the situation.

REFERENCES

Cotton, C. C. Marginality—A neglected dimension in the design of work. *Academy of Management Review*, January 1977, 133-138.

Gardner, B. B., & Whyte, W. F. The man in the middle: Position and problems of the foreman. *Applied Anthropology*, 1945, 4(2), 1-28.

Jacques, E. Social therapy: Technocracy or collaboration? *Journal of Social Issues*, Spring 1947, 3, 59-66.

Lewin, K. *Field theory in social science*. New York: Harper and Row, 1951.

Margulies, N. Implementing organizational change through the use of internal consulting teams. *Training and Development Journal*, July 1971, 25, 26-33.

Margulies, N., & Raia, A. D. Action research and the consultative process. *Business Perspectives*, Fall 1968, 5, 26-30.

Ornstein, R. E. *The psychology of consciousness*. San Francisco: W. H. Freeman, 1972.

Perls, F., Hefferline, R. F., & Goodman, P. *Gestalt therapy*. New York: Delta, 1951.

Tannenbaum, R., & Schmidt, W. How to choose a leadership pattern. *Harvard Business Review*, March/April 1958, 36(2), 95-100.

Ziller, R. G., Stark, B. J., & Pruder, H. O. Marginality and integrative management positions. *Academy of Management Journal*, 1969, 12(4), 487-493.

6

Demise, Absorption, or Renewal for the Future of Organization Development

Noel M. Tichy

One OD practitioner said:

> Implications are that proactive, involved OD persons will be sought after. The accelerating pace of change demands people who are willing to make things happen even if it involves some personal risk.

Another took a counter point of view:

> Frankly, I don't see OD as a profession, and I think the movement in graduate schools and other places to make it a profession is doing more to foster an identity crisis than to build "change agents." The identity crisis is reflected in the following questions: "Well, what the hell is OD anyway? Who really can do it? Where do you really learn it?"

The two quotes reflect the ambivalence that currently exists in the field of organization development (OD). Building on data from interviews with experienced external and internal OD practitioners—many of whom are experiencing doubts about the field of OD—this chapter examines some of the future strategic options open to professionals in the field of OD. Both adaptive and maladaptive responses to self-doubt are presented. One adaptive response is strongly advocated; it proposes that OD professionals move vigorously into human-resource planning and system development. Such a move will require professionals to have a broader knowledge and skill base.

THE PHASES OF OD AS A PROFESSION

Pettigrew (1975) developed a model to explain the evolutionary phases experienced by specialist groups within an organization. This model was based on data collected from studies of both operations researchers and organization development practitioners in several large organizations. The model is summarized briefly below; it is the framework used for analyzing the growth of organization development as a profession.

Pettigrew's Model

The *conception phase* is the time when the profession first emerges. There is a great deal of innovative entreprenuerial activity by a small group, often by one or two key figures. This phase is followed by a *pioneering phase*, during which the profession develops rapidly, often taking on the aura of a religious movement with pioneering professionals portraying themselves as holding the "truth." Pettigrew points out that the overall style during this phase is "of a group of enthusiasts looking inward, concerning themselves with the short term, relentlessly pursuing a task to the exclusion of much of their environment." This eventually leads to problems with the environment, and the once-latent internal tensions between the "missionaries" and "pragmatists" become manifest. This tension, as well as pressure from the external environment, push the profession into a *phase of self-doubt.*

The self-doubt phase is characterized by the group's perception of environmental threats to its existence, causing individuals in the profession to question their own competence and self-esteem. The group begins to exhibit signs of internal conflict and bickering; there are anxieties about careers and a great deal of uncertainty about the future. There is often a crisis of leadership during this phase. A brief view of the OD field, in terms of these three phases of development, is presented below.

Phase I: Conception (Late 1950s to about 1963). The roots of OD clearly existed before the late 1950s, but it was at this point that such people as Herbert Shepard, Robert Blake, Jane Mouton, and Richard Beckhard began to call the consulting work they were doing with organizations "organization development." It was during this phase that these and other behavioral scientists began to move from T-groups to more organizationally focused training and development activities.

Phase II: Pioneering (1964 to about 1973). By late 1964, leadership began to emerge in the field, and a number of key training, consulting, and research projects were carried out in both businesses and schools and other service organizations. People such as Beckhard, Bennis, Schein, Miles, Lippitt, Blake and Mouton, and Shepard were working under the banner of OD. There was a missionary zeal coupled with a great deal of enthusiasm for these activities and a high *esprit de corps.* The mid- to late 1960s witnessed the development of the NTL Institute's Program for Specialists in Organization Development as well as the creation of graduate programs—such as the one at Case Western Reserve—that provided formal training in organization development. In addition, by the late 1960s many corporations had developed internal OD staffs and some had fairly substantial OD departments. By 1969 there was sufficient work in the field to support the Addison-Wesley series of books on OD. During this phase, people in OD straddled two streams. These two streams began in the 1950s; one focused on interpersonal relations and personal and humanistic psychology, and the other focused on organizations as systems, the change process, work, and structural change. By the late 1960s these streams became more differentiated, and OD became clearly identified with the second stream, even though it drew heavily on humanistic psychology, and individual practitioners moved from one stream to the other.

The mixture of these two streams in OD contributed to a phenomenon that Pettigrew identifies as the "single most pervasive source of tension" in the pioneering phase, the tension between the missionaries and the pragmatists. The pragmatists lined up along the system-change stream, while the missionaries ranged along the humanistic-psychology stream. Both groups focused inward.

An interesting indicator of the degree of inward focus on the part of OD professionals is evidenced in the leading books on OD written during this phase. These books ignore much of what behavioral scientists who did not identify themselves with OD were studying and applying in organizations. For example, French and Bell (1973) do not refer to the extensive work on motivation by Porter and Lawler or to work by Vroom on leadership or to work on organization design by James Thompson or Leonard Sayles. In 1975, Huse evidenced a greater awareness of the broader field of behavioral sciences, although one is struck by the narrower outlook on the behavioral sciences reflected in his book than in Porter, Lawler, and Hackman's *Behavior in Organizations*, published that same year. The point is that the field was exhibiting inward-looking behavior both in terms of utilization of relevant knowledge and in terms of a lack of collaboration with other types of behavioral scientists and management scientists.

Phase III: Self-Doubt (about 1973 to the present). Many factors probably have contributed to this phase. The general societal pessimism about social change brought about, in part, by the Nixon era—which ushered in the end of the War on Poverty and, hence, the end of Federal support for large-scale liberal social-change programs—coupled with a major economic recession, has contributed to a less receptive environment for OD-type activities. The result has been increased pressure within organizations on OD people, who had often been advocates of liberal change and had promised a better way of organizational life to prove themselves. This, in turn, exacerbated the conflict between the missionaries and the pragmatists in the OD field.

As early as 1972, self-doubt was in evidence. In a study of nineteen external OD consultants, over 50 percent were found to be in conflict between the goals they espoused for their work and the goals that they actually pursued. This value incongruence was substantially higher for OD-type consultants than for three other types (Tichy, 1974). Other reflections of the self-doubt phase are the assessments of the OD field done by both Friedlander and Burke in 1976.

One of the consequences of self-doubt is an increase in anxieties about one's career. Even though the field continued to grow early in this phase, many organizations that had created OD groups in the late 1960s were now cutting them back, moving them into other functions, or seriously questioning their utility. Many individuals in the field by the mid 1970s were facing a great deal of uncertainty and anxiety about the future of their careers.

A final indication that OD was in a self-doubt phase was the breakup of the leadership system. Through the early 1970s, the NTL Institute was the core association for most of the leadership of the OD field. However, the NTL Institute soon went through its own internal leadership struggles; these resulted in a splintering of the early OD leadership. At the same time, other organizations and institutions began actively to move into the field, carrying out competing professional training and development programs.

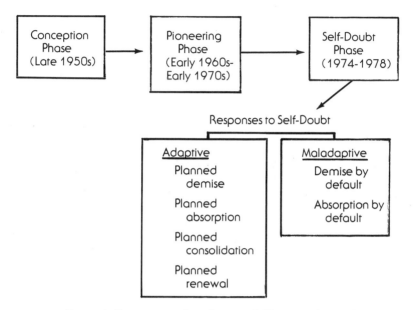

Figure 1. Organization Development's Phases of Growth[1]

Table 1. External OD Practitioner Respondents[2]

Name	Affiliation
Billie Alban	Private Consultant
Clayton Alderfer	University Professor
Chris Argyris	University Professor
Jerry Harvey	University Professor
Steven Iman	Private Consultant
Jay Lorsch	University Professor
William Morris	Private Consultant
Edgar Schein	University Professor
Stanley Seashore	University Professor
Fritz Steele	Private Consultant
Richard Walton	University Professor

[1]Adapted from Andrew Pettigrew, "Strategic Aspects of the Management Specialist Activity," in *Personnel Review*, Vol. 4, No. 1, 1975.

[2]Permission has been obtained from the respondents to list their names in the table.

RESULTS OF CHANGE-AGENT SURVEY

In 1976-1977 a follow-up study was conducted with the group of change agents (Table 1) originally studied five years earlier (Tichy 1974, 1976). One subgroup in this study was a group of organization development consultants. Eleven consultants were randomly selected from the 1971-72 sample of nineteen and were included in the 1976-1977 follow-up study. They were asked about changes in the way they thought about change and in their mode of operation during the past five years. In addition, they were asked about their visions of the future, both in terms of their personal professional activities and in terms of the field of OD in general. Table 1 lists the names of these change agents.

The same questions were asked of a group of eighteen internal OD practitioners (Table 2 identifies their organizational affiliations). These individuals were all participants in the Columbia Business School Advanced Program in Organization Development and Human Resources Management. Another data source is a study carried out by Brian Calvert (1977), in which he compared practitioners in the United States and the United Kingdom. The U.S. respondents were seventeen of the eighteen individuals whose organizational affiliations are identified in Table 2. The interview/questionnaire responses from these sources are used to support the argument that OD is in a phase of self-doubt and to explore some of the possible responses to self-doubt that individuals in the field could pursue.

Table 2. Internal OD Practitioner Respondents

Organizational Affiliations

Aluminum Company of America
American Telephone and Telegraph Company
Canadian Broadcasting Corporation
Citibank
Corning Glass Works
Episcopal Diocese
Ebasco Services, Inc.
Exxon Company, U.S.A. (2)
General Electric (2)
I.C.I. Organics Division
Olin Corporation
Procter and Gamble
Shell Oil Company
Sherwin Williams Co.
Signetics Corporation
Southern New England Telephone
Union Carbide
Department of Veterans Affairs (Canada)

Indicators of Self-Doubt

The responses presented in Tables 3 to 7 and discussed below reflect ambivalence, uncertainty, feelings of impotence, and conflicting views about important issues in the field.

Shifting Goals of OD. Table 3 presents the responses of the external practitioners to a question asking what the goals of a change agent *should* be. The one goal that shows a dramatic shift is "solve social problems"—from ten people in 1972 to only five in 1977. One interpretation of this is that the five who shifted may be reflecting some of the more general societal pessimism about the potential for positive, planned, social change. They may therefore have turned their energies away from the more lofty social aspirations reflected in their 1972 responses. Of more significance is the greater diversity of goal rankings in 1977. Not one goal received over six responses (ranking it as first, second, or third) in 1977.

Where the Organization Is Hurting. Brian Calvert's study of the participants in the Columbia University Advanced Program in Organization Development and Human Resource Management (the Table 2 sample) and of a sample of U.K.

Table 3. Ideal Goals of External OD Practitioners in 1972 and 1977

Goal	Numbers of respondents ranking goal first, second, or third	
	1972	1977
1. Promote technological development, research, innovation	4	1
2. Help insure individual freedom	2	3
3. Insure good human relations	2	3
4. Insure quality, low-priced products for profit	0	0
5. Increase democratic participation	4	5
6. Help organizational efficiency and productivity	7	6
7. Maximize growth and development	0	0
8. Solve social problems	10	5
9. Defend the system of free enterprise	0	0
10. Develop alternative systems	0	0
11. Help increase social and political power of lower levels	2	2

(n=12)

Table 4. Calvert's Study (What Hurts Your Organization Most at the Present Time)

United Kingdom

1. External factors; government pressures
2. The difficulty of managing an increasingly complex environment
3. The trend toward central control
4. Nothing very much
5. Inability to crack the people-productivity problem
6. Price controls
7. Value conflicts (e.g., redundancy)
8. Style conflicts
9. Loneliness among managers at the company center and an inability to know how to deal with such feelings
10. Time pressures on senior management
11. Lack of resources
12. Low confidence and trust between management and employees
13. Inhibiting effect of long time required for participation and communication
14. Negative attitudes about industry in the community
15. An inability to make better use of animate and inanimate assets
16. No consensus about the future and the ideology it contains
17. Living in an old, mature democracy that is breaking up
18. Highly able people unmotivated because of organizational insecurity and personal-life insecurity.
19. Poor system of government (central rather than federal)
20. Excessive control
21. Failure to recognize people's reality, rather than a conditioned response
22. Hundreds of years of running away from interdependence
23. A reward system that stabilizes undesirable and undesired values/behavior
24. People's insecurity about the survival need in a technologically dependent, scarce-resources area.

United States/Canada

1. Failure to understand motivations of people
2. Changing technology
3. Limited understanding of purpose of organization
4. Shift to multi-national corporations with inadequate integrating mechanisms
5. Time devoted to vertical and horizontal integration
6. Environmental pressures that are barriers to a program of finding and developing new energy sources
7. Rapidly changing environment and the import of government intervention
8. Lack of awareness about where the hurts are and options to remedy them
9. Economic cycle
10. National policy on telecommunications
11. Equal employment opportunity and minority groups
12. A perceived lack of a core mission
13. Environmental impact of tough regulations
14. Top-level need for centralized control
15. Arrogance (being told what to do)
16. Old-boy network
17. Lack of funds
18. Aging executive group

practitioners included an item asking respondents to indicate where they felt their organization "hurt" most. Several themes are apparent in Table 4. First, the "hurts" identified are quite deep and they link to serious societal problems. Items such as "economic cycle," "national policy on telecommunications," "lack of funds," "changing technology," "shift to multinational orientation," and "rapidly changing environment" are not problems for which traditional OD technologies of interpersonal dynamics, team building, and data-feedback approaches have much relevance. These issues strike at the core of organizational existence, whereas organization development has historically been applied at the middle of the organization to keep the gears greased and rolling. Second, as a consequence of the first theme, one might speculate that there is a latent theme reflected in the answers in Table 4. This theme is that of impotence. Many of these OD practitioners may feel this because of a lack of ability to deal with what they report as the most serious sources of organizational hurt. If such feelings of impotence exist, they also contribute to self-doubt.

It is interesting to note that almost all the respondents (92 percent of U.K. and 95 percent of U.S. respondents) in Brian Calvert's study rate "productivity" as a real rather than as a mythical issue. They even see themselves as more serious about it than they perceive managers to be (see Table 5). Again, OD literature, training, and practice have not been "bottom line" productivity oriented. This recognition by OD practitioners of the importance of productivity may also add to their self-doubt.

Finally, a more striking reason for expecting self-doubt is reflected in Table 6. Respondents in Calvert's study rated their organization's weakest process and also rated where they were intervening. There are some striking discrepancies that support findings from the earlier study (Tichy, 1974) that change agents often fall prey to the "little-boy-with-a-hammer" problem. Kaplan (1964) noted that "if you give a little boy a hammer he will find that everything needs pounding." Similarly, a consultant with a particular technique or approach will pound everything with it. Table 6 shows evidence of this. Only 6 percent of the U.S. respondents indicate that for their organization the weakest process is "problem solving, decision making, and action planning," yet 52 percent indicate that this is where they intervene most. On the other hand, 44 percent indicate that "superior-subordinate relations" are the weakest process, yet only 11 percent intervene most in this area. In other words, they are not intervening in areas that they report are in most need of help. Providing medicine for the wrong ailments, or not treating those areas most in need, cannot help but foster self-doubt.

Intervention Technology Shifts. One other piece of evidence supporting the self-doubt-phase argument is represented in Table 7, which shows how the external consultants shifted from 1972 to 1977 in their reported use of specific change technologies. These OD practitioners show a most dramatic decrease in the use of techniques in two areas: (a) sensitivity training, and (b) counseling, from ten users in 1972 to only three in 1977. Some techniques remained stable over this time; these are: decision-making structure, team development, survey feedback, interview feedback, and goal setting. These techniques, which appear to be the mainstay of OD, are in many cases hard to link to productivity and the major organizational hurts.

Table 5. Calvert's Study: Do Managers and OD Practitioners Regard Productivity as a Real Issue, a Myth, or a Resolved Issue

| | United Kingdom Respondents | | United States and Canadian Respondents | |
	Perceptions of Managers	OD Self-Rating	Perceptions of Managers	OD Self-Rating
A real issue	62	92	89	95
A myth	31	8	11	5
A resolved issue	7	0	0	0
	100%	100%	100%	100%
	(n = 13)		(n = 17)	

Table 6. Calvert's Study: Organization Processes in Which Respondents Most Often Intervene and the Organizational Process That Is Weakest

| | Weakest Process | | Process in Which Respondents Intervene Most | |
	United Kingdom	United States	United Kingdom	United States
Communication patterns, styles, and flows	0	11	0	13
Goal setting	0	6	4	11
Decision making, problem solving, action planning	0	6	38	52
Conflict resolution and management	18	11	33	5
Managing interface relations between groups and subsystems	73	22	25	8
Superior-subordinate relationships, leadership styles	9	44	0	11
	100%	100%	100%	100%
	(n=13)	(n=17)	(n=13)	(n=17)

Table 7. Organization Development Type's Use of Change Tactics:
Study I and Study II

Change Tactic	Number using technique Study I	Number using technique Study II	Number of changes from first to second study More	Less
Mass demonstrations	0	0	0	0
Confrontation	12	10	0	2
Decision-making involvement	11	11	1	1
Survey feedback	11	9	1	3
Interviews and feedback	11	10	1	2
Job training	5	2	1	4
Behavioral-science training	11	9	1	3
Executive search	6	3	0	3
Goal setting	11	10	1	2
Long-range planning	9	7	2	4
Action research	10	10	1	1
Sensitivity training	10	3	0	7
Counseling	11	3	0	7
Team development	12	11	0	1
Change authority structures	10	8	0	2
Change decision making	11	11	0	0
Technological innovations	7	5	0	2
Change in reward structures	8	8	2	2
Role clarification	12	8	–	4
Selection system	6	6	3	3

In summary, evidence for OD being in a self-doubt phase includes:

1. A goal shift by half the external OD consultants (no longer espousing that solving social problems should be a high-priority goal). In addition, the 1976-1977 goal ratings showed much diversity, with no goal being rated as important by more than six of the eleven respondents.
2. A large number of the major organizational "hurts" reported by internal OD practitioners were societally related and focused on the interface of organizations and their environments.
3. There was a poor match between what respondents indicated were the weakest areas in their organizations (implying those that were most in need of intervention) and those areas that they most often worked on to improve (applying medicine for minor ailments while the major ailments go untreated).

4. The lack of clear linkage of mainstay OD technology to both organizational productivity and major organizational hurts.

Responses to Self-Doubt

There are alternative ways out of the self-doubt phase. Six major ones will be considered for OD practitioners and the field of OD. They are divided into what Pettigrew defined as maladaptive and adaptive responses to self-doubt.

Maladaptive Responses to Self-Doubt. Pettigrew (1975) identified the characteristics of maladaptive responses to the self-doubt phase.

1. Reacting to the symptoms, e.g., selling OD harder, rather than diagnosing why organizations are disillusioned.
2. Withdrawing from the threat rather than confronting it, e.g., not actively engaging and confronting skeptical and attacking managers and behavioral scientists.
3. Living off existing capital rather than developing new capital. One sign of this is the paucity of cross-fertilization from other behavioral science and management science areas into the OD field; another is the lack of OD research and development activity being undertaken presently.
4. Developing singular plans rather than a number of contingencies. There appears to be little strategic contingency planning being carried out by the profession or by departments of OD in corporations.
5. Defensively stigmatizing and labeling the enemy. The enemy might be managers who just do not understand the importance of OD, other consultants who see OD as worthless, or factions within the OD field.

Two likely consequences of following these responses to self-doubt are (a) *demise by default*, in which the field would disappear because of lack of response to external threats and (b) *absorption by default*, in which various aspects of OD would be taken over by other functions within the organization or incorporated into other disciplines.

Adaptive Responses to Self-Doubt. Pettigrew (1975) provides an alternative scenario:

> If maladaptive responses are dominated by the psychological and system state of approach-avoidance, of evasion, adaptive responses are concerned with building processes and relationships whereby the causes of self-doubt and uncertainty are understood and confronted. Processes of adaptation recognize that the ways in which responses or strategies are formulated are as important as the appropriateness of the strategies themselves. . . . (p. 10)

The adaptive response is clearly to apply some of OD's own action-research medicine to itself as a profession. Self-doubt is a time of uncertainty and results in high anxiety and conflict. Managing this uncertainty in a diagnostic, problem-solving, and confronting way can increase the probability of OD responding in an adaptive way.

Four basic adaptive responses are discussed in this chapter:

1. *Planned demise*, in which the field plans its own death. It is conceivable that this could come about as an adaptive response if an assessment were made that the needs of organizations no longer call for the use of OD.
2. *Planned absorption*, in which OD theory and practice fold into other activities, such as human-resource management, corporate planning, systems design, or quality-of-work-life efforts.
3. *Consolidation*, in which OD activities are improved—in some cases merely fine tuned, in others completely overhauled—yet the scope and approach are basically left unchanged.
4. *Renewal*, in which a major overhaul of focus and approach is undertaken. The activities associated with OD could broaden and shift to new applications, resulting in new vigor to the field and the bringing in of new resources.

The Future of OD

Respondents in the study were asked to describe any personal changes that they felt would occur for themselves over the next several years and also to predict changes for the profession. The responses were divided into adaptive and maladaptive responses to self-doubt. For example, one respondent predicted that the field would "disappear and be absorbed into a total systems approach, and that furthermore it is not a profession because it is too disconnected from reality." This response was put into the "demise by default" category. The categorization of responses obviously reflects the author's subjective judgment and can be questioned. However, the categories provide a useful device for thinking about where a number of key practitioners in the field are personally headed and where they think the field is headed.

Some overall observations can be made from the study.

1. A great deal of variability exists among respondents. There are contradictory views; one respondent feels that the field will disappear; another feels that it is finally coming of age.
2. Human-resource management is a theme for many of the internal respondents, but is not mentioned by any of the external respondents.
3. Many individuals see their future moving in directions that are quite distinct, sometimes contrary to the field in general.

Examination of Strategic Alternatives for OD

Demise by Default. There are no responses for either internal or external practitioners that indicate that this will happen in the future. However, a number of predictions for the future of OD are included in the "demise by default" category. These include predictions about "no more internal OD people," "more marginal people," and the "dysfunctional professionalization of the field." If these predictions were to come true, there is a rather high probability that the field would fall into demise by default. My personal view is that this is a rather remote possibility.

Absorption by Default. Individuals reported personal futures that indicate a high potential for nonplanned absorption into other activities. For example, doing group work (and T-groups) is likely to result in isolation from the rest of the OD field and in eventual absorption by default into counseling or some related field. This is also true of the respondent who indicated evaluation research for his personal future. Several predictions about OD's future also indicate that bits and pieces of OD technology may be absorbed and used by other functions or disciplines while the field of OD slips away.

Planned Demise. None of the internal OD consultants are planning their own demise as OD practitioners. One external consultant has already done so, since, he declares, "the behavioral sciences are bankrupt." He also predicts the demise of what he calls the "lunatic fringe" and the "human relations types." Planned demise, however, is a very unlikely future for OD.

Planned Absorption. For the internal practitioners there are several avenues leading to planned absorption. One way is to become absorbed into line management. This may be through line managers who rotate in and out of OD assignments, through the promotion of OD people into line positions, or through the transfer of OD skills to managers. The result might be that OD disappears and becomes absorbed into management.

Another planned absorption is the moving of OD into human-resource management, and/or quality-of-work-life activities. The move to human-resource management would mean that OD would become more directly related to manpower-planning systems, incentive systems, employee benefits, and many of the traditional personnel functions. A move into quality-of-work-life activities would put OD into the industrial-relations field, since unions are actively involved in many quality-of-work-life ventures. Finally, another avenue for planned absorption is to move OD under the wing of equal employment opportunity-affirmative action concerns.

Planned Consolidation. The theme in this category is to pull together and strengthen specific aspects of OD. The internal practitioners report such options as work at higher levels, broader emphasis on systematic diagnosis, and systems thinking. The profession may be more valued by the line and the top management and clearer about its generalist and specialist competencies. Two of the external practitioners were planning to emphasize interorganizational work. In all cases, the individuals and the field would be building on existing competence and existing approaches.

Planned Renewal. There were only a few responses that seemed to reflect planned renewal, and these were both from internal practitioners. The personal thrust is toward such things as total system change, more proactive orientation, and quality of work life. For the field, there are several predictions that human-resource management and quality-of-work-life projects are going to be subsumed under OD. Two other themes about the future and planned renewal for the OD field emerged. These are (a) that it will become more directly tied to the mission of the organization and (b) that there will be better theory and higher quality people in the field.

A CHALLENGE FOR THE FUTURE OF OD

It is unlikely that OD practitioners will follow any one strategic alternative for the future. It may be that there is not even one dominant future strategy. I would, however, like to challenge the practitioners in the field to mobilize along each of the following avenues:

1. Strategic planning and organization design;
2. Line management; and
3. Personnel or human-resource management.

A Plan for Absorption and Renewal of OD

My survey of the terrain compels me to focus on the following elements of organizational topography:

1. The lack of linkage between human-resource-management systems with the mission of most complex organizations. For example, how does being in business to develop comprehensive communication systems relate to IBM's human-resource system? Very few organizations directly involve systematic human-resource-management considerations in strategic planning, and when they do, it is not generally done by the personnel, human-resource management, or organization development staff but by line management. The question is who should be providing the substantive input on human-resource management at the corporate strategy level.
2. Productivity concerns are real, yet they are dealt with only in a piecemeal fashion by OD practitioners. Who is providing the overall guidance with regard to productivity, and who should be?
3. Quality of work life is a catchword meaning a variety of programs in the work redesign and labor management area. Some OD practitioners appear to be along for the ride, yet the lead in this area is being taken by others. What should OD's involvement be with quality-of-work-life endeavors?
4. Pay and incentive systems are out of whack in much of the Western world. When Edward Lawler ran a session for advanced OD practitioners at the Columbia Program, it was surprising to discover that most of the OD practitioners present knew little about pay and incentive systems and considered them to be something that someone else in their corporation was concerned with. Given their importance in relation to motivation and human resources, one might ask why OD does not involve itself more with such critical change levers.

My view is that OD in general is largely tinkering at the margins. The organizational levers that it tends to pull are not the core, strategic ones. For example, many OD practitioners whom I have encountered talk about implementing and effectively operating complex matrix structures. This is done, however, after a strategic decision is made at the top of their organization to go with a matrix structure. The core strategic lever is not implementing the matrix but helping top management determine whether the structure is appropriate to the organization's strategy—an arena in which few OD practitioners find themselves equipped to operate. Other examples of OD performing a follow-up role are helping with the introduction of a new pay system, helping with the planning for a new plant opening, working on interdepartmental conflict without questioning the existence of the departments, or accepting the organization's mission without questioning how human-resource management is tied into it.

In order to move OD into the mainstream of organizational life, three avenues are presented as alternative routes.

1. *Planned absorption into strategic planning and organization design.* For some OD practitioners, being absorbed into the strategic-planning and organization-design functions of the organization may be a high-impact route. This means that the practitioner must be not only a process consultant to these activities but also a substantive expert. This avenue implies learning more about business policy, strategic decision making, and corporate planning.

2. *Planned absorption into line management.* Other OD practitioners may take the avenue of becoming line managers and attempt to have OD approaches absorbed in that fashion. The practice of rotating managers in and out of OD assignments is one organizational mechanism for accomplishing this. Incorporating OD skills in management-development programs is another approach.

3. *Planned absorption into human-resource management.* The final avenue is one that has the greatest potential for significant impact on organizations: to have OD absorbed into human-resource management. By human-resource management is meant all the employee-centered systems in the organization. They can be divided into the following categories:
   (a) manpower planning (forecasts, affirmative action planning);
   (b) selection and placement (recruitment, selection, placement, transfer, promotion);
   (c) reward systems (benefits, salary structure, extrinsic and intrinsic rewards);
   (d) performance evaluation and appraisal systems; and
   (e) development (training, rotation, counseling, career planning).

The goals of OD absorption into human-resource management are:

1. To begin more explicit and carefully conceptualized linkage between human-resource management and corporate-level strategic planning.

2. To develop integrated human-resource-management systems that are grounded in behavioral-science theory and knowledge regarding human motivation and organizational behavior.

3. To develop organizational capacity for personal and organization development.

Ironically, to accomplish these goals means that OD, which in many organizations struggled for years to dissassociate itself from personnel, will have to come home to roost. Personnel, or what some organizations are changing to human-resource management, is increasingly becoming the area where a great deal of corporate strategic action is taking place. To a large extent this is because of external factors such as those listed by one of our internal OD practitioners:

1. The need to cope with limits to growth in the industrialized world;
2. An increased emphasis on human values;
3. High pressure for productivity;
4. A highly educated (probably overeducated) work force;
5. The European emphasis on industrial democracy;
6. World interdependence.

Organizational survival is tied directly to more sophisticated human-resource management in the future. It is currently being undermanaged in most large corporations. No one group—personnel, line management, or OD—has successfully undertaken the immensely complex task.

The potential for impacting organizational life and effectiveness through strategic human-resource management is considerable. The major avenue for this is through personnel. To underscore the potential for impact, consider for a moment the numbers involved. There are about 1500 members of the OD Network operating in from 600 to 1000 organizations. This is minimal when one considers that there are over 300,000 corporations in this country, about 100,000 of which have personnel departments. These personnel departments will, by default, be defining human-resource management in most corporations. There is an opportunity for OD to move in and either be absorbed or take over. I propose absorption and, at the same time, renewal—with new perspectives, knowledge, and skills. The results would be an amalgamation of OD and traditional personnel functions, creating a more systems-directed human-resource-management approach.

In order for the profession to be able to tackle human-resource management, it needs:

1. *Broader management and organizational perspectives.* OD practitioners will have to learn more about the business functions of the organization, about strategic planning, about management-information systems, and about organizational design.
2. *A broader working-knowledge base.* The OD profession has been inward looking even in the behavioral sciences. In order to work on human-resource management problems such as manpower planning, career pathing, training, selection, recruitment, pay and incentive systems, industrial relations, quality of work life, etc., a great deal of homework will have to be done to learn what is being done in the field of organizational behavior. Also, many OD professionals lack basic knowledge in marketing, accounting, management science, production, and finance. Working at the top of the corporation with top management will require new

understandings in these areas. Finally, most OD professionals, unless originally from personnel, have a very superficial understanding of traditional personnel functions.

3. *More sophisticated political awareness.* Dealing with top-level strategy in a large organization is a very political process. OD professionals often shy away from "organizational politics." In order to have a large impact on an organization in the human-resource area, one has to step into the political arena and deal with the organizational power where it resides.

The challenge is for OD to find enough good practitioners to tackle the big issues. It is risky; it will require bold moves; but if it is not undertaken, the issues will be tackled, by default, by some other discipline or function, and that function will have a major impact on people and organizations.

CONCLUSION

Some practitioners in the field of OD are exhibiting symptoms of self-doubt. An argument has been made that this is reflective of the broader field of OD and that the field is, in fact, in a phase of self-doubt. Alternative responses to self-doubt include both adaptive and maladaptive ones. The maladaptive responses will happen if individuals in the field become defensive, look inward, and avoid risks. The result could then very well be the demise or absorption of the field by default.

On the other hand, if significant numbers of OD practitioners mobilize and subscribe to the OD philosophy of proactive diagnostic-action-research behavior, they can make adaptive responses. Three such responses are (a) planned absorption into strategic planning and organizational-design activities; (b) planned absorption into line management; and (c) planned absorption into human-resource management, which seems to be the most promising response.

REFERENCES

Burke, W. Organization development in transition. *Journal of Applied Behavioral Science*, 1976, *12*(1), 22-43.

Calvert, B. *A comparison of U.S. and U.K. organization development consultants.* Unpublished working paper. London, England, 1977.

French, W., & Bell, C. *Organization development.* Englewood Cliffs, NJ: Prentice-Hall, 1973.

Friedlander, F. OD reaches adolescence: An exploration of its underlying values. *Journal of Applied Behavioral Science*, 1976, *12*(1), 7-21.

Huse, E. *Organization development.* St. Paul, MN: West, 1975.

Kaplan, A. *The conduct of inquiry.* San Francisco: Chandler, 1964.

Lawler, E. Address to the Advanced Program in Organization Development and Human Resource Management, Columbia University, February 6, 1977.

Pettigrew, A. Strategic aspects of the management specialists activity. *Personnel Review*, 1975, *4*(1), 160-175.

Porter, L., Lawler, E., & Hackman, R. *Behavior in organizations*. New York: McGraw-Hill, 1975.

Tichy, N. Agents of planned change: Congruence of values, cognitions and action. *Administrative Science Quarterly*, June 1974, 164-182.

Tichy, N., & Hornstein, H. Stand when your number is called: An empirical attempt to classify change agent types. *Human Relations*, 1976, 29(10), 945-967.

Tichy, N., & Sole, K. Working paper #164, Graduate School of Business, Columbia University, 1977.

Section II:
CURRENT THEORY AND RESEARCH IN ORGANIZATION DEVELOPMENT

OVERVIEW

The field of organization development continues to stimulate thinking, but this does not always produce conceptually coherent writing. When people do write coherently, we sometimes call it "theory," albeit most of the time we are using the term loosely. There is no single theory on which OD is based. In fact, there may be as many OD theories as there are practitioners. Those, such as Argyris, Bennis, Likert, Levinson, Lawrence and Lorsch, and some others, who have systematically and theoretically written about OD are indeed few, and much of their writing is based on either Lewin or Freud. Argyris (1971) advocates individual, behavioral change starting with top management. The direction of the change stems from McGregor's original ideas regarding Theory Y assumptions of human behavior. The Bennis (1969) approach is an educative one; Likert (1967) argues for participative management; Levinson (1972) emphasizes stress and the psychoanalytic framework; and Lawrence and Lorsch (1969) say that the direction of change for an organization depends on many variables, especially the nature of the organization's environment. At the risk of oversimplification, we can classify all these theories as either normative (a specific direction for change is advocated) or contingent (there is no single best way). Likert, for example, clearly is normative, and Lawrence and Lorsch are contingency theorists.

In the previous section, Tichy states that OD is in a phase of self-doubt, at what might be a crossroads. I think he is probably accurate about there being one or more choice points, but I do not agree with the nature of the choices. In any case, I am certain that one choice is normative versus contingency, for example, whether to advocate participative management or to take a Hersey-Blanchard situational approach (see Chapter 15). The adherents of the normative approach are fewer, the contingency approach is more widespread and more popular. Whether there is a further contingency depends on the nature of the OD project or it is a matter of whether one is diagnosing or intervening.

Davis, in Chapter 7 of this section, believes that we are entering the contingency era, the human relations (a specific normative theory) era—its predecessor—having already begun to fade. He does not debate the issue. He assumes that contingency theory is here to stay, and he discusses ways to bridge the gap between theory and practice within that context. He contends that practice is ahead of (contingency) theory, and he presents the matrix way of organizing and managing to show how theory and practice can be brought closer together. In this case, theory has to do with unity of command and balance of power and with the practice of managing complex organizations in which balancing power is a constant necessity. We also learn from Davis some important conditions for determining whether an organization should pursue a matrix structure.

Remaining with a systems viewpoint and, more specifically, continuing to focus on organizational design, Egan, in Chapter 8, provides two working models of organizational change. Model A describes the logic that underlies organizational *design*, and Model B provides the logic for organizational *change*. In other words, to change an organization one must first understand how it works and why it works the way it does and, second, understand the step-by-step process of planned change. Thus, Egan's models provide the OD practitioner with a systematic way of effecting change.

In Chapter 9, Gibb is theoretical, but beyond that obvious point the similarities between his chapter and the previous two quickly disappear. He clearly is in the normative camp. Over the years Gibb has argued consistently that trust is critical to organizational effectiveness; in this chapter, he argues that increasing the level of trust is a (if not *the*) central issue in OD efforts. He discusses this issue within the concept of environmental quality, a term that is akin to climate (see Litwin, Humphrey, and Wilson, Chapter 13). Gibb contends that organizations evolve through ten different trust levels or stages. These stages represent an evolution of environmental quality from punitive, the most primitive level, to what he calls the cosmic state, a mystical if not nirvanic quality of organizational life. He then discusses how the OD practitioner can use these environmental-quality stages diagnostically and what should be considered in an intervention.

If one reads this section in order, one may be jolted back to the "hard" world of objectivity, quantitative data, and scientific method by the research of King, Sherwood, and Manning (Chapter 10). And although I may not agree with their claim that OD "must become a research-based science," they do show the clear need for OD to be on more solid, empirical ground. It is easy to agree with them regarding not only the need for more research but also for more methodological rigor and for reducing the gap between scientific achievement and practice. This last point is perhaps the most important. These authors and researchers found that even though OD practitioners apparently read the literature, it does not seem to impact them in any clear, applicable way, and, if it does, the degree of individual differences regarding this impact is remarkable. Perhaps OD as a field is still not coherent or systematic enough to affect most people the same way.

The chapter by Fullan and Miles (Chapter 11) presents considerable information regarding (and contributes significantly to the knowledge of) the state of organization development in schools. Relying on questionnaire data from a comprehensive survey, the authors show, not surprisingly, that OD remains active in schools after more than fifteen years. What is surprising, however, is the pervasiveness of OD in schools. It appears that a sustained (eighteen months or more) effort has occurred in more than seventy-six school districts in the United States and Canada.

This second section indicates that:

1. OD continues to stimulate people to think and to act.

2. Although research on OD efforts is difficult to do, some continue to try, and that is good. To say more is needed is a cliché, but true nevertheless.
3. Even though OD does not have a unified theory base, people like Gibb, Golembiewski, Weisbord, and others continue to conceptualize. In time, much of this conceptualization may begin to connect and develop into theory.

REFERENCES

Argyris, C. *Management and organization development*. New York: McGraw-Hill, 1971.

Bennis, W. G. *Organization development: Its nature, origins, and prospects*. Reading, MA: Addison-Wesley, 1969.

Lawrence, P. R., & Lorsch, J. W. *Developing organizations: Diagnosis and action*. Reading, MA: Addison-Wesley, 1969.

Levinson, H. *Organizational diagnosis*. Cambridge, MA: Harvard University Press, 1972.

Likert, R. *The human organization*. New York: McGraw-Hill, 1967.

7

Matrix: Filling the Gap Between Theory and Practice

Stanley M. Davis

All forms of social organization have two simultaneous needs that are often at odds with each other: freedom and order. Freedom springs from intuition and leads to innovation. Order stems from intelligence and provides efficiency. Both are essential, but they are not always compatible with each other. Within organizations, these requirements are translated into structural terms: freedom is translated as the specialized interests of different parts of an organization—its optimal goal is decentralization; order is represented as the regulation and integration of all elements in harmonious and common action—its optimal goal is centralization. The problem with the centralization/decentralization issue is that the more you realize the benefits of the one, the less you realize the benefits of the other. The dilemma of organization is the dilemma of an either/or world and of being either a boss or a subordinate.

In recent years, contingency theory has largely replaced classical and human-relations approaches and, in so doing, has helped to eliminate much of the "either/orness" in issues of management and organization theory. The logic of contingency theory is that one must manage and organize to meet the particular needs of each business, and if different businesses have different needs, then one style of management and one structural design for all is bound to be inadequate.

Major theoretical shifts do not occur with great frequency. Realistically, there have been only three major schools of organization thought in this century: the classical and the human-relations theories being the first two, and the contingency theory being the third. This third approach is only about a decade old and still is not a complete formulation. It is my opinion that it will take another decade before it can or will be a "mature" theory. At present, however, it seems the most useful approach to issues of organization development, and current theory and practice appear to be moving in the direction of wider acceptance and application of it.

It has been my observation that, through trial and error, managers evolve new ways of managing and organizing, and that academics and consultants then come along and develop these new methods in a more articulate and generalizable form. However, practitioners do not invent new theory when the old or current theory does not meet their current needs. Either they ignore existing theory or

95

they bend it. However inventive they are, they nevertheless will be constrained by the limitations of the theory on which their beliefs are premised. In fact, the more inventive they are, the more their practices will conflict with the theoretical premises they carry around—however unconscious and implicit these are. We can speed up the evolution of theory and practice, then, by reducing the lag that occurs between the two. Many managers find themselves practicing in reality what they reject in theory, and we can advance the boundaries of organization development by providing them with theory that is at the same time both acceptable and consonant with their behavior.

I want to underscore the distinction between accurate theory and acceptable theory. I am struck by the fact that contingency theory is, or at least has been, more *accurate* than *accepted*. What appears obvious and logical will not necessarily be employed in the next day, year, or decade. A striking example of this can be found at General Electric, which is accepted by most as a very well-managed and organized corporation. Despite the diversity of its businesses, however, for decades G.E. used one basic structure throughout its organization (Figure 1). Members of G.E.'s organizational planning department told me that after reading Alfred Chandler's *Strategy and Structure* (1962) more than ten years ago, they understood the logic of contingency theory: fit the particular structure and management to the particular strategy. But they said that no one in G.E. was interested. For decades, managers' careers were built on the principle of the pyramid; the planning, control, and reward systems were geared to the pyramid; and the culture was not to be changed. During the past decade, more of G.E.'s groups, divisions, and departments have moved away from the pyramid structure in practice, but the supporting culture was still the singular traditional form. Now, those who have adopted alternative forms of managerial behavior and structural design consider the others as "dinosaurs" and those who maintain the classical form are resentful of the light in which they have been cast. Even though representatives of the "new" and "old" forms acknowledge that each is probably right for their particular businesses, there is nonetheless an air of radical/reactionary tension when the topic is discussed. Contingency theory may be accurate, but it is only beginning to be accepted. Practice is ahead of theory, and the lag between the two holds back the development of each proportionately.

Organization development lies somewhere between the extremes of the practical manager who seldom thinks in theory and the academic who elaborates through theory. As such, the field is an appropriate means by which to reduce the gap between the two. I have attempted to do this during the past few years, specifically in a book, *Matrix*, written with Paul Lawrence (1977). After writing the book, I saw that it is directed at reducing the gap between theory and practice, particularly between the dominant theory of a unity of command and the less-clear reality of balanced power as basic alternatives in the management and organization of large and complex corporations.

This paper therefore focuses on the effects that theory and practice have on each other in the development of management and organizations. First it discusses the derivation of theory from what is practiced, though not preached, in organizations. Then it addresses the question of how to help managers accept theories that more accurately reflect their practices, rather than their beliefs.

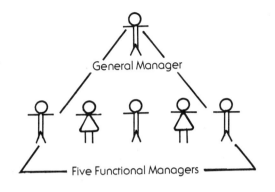

Figure 1. The Pyramid Structure

THEORY BASED ON PRACTICE

The following statements of theory (a) help managers to accept a conceptualization that accurately reflects their reality and (b) help theoreticians to develop contingency theory further. Specifically, they elaborate the balance-of-power model of management and organization and, more particularly, the application of that model in the process and form of *matrix*.

A Multiple Command System. The critical identifying feature of a matrix organization is that some managers report to two bosses rather than to the traditional single boss; there is a dual rather than a single chain of command. While the one-boss model accepts the greater authority of those higher in the hierarchy as given, the two-boss model does not relinquish the subordinate's autonomy quite so easily. Hierarchy of power and status is not denied, but it is made plural.

Three Necessary and Sufficient Conditions. For matrix to be the preferred managerial and organizational choice, three basic conditions must be present simultaneously. These conditions may be experienced as environmental pressures; each triggers an internal response within the organization (Figure 2).

It is easy for managers from all kinds of organizations to read these three conditions and readily nod their heads in quick agreement that all three conditions are present in their situations. Such an initial reaction is understandable. After all, most managers feel pressured from multiple sides and swamped with information. If they felt otherwise, they would have trouble justifying their salaries. But a facile reaction is dangerous. Organizations do, in fact, vary in the extent to which they experience these pressures. Until these three conditions are overwhelmingly present—in a literal sense—the matrix structure will almost certainly be an unnecessary complexity. Caution should be exercised in judging the presence or absence of these conditions, and one is well advised to err on the conservative side. Clearly, only a limited—even if growing—number of organizations really need a fully evolved matrix.

	Environmental Pressure	Behavioral Linkage
Condition 1	Two or more critical sectors, functions, products, services, markets, or areas	Balance of power, dual command, simultaneous decision making
Condition 2	Performance of uncertain, complex, interdependent, and changing tasks	Enriched information-processing capacity
Condition 3	Economies of scale	Shared and flexible use of scarce human resources

Figure 2.   Necessary and Sufficient Conditions for Matrix Management

The threefold behavior that the matrix tries to induce is: (a) the employment of undivided human effort on two (or more) essential organizational tasks simultaneously, (b) the human processing of a great deal of information and the commitment of the organization to a balanced, reasoned response (a general management response), and (c) the rapid redeployment of human resources to various projects, products, services, clients, or markets.

Balance of Power: More Flexible than Stable. An advantage of the traditional unity-of-command model is its stability, but it is a stability that is built into the formal design, not into the behavior of the people within its framework. A corollary of this stability is its rigidity. If there is to be any flux or change, it can occur either in one manner or another, but never in several forms simultaneously. It is an either-or model—a clear but often oversimplified view of the practice of power in organizations. The model has the strength of success; it has proven itself worthy and has withstood the test of time. There is an air about it of simpler times, of an unquestioned and everlasting order. It is a model that outlasts the individuals who practice it, just as the physical pyramids have survived the kings who built them.

The balance-of-power model is more fragile. It has the adaptability of fabric; the matrix is a grid like the warp and woof of cloth.

The environmental pressure to give attention to two or more critical sectors (condition 1 in Figure 1) is largely a question of how to give form to required behavior and how to create appropriate frameworks for work relationships. Dealing with uncertain, complex, and changing tasks (condition 2), however, requires the flexibility of response that the theoretical model must reflect.

Although power balancing is practiced in organizations all the time, a theory about the balance of power in organizations has never been well developed. Related theory has been limited to the political science of government and has not extended to the social science of corporations. An adequate theory would have to focus on process more than on form because the form of power in organization structures changes with the shifts in behavior of the members and the coalitions they create with one another.

KEY ROLES IN THE MODEL

There are three key roles in the balance-of-power model: (a) top leadership, (b) power-sharing (matrix) managers who have common subordinates, and (c) subordinate managers with two bosses. These roles are generally standard in form, position, and nomenclature, reflecting the traditional unity-of-command hierarchy. What makes them different in the balance-of-power hierarchy is the behavior that is necessary if the theory is to be put into practice or accurately reflect existing behavior.

The Top Leadership. The top leadership is outside the matrix (Figure 3). It is not generally recognized that even in matrix organizations, the top executives are not *in* the matrix. They are, however, certainly *of* it; it is the top executives who oversee and guarantee the balance of power. In a corporate-wide matrix, this is the chief executive and/or a few other key individuals; in a product-group or division matrix, it is the senior manager. This individual does not share power with others, and there is no unequal separation of authority and responsibility.

One of the several paradoxes of the matrix, then, is that it requires a strong unity of command at the top to ensure a balance of power at the next level down. In some ways this is the benevolent-dictator model: "You will enjoy democracy (shared power) and I will enjoy autocracy (ultimate power)"; or "I'm OK, you're OK; but I'm still the boss."

The Matrix Boss. This senior-management person reports in a direct line to the top, but does not have a complete line of command below (Figure 4). The matrix boss is in charge of an entire function, product, area, business, or service, but is not in full command over the individuals reporting to him. Matrix bosses share power with equals, often over the same subordinates and usually over information and issues. They are the recipients of the unequal distribution of authority and responsibility. The boss who shares subordinates with other bosses is asked to represent a major portion of an organization's activities and also to have an institutional perspective—the corporate point of view.

Since the heir to the chief executive is likely to be found in these ranks, there is generally a great, though diplomatic, battle going on for supremacy among the matrix bosses. The statesman's posture is an essential ingredient to success. The appearance of being threatened by the sharing of subordinates is fatal; it is not top-management behavior. Top leadership often uses such power sharing to allow the candidates for the top to spar with each other in a constructive arena. The balance of power (matrix) is a better format than the unity of command (pyramid) for testing the strength of managers' personalities, perceptions, and abilities to lead.

The matrix boss is aware that his subordinates have other voices to attend to, other masters to please. Orders that seem irrational or unfair can be circumvented more easily under the protection of the other boss than they can in a single chain of command. More care, therefore, is given to making sure that the logic and importance of a directive are clear.

For senior managers who must share their people with other senior managers, a power-balanced model is both a training ground for assuming the institutional reins and an incentive for not having to share those reins so much.

Figure 3.   Top Leadership

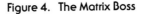

Figure 4.   The Matrix Boss

The Two-Boss Manager. The rule to success in this role (Figure 5) is to accept the fact that, while it can place contradictory demands on people, it is the best way to accommodate simultaneous, competing demands. If this person assumes that each of his bosses has equally important claims, the correct choice is both—in varying proportions. This manager is at the apex of his or her own pyramid; subordinates to this role need not be shared. It is the multiple demands from above that must be managed. But this formulation is not so different from the top role: both must pay heed to competing demands, make trade-offs, and manage conflicts that cannot be resolved. Any skillful politician knows that alternative sources of power increase one's flexibility. It would be a nonimaginative two-boss manager who would trade extra degrees of freedom for finite and singular sources of action.

A theory that legitimatizes this role more adequately would be of great service to practicing managers. Currently, many are engaged in behavior that mirrors the role, but there are no principles to turn to for conceptual support. The tensions they feel are heightened because accepted principles tell them that their behavior is unusual. The corridors of power allow only for a unity of command in the organization's hierarchy. But there are also closets of power—illegitimate spaces where the reality of shared power is reinforced daily. If conceptual models were developed that would bring the shared-power model out of the closets and into the corridors of power, both practitioners and theorists would be better off. The practitioners would benefit because they would have legitimate roles on which to model their existing behavior, and the theorists would gain because their models would be based on the reality that different tasks and environments call for different models of management and organization.

Figure 5. The Two-Boss Manager

PRACTICAL OBSERVATIONS ON THE ACCEPTANCE OF THEORY

There are several practical arguments that can be used to help managers accept a theory that more closely resembles their actions than the one to which they currently subscribe.

There Is a Choice. The spectrum of human institutions offers us choice in regard to organization models. Different institutions can and do use the same model for different purposes, and business models have come largely from the military, the church, and the monarchy. Other institutions—particularly the family and our government—provide alternative models. We all had a mother *and* a father. Because the traditional pattern has been so nearly universal in contemporary business management, awareness of alternatives (or the fact that any choice exists) is important.

You Feel Better and Perform Better When You Do What You Say and Say What You Do (Accurately). We use the term "cognitive dissonance" to describe the reasons for managerial actions that do not conform to traditional theory. There is a definite appeal in behaving consistently with stated beliefs. Difficult periods of adjustment are more likely to be worth the price when fundamental principles can be used to support actions.

Grow It Internally; It Cannot Be Copied. It is hard to find organizations that have successfully jumped in one dramatic leap, structurally or managerially, from a single chain of command to a mature matrix. A lot of learning is needed before an organization can achieve a fully functioning matrix, and learning takes time and effort. Although there are some common patterns that have evolved to full-blown matrix organizations, the pattern followed, not surprisingly, seems to be largely determined by the type, size, history, etc., of the organization. Tracing various paths toward a matrix has more than historic value since it tends to point out that a matrix, to be successful, needs to be "grown" through successive phases. A higher probability of failure occurs when an organization sees a comparable enterprise that has apparently answered mutual problems by using the matrix and then copies it. Matrix is not like an appliance that can be purchased and plugged in. The most successful outcomes, I find, are in organizations that evolve a matrix without realizing what is happening—like Molière's gentleman who was surprised to find that he had been speaking prose all his life.

Never Sell. The promise of management and organization based on a balance of power is the promise of a release from the dilemma of an either/or perspective. It promises the flexibility of both decentralization and centralization, specialization and integration, freedom and order, at the same time. But there are prices to pay, especially when the process and form of shared power are not called for by the particular situation. Even when they are called for and/or when a multiple command system is being used but denied, it seldom helps to push the acceptance of matrix forms and processes on an organization. It must be understood as a process, not forced on an organization as a panacea.

Use Only as Directed. Matrix management is truly a significant change from traditional forms. It is definitely not just another passing fad. It is also an exceedingly *complex* form and a process that is not for everybody. It should be used only when it is needed and appropriate.

It Is Prone to Pathologies. To accommodate competing needs simultaneously, matrix has evolved as a design that is paradoxical and contradictory. It is prone to pathologies—problems that develop because of the design or its application. Classical theory says that conflict results from inappropriate or inadequate form; human-relations theory acknowledges conflict but tries to eliminate it (the body of work in the 1960s on conflict resolution). Matrix—as an application of contingency theory—allows that conflict is built into the process of management, and purposefully so, by its form. Conflict is not eliminated; it is managed. Some of the common pathologies are:

1. *Anarchy:* A formless state of confusion in which people can identify no "boss" to whom they are responsible.
2. *Power Struggles:* A common problem in many organizations, these are built into the matrix design.
3. *Too Much Grouping:* There is a mistaken belief that matrix management necessitates group decision making.
4. *Collapse During Economic Crunch:* The matrix is used as a scapegoat or a smoke screen for bad management.
5. *Excessive Overhead:* Fear of the high costs associated with a matrix.
6. *Sinking:* The tendency for matrices to fail at high levels in an organization, but to sink lower down and then thrive.
7. *Layering:* Matrices within matrices within matrices.
8. *Decision Strangulation:* Too much democracy, too little action.
9. *Navel Gazing:* Excessive preoccupation with internal issues; loss of touch with the marketplace.

Reform, not Revolution. If it can be demonstrated that the matrix theory is not a radical departure from the older, more comfortable one, it is more likely to be accepted and pathologies are more likely to be avoided. Reform is more palatable than revolution. Managerial behavior is most easily changed if the changes are perceived as logical extensions and incremental development, rather than as drastic turns, whatever the direction.

A Familiar, Simple Approach. Although balance-of-power theory is more recent than theories premised on unitary command, both are centuries old. The terms it utilizes—teams, project management, brand managers, coordinating committees, dotted lines—are all familiar. This use of nontechnical language helps to reduce resistance.

In describing the theories, unity of command can be referred to as the one-boss model and the balance of power can be referred to as the two-boss model. In effect, the diamond becomes the alternative to the pyramid (Figure 6). Such imagery has been helpful in explaining many elements of the theory as well as in translating the theory into practical action. The connotation of the diamond— both in terms of value and in a baseball "team" sense—is positive. Biblical and sexual (not sexist) images also have been effective. For example: "One of the commandments in the Old Testament of Management states that 'thou shalt have but one boss above thee,'" or "We have all lived with solid- and dotted-line reporting, similar to one open and legitimate relationship and one that exists but is not quite acceptable. I am suggesting that the second relationship be brought out of the closet." This is not how theorists speak or write, but it may be one way to translate theory into practice.

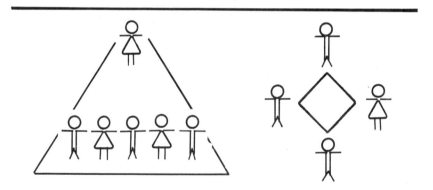

Figure 6. One-Boss and Two-Boss Models

Matrix Is a Verb. Most managers do not want to wade through entire theories; they want to receive the message in one sentence. The answer to this is that matrix is a verb. More importantly, this means that matrix is essentially *a process more than a form;* it refers more to behavior than to structure. The field of organization development has preferred process over form, relationships over structure, and micro focus rather than macro focus. It should be heartening, then, that in the matrix, the process is what counts. More accurately, structure channels behavior or, at least, it channels expected behavior. The appropriate structure is a reflection of intended outcomes. The outcomes are the ways in which the inhabitants respond to contextual cues. If you want people to practice and apply the lessons of contingency theory, you are more likely to succeed if their environment is structured to facilitate their doing so. The gap between current theory and practice in organization development would be lessened substantially if more attention were paid to the interplay between processes (macro and micro) and form.

Matrix Organization = *Matrix Structure* + *Matrix Management* + *Matrix Systems* + *Matrix Culture.* The structure involves dual chains of command. The system must also operate along two dimensions simultaneously; planning, controlling, appraising, rewarding, etc., must be carried out along both functional and product lines at the same time. Moreover, every organization has a culture of its own, and for the matrix to succeed, the spirit of the organization must be consonant with the new form. Finally, the behavior of people, especially those with two bosses and those who share subordinates, must reflect an understanding of an ability to work within such overlapping boundaries.

The change from a unity of command to a balance of power cannot be accomplished by issuing a new organization chart. People are brought up, by and large, to think in terms of "one person, one boss," and such habits are not easily changed. People must learn to work comfortably and effectively within a different way of managing and organizing.

These points are offered to demonstrate that matrix is a suitable alternative to unity of command in both organization *behavior* and *design*. The gap between the two will be reduced when practice and theory are made more consistent with each other.

REFERENCES

Chandler, A. D., Jr. *Strategy and structure.* New York: Anchor Books, Doubleday, 1966. (Originally published by The M.I.T. Press, Cambridge, MA, 1962.)

Davis, S. M., & Lawrence, P. R. *Matrix.* Reading, MA: Addison-Wesley, 1977.

8

Model A: The Logic of Systems as OD Instrument

Gerard Egan

Galbraith (1977) discusses the question of whether there can be a *science* of organization design. If, as managers often claim, the problems in their organizations are unique, then, Galbraith points out, there can be no science of organization design. Behavioral scientists can be only process consultants who help individual managers to design completely unique organizations. However, Galbraith's experience and his reading of current research relating to organization development both suggest that this is not the case. Figure 1 illustrates his point. Each circle represents an organization. The black area indicates what all organizations have in common, the striped areas indicate what some organizations have in common with some others, and the white areas indicate what is unique to any given organization. Galbraith estimates that 50 percent to 75 percent of the variance in organization design is represented by a combination of the black and striped areas. He concludes, therefore, that there *can* be a science of organization design.

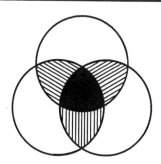

Figure 1. Commonalities Between Organizations

---

[1]The figure was suggested by John Dutton at the Kiev Seminar on Organization Design, USSR, May 29-June 2, 1972. See Galbraith, pp. 7-9.

This paper addresses itself to the fundamental similarities that exist among organizations, that is, to what is represented by the black area in Figure 1. An OD instrument that takes the shape of a working model (Egan & Cowan, in press) is based on these similarities.

SOME REFLECTIONS ON WORKING MODELS

A model, as the term is used here, is a visual portrayal of how things actually work or how they should work or might work under ideal conditions. A model is a cognitive map that enables people to see how something is put together or gives them an overview of the steps in a process, showing them how one step follows from another.

A working model is one that enables the user to *do* something, to achieve behavioral goals more effectively. For instance, if a piece of furniture is received unassembled by a buyer, a set of assembly instructions with pictures usually accompanies it. The buyer, then, has a working model that enables him or her to put the furniture together. Working models provide frameworks for action or intervention, i.e., they help people to *do* something.

Obviously, models that help people to *understand* organizations ultimately can be very useful, but they are often too complicated or too abstract to serve as frameworks for action. For instance, Blake and Mouton's (1976) Consulcube℠ is too complicated to serve in an immediate way as a working model.

Two criteria characterize working models: (a) they are *complex* enough to account for the reality they attempt to describe and portray, and (b) they are *simple* enough to use. A model that meets only the first criterion is likely to be of interest only to theoreticians and researchers. A model that meets only the second criterion would tend to be simplistic rather than merely simple, and would therefore be useless as a working model. Lippitt (1973) suggests that models for practitioners need to be two dimensional, linear, and basically nonmathematical. Blake and Mouton's Consulcube℠ violates the two-dimensional criterion. Complex and sophisticated three-dimensional models, such as the Consulcube℠, can be powerful instruments in the hands of theoreticians, researchers, and advanced practitioners, but they do not help less-sophisticated practitioners or the ordinary members of organizations who are involved in change processes—at least not until they are translated into simpler forms.

In summary, working models—as opposed to models devised primarily to understand systems:

1. Provide a vehicle for translating theory and research into a visualization of how things work;
2. Constitute a framework for action or intervention (delivery);
3. Suggest the technologies and skills needed to do the work;
4. Are two dimensional, linear, and nonmathematical.

MODEL A AND MODEL B

All those involved in organization development efforts—consultants, mediators, and the members of the target group who are expected to cooperate actively with change—would do well to acquire a thorough working knowledge of two organization-related models (Model A and Model B) and of the basic skills needed to use them in the process of organizational change.

Model A: The Logic Underlying Organization Design

Model A does not provide the principles of organization design but, rather, the *logic* that underlies design efforts. Model A provides the skeleton or the outline to which design must conform. Model A, then, is a prescriptive model. It provides systematic answers to such questions as: What are the essential elements of an organization? How do these elements fit together? How does an organization operate?

Model B: The Logic of Organizational Change

The second model, Model B, is an expanded version of the basic human problem-solving model that has been with us at least since Aristotle. Model B answers such questions as: What are the basic steps in any change process? How are these steps applied so that an organization conforms more to the logic of Model A? How do we choose from among the many different ways of redesigning and improving organizations?

Model A presents the logic underlying a well-designed and well-functioning organization; Model B provides the logic of a step-by-step process of change. Galbraith (1977) implies the need for both models.

> Organization design consists of two choices. The first is what kind of structure, process, and reward system package should we adopt. . . . The second is how do we get from where we are to where we want to be. (p. xi)

Whatever structures, processes, and reward systems (all elements of Model A) are adopted must conform to the logic of organizations described in Model A.

THE ELEMENTS OF MODEL A

The following is a summary of the elements of Model A (Egan, in press).
1. An assessment of the needs and wants of the receiving system;
2. The construction of mission statements related to the needs and wants of the receiving system;
3. The translation of mission statements into behavioral goals;
4. The development of programs to achieve these goals;
5. The education and training of people to execute these programs;
6. The provision of whatever other resources are needed (beside the knowledge and skills of workers) to execute the programs;
7. A division of labor that facilitates program execution;
8. The establishment of clear relationships based on program-oriented division of labor;
9. The development of communication processes, including information sharing and feedback, that facilitate relationships and program execution;

10. The development of a human climate—one that meets the legitimate needs of organization members;
11. The human use of the basic principles of behavior in establishing and executing the entire process;
12. Control of relationships between the environment and the organization so that these transactions are mutually constructive.

The Needs/Wants of the Receiving System

Organizations take certain inputs such as raw materials and/or the abilities of their members and transform them into outputs that meet the needs and wants of a receiving system. General Motors transforms raw materials into automobiles that meet the needs and wants of the general public for personal transportation. It is essential that an organization first assess the needs and wants of the receiving system.

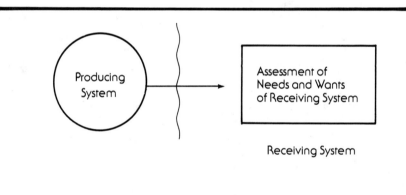

Receiving System

Figure 2. Model A Including Needs and Wants

Since, in a fundamental sense, the organization exists to meet the needs and wants of the receiving system, well-designed and functioning organizations assess these needs in order to establish a mission and goals. Each organization develops whatever instruments it needs to assess these needs and wants as accurately as possible. Consumer surveys and analyses of population shifts are examples of ways to assess needs.

The Mission of the Producing System

Obviously, the overall mission of any organization is to meet the needs and wants of the members of the receiving system. If an organization does not meet these needs and wants, it cannot meet its own. The logic of organization design, then, demands that the organization elaborate mission statements that are reflections of the needs and wants of the receiving system.

An effectively functioning organization knows, explicitly, why it is in business. Mission statements are statements of the general purpose and the wide-ranging goals of the organization. Very often mission statements include the philosophy and the values of a system, that is, they indicate in what spirit and under what conditions products and services are to be delivered. Organization development efforts can be directed toward helping an organization to develop mission statements that are clearly related to the needs and wants of the members of the receiving system and toward helping an organization become aware of its values. Ideally, these statements are written out and communicated to the members of the organization itself and to the members of the receiving system.

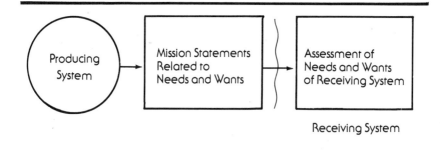

Figure 3. Model A Including Mission Statements

Since a mission can change with changing environments, organization development efforts can be directed toward such fundamental issues as the reasons why an organization exists. Organizations can learn the skills of writing and communicating clear and accurate mission statements.

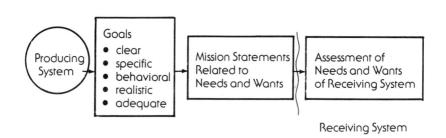

Figure 4. Model A Including Goals

Setting Behavioral Goals

Goals are behavioral translations of mission statements. They are the concrete ways in which the needs and wants of the receiving system are to be satisfied. If they are vague, the work of the entire organization suffers. Well-designed and well-functioning organizations have goals that are clear, measurable (or at least verifiable), realistic (not set too high), worthwhile (not set too low), and adequate (substantial translations of mission statements). If larger goals are subdivided into subgoals, the same qualities should characterize these subgoals. Furthermore, both goals and subgoals should be communicated clearly to the members of the organization and members should be committed to their attainment. Achieving goal clarity—especially in human-service-delivery organizations such as governmental agencies, the helping professions, churches, and educational enterprises—is often very difficult. Consequently, organization development efforts often are centered on setting behavioral goals and training system members in the skills of behavioral goal setting.

Program Development: The Means of Achieving Goals

In an effectively operating organization, systematic, step-by-step programs (means) are established to achieve clear behavioral goals (ends). The key behavioral term with respect to program development is "shaping." It means that: (a) each program moves step-by-step toward the goal or subgoal; (b) no step is too complicated; and (c) the connection between one step and the next (1 through n in Figure 5) is logical and clear. Organization development efforts often are centered on the development of well-shaped programs. Since some organizations, especially human-service-delivery organizations, move too quickly from mission to programs, consultants to organizations provide an extremely useful service by helping a system to make sure that its programs respond to well-thought-out behavioral goals. Effectively operating systems avoid any kind of "functional autonomy" of programs, i.e., programs that look good in themselves but are not related organically to the needs and wants of the receiving system, the mission of the organization, and specific, operational goals. Programs must be justified by the logic of the organizational system.

Working Knowledge and Skills for Program Implementation

In a properly functioning organization, those responsible for carrying out programs have both the working knowledge (relevant operant information) and the skills needed to move through programs efficiently.

The system, therefore, either selects people who already possess such working knowledge and skills or sets up educational programs to prepare organizational members for the programs in which they will participate. In an organization that respects the logic underlying system design, program-oriented working knowledge and skills are not taken for granted.

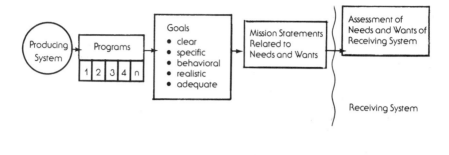

Figure 5. Model A Including Programs

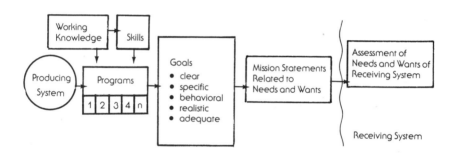

Figure 6. Model A Including Working Knowledge and Skills

Organization development programs often are based on training programs. From time to time there is a need to develop new training methodologies to meet the changing needs of the organization. The term "training methodologies" refers to both technical and interpersonal knowledge and skills. However, education for working knowledge and training for skills should never be taken out of the systemic context of the organization. Human relations training will help an organization little if it suffers from fuzzy goals or an inadequate assessment of the needs and wants of the receiving system. The entire logic of organization design and functioning must be kept in mind despite the particular focus of given organization development effort.

Other Resources Needed for the Implementation of Programs

In an effective organization, the resources other than working knowledge and skills that are needed by system members to execute programs efficiently are provided at the time that they are needed. For instance, highly *skilled* typists who have a *working knowledge* of the format in which letters are to be typed also need decent typewriters, desks, chairs, paper, and other resources. These other resources will differ greatly from organization to organization. In organizations of any complexity, programs revolve around the delivery of resources to implement goal-related programs. In this case, organization development efforts relate to the coordination of resources. Other resources, too, must be seen in the light of the entire system. For instance, if some of the teachers in a school do not have adequate teaching and human relations skills, then other resources such as videotape equipment, aesthetic buildings, high-quality multimedia packages, and the like are not going to make up for their basic deficiencies.

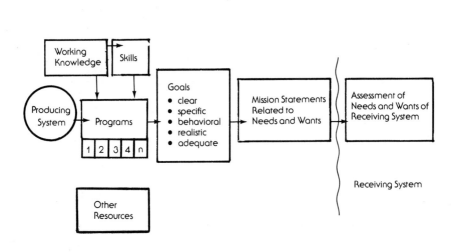

Figure 7. Model A Including Other Resources

Structure: Dividing the Work of the Organization

Since an organization has many tasks, the work of the organization must be divided. "Structure" means the way in which the work or tasks of a system are divided. Structure leads to different roles within the organization. In Figure 8, A and B must cooperate in order to carry out Task 1, but they work individually in order to accomplish the rest of their tasks. The function of C is managerial: to coordinate the interactions between A and B and to coordinate all work toward the achievement of organizational goals. Organization development efforts often revolve around the clarification of roles in organizations and the coordination of these roles (management functions). In an effectively functioning organization, roles are needed, and they are clear. Structure, too, is a systemic variable, i.e., roles exist in order to get the work of the system done.

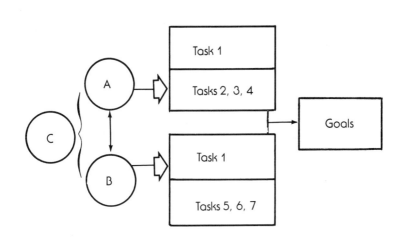

Figure 8. Organizational Structure

Relationships: The Consequence of Structure

As we have seen, structure creates a diversity of roles within an organization. But these roles are related. People in different roles must relate to one another. In an effectively operating organization, not only are individual roles clear, but the relationships among these roles are also clear. In larger organizations, of course, there are vertical and horizontal relationships of increasing complexity, and coordination becomes critical. The logic of systems calls for coordinating or managerial roles. However, relationships among roles exist primarily in order to pursue interrelated programs toward clear behavioral objectives and goals. Managerial leadership is not a goal in itself; it exists for the benefit of the system.

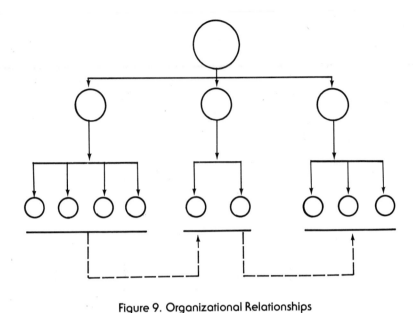

Figure 9. Organizational Relationships

Organization development efforts such as relationship clarification, team building, and the development of managerial style relate to this area (the logic of systems); however, these interventions must be evaluated in terms of the entire system. Attempts at improving managerial skills in an organization with fuzzy goals or poor training procedures will probably not improve system functioning. *System* leadership exists if the organization is achieving its goals. All the members of the organization participate in system leadership. Managerial leadership is an important part of and relates to system leadership, but it is a mistake to equate the two.

Because people relate to one another in an organization, conflict can arise. The *content* of the conflict can relate to any of the elements of the organization under discussion here—from the assessment of the needs and wants of the receiving system on down. This "relationship" category therefore calls for organization development techniques such as negotiation and conflict management.

Communication in the Service of Relationships and Decision Making

Structure involves interacting roles, and such relationships demand that these be effective communication processes within the organization. In an effective organization, communication is related to goals and program execution. There is neither too much communication nor too little. And the quality is high; communication is clear and accurate. In an organization that respects the logic of systems on which it is based, communication processes and patterns are chosen because of their relationship to the interacting roles, the programs, and the goals of the organization and not because of idiosyncratic needs of individual members of the organization, whether they happen to be in managerial roles or not.

Organization development efforts often center around two central communication issues: information sharing and feedback. In an effectively operating organization, all members receive whatever information they need to participate in program execution. Every person who must make decisions receives whatever *information* he or she needs to make the decision well. Such an organization creates all necessary communication channels, whether vertical or horizontal. Information processing is program and goal related.

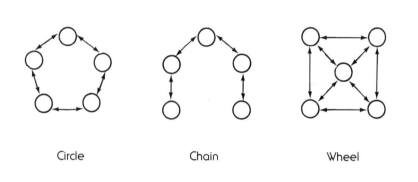

Circle   Chain   Wheel

Figure 10. Communication Patterns Possible in a Five-Person System

Each member of the organization also receives the *feedback* that he or she needs to do the job well. Feedback is an ongoing process that is related to program execution. Ongoing feedback is necessary to evaluation processes. Therefore, evaluation, too, is an ongoing process based on effective feedback and not merely a judgment at the end of a process. If goals and programs are clear, each member should be able to engage in self-evaluation as part of the overall evaluation process.

OD efforts related to this category center around information processing, decision making, feedback, and evaluation.

Environment: Social Influence and Systems

An effectively operating organization is aware of the significant ways in which other systems in the environment are affecting it and its relationship to the receiving system. It is aware of its impact on both the receiving system and the other systems in the environment. It knows how to protect itself from harmful environmental influences, how to utilize helpful environmental resources, and how to accomplish its work without damaging the environment. Ideally, a good organization contributes to the development and well-being of other systems in the environment.

OD efforts sometimes fail, not because they are not good in themselves, and not because they fail to face the internal problems of the organization, but because they fail to take into account the limitations that arise from the environment.

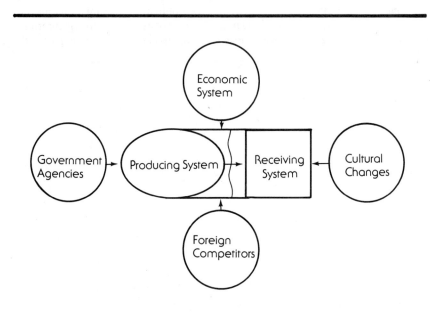

Figure 11. Environmental Influences on a Producing System/Receiving System Unit

The Effective Use of the Principles of Behavior

Well-functioning organizations have a working knowledge of and a respect for the basic principles or laws of human behavior and they have the ability to apply these principles in every phase of their structure and functioning (Luthans & Kreitner, 1975). This includes such principles as shaping, reinforcement, punishment and its effects, aversive conditioning, modeling, and the like. If an organization does not use these principles actively, they will work against it.

Organization development efforts that center around such issues as motivation, reward systems, job satisfaction, and job enrichment are all based on the principles of human behavior. Consultants, mediators, and members of target change groups all benefit from both understanding and using these principles.

A Climate that Balances System Needs and Member Needs.

Systems have both external and internal environments. Climate refers to the internal environment—or what is sometimes referred to, somewhat drably, as the "working conditions" of an organization. Well-designed and effectively functioning organizations provide both support and challenge for their members. The relationships between productivity and the human needs of the members of the organization are understood, and neither is overemphasized at the expense of the other. Values that promote human dignity and human development are pursued without being interpreted as "giving in" to workers or as inimical to organizational values. Effective organizations face issues relating to climate openly, as part of the ordinary business of the system.

Argyris (1976a, 1976b) has elaborated models and technologies for assessing the climate of an organization and for helping organizations to move from highly controlling, authoritarian, win-lose systems to more open and supportive systems. He calls the former Model-I systems, the latter Model-II systems. He notes that the world is filled with Model-I systems, and that it is extremely difficult for Model-I systems to move toward becoming Model-II systems, even when top management is committed to such a change.

Organizational climate, then, offers serious challenges to OD efforts. Participative management and decision making, the freedom to challenge decisions that are based on inaccurate or inadequate information, the creation of a climate of learning in the organization—these and similar issues relate to the element of system logic. They are the elements of Model A (as I presently conceive of them), together with some indications of how the model relates to OD interventions.

THE USE OF MODEL A IN OD INTERVENTIONS

Organizations, like people, fall short of ideals. They can always be better. Like people, they are in constant need of renewal—some more than others. There are many ways in which Model A relates to this process of renewal, and these possibilities are interrelated.

Giving OD Away. Miller (1969) suggests that psychologists learn to "give psychology away," that is, to equip the people they serve with the kinds of working knowledge and skills that enable the people to achieve greater mastery over their own lives. This is the meaning of the popular self-help movement (Gartner & Riessman, 1977). Havelock (1973), in discussing OD interventions in educational systems, notes that these interventions are incomplete if the system is left without the capacity to renew itself. Egan and Cowan (in press) have elaborated a model for giving the social sciences away through education and training that would begin early in life. Model A, perhaps in an expanded and developed form, could be a first step in giving OD away to the systems with which consultants work. The number of managers, especially those involved in human-service-delivery systems, who have not developed a Model A of their own is quite large. Sharing Model A with managers has been, for me, a most useful first step.

A Common Understanding of the Logic of Systems. Sharing some variation of Model A with those who have the responsibility for directing OD processes helps to develop a spirit of cooperation. If managers have elaborated their own version of Model A, comparing it with the consultant's is often a mutually helpful process. Such sharing also enables the parties in a change process to speak a common language. Managers, in turn, can profitably share Model A with all those who are expected to cooperate in change efforts. Again, a common understanding of the logic of the organization and a common language help the process of change to happen more smoothly.

A Cognitive Map of the Organization. Model A provides a "geography" of the organization. In the case of OD interventions, it makes the point or points of entry into a system visually clear. It also makes it quite clear that OD interventions are systemic even when they relate to one specific area in the system, for instance, the assessment of the needs of the receiving system or the establishment of more effective information-processing systems. Change efforts directed at any part of an organization ripple throughout the system. Model A enables people to understand the logic behind this ripple effect and even to visualize it.

A Primary Diagnostic Tool. A working knowledge of Model A helps the members of organizations to discover the illogical aspects of their organizations. As Weisbord (1976) suggests, Model A can be placed over an organization like a radar screen. The "blips" are the inconsistencies, the trouble spots, the danger points, the "soft" areas needing attention and change. Model A, then, is the first step in Model B (the step-by-step process of change). It provides a comprehensive framework for the diagnosis of an organization. Reviewing Model A with a manager constitutes an organizational checkup. The more people in the organization who are conversant with some form of Model A, the more possible participants there are in the diagnostic process.

Identifying and Organizing OD Technologies. Model A can be used to help identify the specific OD technologies that are needed to handle the problems of an organization. For instance, if relationships and communication are poor within a specific team, team building is called for. If workers in the organization are making mistakes in attempting to execute well-shaped programs (and other blips, such as fuzzy goals, do not show up on the screen), more effective education and training programs may well be called for. If the sales and production departments are fighting over delivery schedules, some form of conflict management, and perhaps even a redesign of the system, is called for. Model A does not allow for the use of pet technologies that are not appropriate. For instance, even though one may be an expert in team building, Model A clearly indicates that team building does little good in an organization that suffers from unclear goals. All too frequently, consultants do what they do best, no matter what is called for by the organization. Model A and Model B provide a context into which OD interventions may be fit. This kind of clarity can be invaluable.

REFERENCES

Argyris, C. *Increasing leadership effectiveness*. New York: John Wiley, 1976. (a)

Argyris, C. Theories of action that inhibit individual learning. *American Psychologist*, 1976, *31*, 638-654. (b)

Blake, R. R., & Mouton, J. S. *Consultation*. Reading, MA: Addison-Wesley, 1976.

Egan, G. *Change agent skills: Models and methods for improving systems*. Monterey, CA: Brooks/Cole, in press.

Egan, G., & Cowan, M. *Human development in human systems: A working model*. Monterey, CA: Brooks/Cole, in press.

Galbraith, J. R. *Organization design*. Reading, MA: Addison-Wesley, 1977.

Gartner, A., & Riessman, F. *Self-help in the human services*. San Francisco: Jossey-Bass, 1977.

Havelock, R. G. *The change agent's guide to innovation in education*. Englewood Cliffs, NJ: Educational Technology Publications, 1973.

Lippitt, G. *Visualizing change*. La Jolla, CA: University Associates, 1973.

Luthans, F., & Kreitner, R. *Organizational behavior modification*. Glenview, IL: Scott, Foresman, 1975.

Miller, G. A. Psychology as a means of promoting human welfare. *American Psychologist*, 1969, *24*, 1063-1075.

Weisbord, M. R. Organizational diagnosis: Six places to look for trouble with or without a theory. *Group & Organization Studies*, 1976, *1*, 430-447.

Improving Organizational Effectiveness Through Focus on Environmental Quality

Jack R. Gibb

TORI (Trust Level) Theory is based on the assumption that trust level is the key catalytic and synergistic variable in organizational effectiveness (Gibb, 1972, 1978). When trust is high, relative to fear: systems function well; productivity and creativity are high; energy is focused; the creative processes are heightened; consciousness is awakened; persons and systems transcend apparent limits and discover new and awesome abilities and talents; and outcome measures are positive.

When fear levels are high, relative to trust: personal and organizational processes are impaired; life forces are mobilized in defense against perceived, anticipated, or fantasied dangers; consciousness is restricted; perspective is narrowed; energy is diverted from problem solving and creativity; organizational processes become segmented and discordant; and outcome measures are negatively retarded.

THE EVOLUTION OF ENVIRONMENTAL QUALITY

If trust level is so critical in organization development, then changing the level of trust is a central issue in OD efforts. TORI theorists working with large systems have discovered that trust level is directly related to *environmental quality* and that of all the options open to the OD specialist, the one with the greatest leverage is *environmental design*. To talk meaningfully about this approach to OD, it will be helpful to look first at the evolution of environmental quality. Systems evolve through the following ten stages in the evolution of trust level.

EQ I—Punitive

Punishment is a dominant and visible process. In early and primitive stages of fear and distrust, people attempt to reduce visible or prospective chaos and danger through punishment. In spite of overwhelming evidence that it accomplishes little or nothing of value and that it does produce massive negative effects, punishment is amazingly persistent in the modern organizational world. Punishing behavior is sustained by guilt and hostility and is easily rationalized. In turn, it produces more guilt and hostility. Managment often elects to continue a punitive program because of fear of rebellion and loss of control. The focus is on survival and retribution. EQ (environmental quality) I management is seen in some prisons, mental hospitals, and prison camps. Residual forms are evident in some schools, churches, and businesses.

EQ II—Autocratic

Autocratic management uses power and authority to maintain control and order. This provides order and structure and some security. The primary weakness of autocratic management is that it creates passivity and dependency. The focus of energy is on maintaining power, keeping control, and securing obedience. The mode is sustained by easily aroused, primitive fears of ambiguity, disorder, and powerlessness. An autocratic environment is associated with a moralistic view of responsibility and obedience. It fosters linear relationships, a hierarchy of power and responsibility, a span of control, and rational relationships.

At the intrapersonal level, autocracy is represented by tight inner controls, suppression of feelings and impulses, rationalization as a defense mechanism, low tolerance for ambiguity, and an authoritarian character structure.

EQ III—Benevolent

The primary and most characteristic theme of EQ III is nurturing and caring. This "parental" environment is common in the school, the church, and the home. Because the paternalism provides security and affection and seems to meet many of the emotional needs of others, the dependence and resistance that result are unperceived or tolerated by management, which uses rewards and punishments as a control system.

The high cost of paternalism is in apathy and emotional dependencies. The benevolent person is likely to see the world in terms of punishment and reward, praise and reproof, winning and losing, and acceptance and rejection. Something good is seen as a "win-win" situation, rather than as a natural, intrinsically rewarded event.

EQ IV—Advisory

This stage focuses on giving consultative help, collecting data, expanding the data base, and enriching communication at all levels. As fear and distrust decrease, there is a movement away from considering the management group to be the primary source of motivation, wisdom, and decision making. Management uses survey data, rational communication nets, training programs in decision making, and external consultants to make managing a rational, scientific process.

EQ V—Participative

As trust levels increase, the management focus shifts to participation, consensual decision making, and choice. Participatory management is seen by many as the highest form of management and as an ideal form of social environment.

From the standpoint of trust formation, participatory organizational life is seen as a significant transitional form. However, the first five EQ levels represent *leader-centered* environments, although the role of the leader becomes less and less critical from one level to the next. The participative level is as effective and advanced as an organizational environment can become within the limitations of leadership forms (action and decision making are only as effective as the leader is effective). At this level, the costs of being leader centered are muted but still present.

EQ VI—Emergent

Level VI, the emergent environment, is a quantum jump away from participatory leadership. The emergent form of group, community, or organization is a new and leaderless level of reality and interaction. There are vestigial remains of the dynamics of power, control, and influence, but these concerns are replaced by concerns about interpersonal skills, being, awareness, experimentation, and empathy.

TORI theorists have pioneered in the development of leaderless T-groups, consultantless team training, leaderless communities, teacherless classrooms, therapy groups without therapists, and work groups without supervisors. In general, the results have been highly successful in terms of productivity, profit, personal growth, and a variety of outcome measures. Although there are obvious advantages of such groups, full development of effective leaderless groups depends on a cultural evolution in values and beliefs, evolution in management theory, the acquisition of new skills, and more experimentation in organizational settings.

The emergent organization or group reduces dependency, adds functional resources, reduces dysfunctional focus of energy on power and authority, and increases creativity and feelings of freedom.

EQ VII—Organic

With the evolution of trust and a greater familiarity with leaderless freedom and creativity, a reliance on empathic and intuitive modes of being and communicating develops. There is a move away from dependence on words and verbal interaction and a focus on sensory awareness, touching, and nonverbal communication.

With the recognition that defensive life is embodied in words, verbal communication, and the word-related conflicts of the relatively stormy environments V and VI, come the learning of nonverbal cue systems, the satisfactions of silence, the deep-sensing reality of touch, and the new awareness of trust and its significance.

I have seen these environments in children's informal games, small work groups that have been together for long periods, therapy groups, five-day and seven-day TORI communities, hunch-valuing executive groups, and alternative communities, as well as in isolated instances in a variety of organizations with which I have consulted. It occurs often enough for me to know that such groups are possible, that experience with such groups can change lives in significant ways, and that such integrated living is the wave of the future. Many managers in current business organizations are intrigued with this kind of environment, and organizations are much more ready for this than is commonly thought.

EQ VIII—Holistic

In the holistic environment there is an integration of the unconscious and archetypical elements of life into all personal and organizational action. There is new creativity, growth of synergy, and integration.

Experimentation with this form of environment is furthered by personal-growth experiences with psychosynthesis, hypnosis, dream analysis, holistic healing, prayer, guided fantasy, depth therapy, and a wide variety of other ways of integrating the unconscious and the foreconscious into everyday living.

In the organization we see many instances of the unconscious at work and play: collusive work slowdown, hidden agenda, the following of charismatic persons, the collective punishment of deviants, the Peter Principle, displacement of guilt, leadership martyrdom, sibling rivalry, and a wide variety of recurrent quasi-conscious processes.

EQ IX—Transcendent

This environment is another key transition in which quantum leaps are made into new areas of being. This state brings the integration of altered and extrasensory states into being and consciousness. Environment IX taps new sources of energy and goes beyond the familiar world of organizational reality and management systems into a highly controversial world of mystical events, clairvoyance, out-of-the-body trips, extrasensory perception, faith healing, and a number of phenomena that transcend everyday experience. How much effect this new world of experimentation and discovery will have on the organizational realities of decision making, productivity, choice, and management is a significant question. I believe that the next decade or so will bring amazing changes paralleling the magnitude of the industrial revolution.

EQ X—Cosmic

The cosmic state is a step beyond transcendental environments. Many people have reported being in mystical states they describe as nirvanic, beyond the limitations of the body, fear-free, or cosmic. Although they are controversial and speculative, these reports are highly significant, indicate *further states of trust* beyond the awareness of most people, and give an indication of what expanded awareness of extremely augmented trust might bring to the field of organization development. I have personally had four distinct experiences in the past three years that I would call "cosmic" and that have expanded my trust, perceptivity, perspective, and effectiveness in life situations, including organizational consulting. The practical implications of such experiences for organizational environments are as yet unclear. A more comprehensive discussion of the implications of cosmic experiences for organization development may be found in Gibb (1978).

So far, my extrapolations of the fear-trust constructs seem to hold up well in integrating new developments in theoretical physics, holistic medicine, cosmic speculations, and a variety of marginal and speculative "scientific" readings. Trust seems to be a unitary concept that integrates all environmental levels very well. Fear may be dependent on bodily and sensory states and of less use in post-cosmic environments.

FUNCTIONAL USE OF THE ENVIRONMENTAL-QUALITY SCALE

Tables 1 through 4 summarize some of the analytic uses of the EQ scale. Space limitations allow me to discuss only a few such uses for internal and external OD consultation.

To have long-range effects on the system, the OD effort must be based on the EQ level toward which the system is moving, rather than on the level from which it is moving. OD efforts tend to prepare the system for retrospective living. "Power laboratories," and "assertiveness training," for example, are directed toward functional living in EQ levels II-IV, but are of little relevance at EQ V and are irrelevant at levels VI and VII. Most contemporary systems that hire consultants are moving through EQ levels IV, V, and VI. Programs focused on experiences in intuition, empathy, nonverbal communication, and similar processes relevant to EQ VI and VII will have a more direct and enduring effect on the system.

Each level sets up new forces that provide for its own demise and provide energy to transcend the phase and move to new levels of integration. Although we see many instances of regression to lower levels of integration (recurrent waves of conservatism in beliefs, attitudes, practices, and theory), these regressions seem to be temporary holding patterns. Growth seems to be a directional process.

Something is worked through at each level, by the person and by the system, that provides strength of resources for new movement in the evolutionary process. Each stage has its own limitations, some of which are listed in column two of Table 2. Each primary-need system seems to have its day, its time, its season, its period of centrality.

Each stage transcends a prior dependency. Thus, the punitive stage produces guilt and hostility; autocracy breeds dependency and apathy; benevolence produces parent-child dependency; the consultative system produces an overemphasis on rationality; participatory climates focus too much energy on process; and emergent climates show an overreliance on rational and verbal processes. The consultant's task is to help the organization move into its next stage.

Each level of integration provides nurturing for a newly-emerging central function (see Table 1).

Table 1. Development of Environmental Quality

	Theme of Phase	Definitive Nature	Key Function Best Nurtured
I.	Punitive	Punishment as a form of control and socialization	Reduces frightening chaos and apparent danger
II.	Autocratic	Power and authority to maintain control and order	Provides order and structure
III.	Benevolent	Parental nurturing and caring as a primary theme	Provides security and affection
IV.	Advisory	Focus on consultative help and data collection	Expands the data base and enriches communication
V.	Participative	Focus on participation, consensual decision making, and choice	Increases involvement, loyalty, and group strength
VI.	Emergent	Rise of group and community as new and leaderless level of reality and interaction	Reduces dependency, adds vitality, and increases functional resources
VII.	Organic	Rise of empathic and intuitive modes of being and communicating	Taps intuitive and sublinguistic sources of creativity and being
VIII.	Holistic	Integration of unconscious, archetypical, and latent processes into enriched living	Releases wellsprings of energy and creativity
IX.	Transcendent	Integration of altered and extrasensory states into being and consciousness	Taps nonsensory sources of being and energy
X.	Cosmic	Focus on cosmic, universal, and nirvanic states of community and being	Taps into largely unexplored universal energy and being

Table 2. Dynamics of the Environmental-Quality States

	Theme of Phase	Key Limitation	Primary Fear	Focus of Energy
I.	Punitive	Guilt and residual hostility	Fear of rebellion and loss of control	Survival and retribution
II.	Autocratic	Passivity and dependency	Fear of ambiguity, disorder, and anarchy	Power, control, and obedience
III.	Benevolent	Multiple emotional disorders and apathy	Fear of emotional weaning	Reward and punishment
IV.	Advisory	Failure to tap energy and action and to distribute responsibility	Fear of conflict, diversity, and action	Communication and validity of data processing
V.	Participative	Ambiguity of leader role	Fear of leaderlessness and responsibility	Influence, choosing, and resolving conflict
VI.	Emergent	Overreliance on rational and verbal process	Fear of nonrational and nonverbal states	Being, freedom, and searching
VII.	Organic	Overreliance on conscious processes	Fear of mysteries of unconscious and primal	Expression, integration, and sensing
VIII.	Holistic	Overreliance on sensory data and experience	Fear of loss of conscious and voluntary control	Creativity and spontaneity
IX.	Transcendent	Overreliance on mind and body	Fear of leaving security of bodily and sensory base	Transcending sensory and body states
X.	Cosmic	Little or no data available	Fears may be transcended	Cosmic being

New need systems are predominant at each level. Recognition of this process helps the consultant to gain perspective on the evolutionary process and not block processes of growth and development. Table 3, which describes this need and want hierarchy, is especially helpful for understanding what is happening in changing organizations.

Movement up the scale of trust is limited by fears that are unintegrated, displaced, unrecognized, or repressed. Table 2 lists the primary fears that block the flow of new growth. The consultant's task is to relate to these fears in productive ways that do not escalate them.

A fear-bred impasse occurs at the interface between levels, creating a state of tension and transition. This lack of equilibrium may cause pain, fear, and ambiguity. It is often a time of optimal learning, and a point at which the consultant can be most effective and useful. The nature of the impasse is related to the list of key limitations in Table 2.

Dysfunctional perseverance occurs when concepts and modes appropriate at one level of evolution persist beyond that level. Power strategies are useful and effective at levels I, II, and III, but dysfunctional later. Punishment as a strategy is probably not effective after level I. Leadership concepts and theories are useful in levels I through V, but are not useful, and are probably confusing, at levels VI and beyond. Experiences that strengthen the ego may be useful at levels I through VIII but are dysfunctional at levels IX and X, for which ego-free states are essential.

Each new level provides an environment for the focus and release of new energy. Table 4 indicates some of the sources of energy available at each level. The primary energy is available, but not released because of fears that arise as new levels of integration are reached. The consultant can be very useful as a catalyst for this release.

Any relevant segment of the environmental analysis can be used by the consultant or by management for diagnosis. For instance, most management systems struggle through environments II through V, which roughly parallel Likert's System I, II, III, and IV managment styles. By seeing other viable management options in EQ levels VI and VII, management can devise useful experiments for subsystems that demonstrate the power and productivity of emergent and organic modes.

Most environments include overlapping elements of about three adjoining phases. The system can tolerate this much spread and dissonance, but a larger range produces too many communication problems and the gap is too large to be bridged by empathy. A consultant is probably most effective if his or her customary internal environmental state is within two levels of the customary level of the client system. One significant contribution that a consultant can bring to another person or to a system is an expanded perspective.

Individuals or human systems produce more effective movement from one stage to the next through environmental design than through external intervention. Table 5 summarizes the distinctive characteristics of these two alternative styles of life management. An understanding of these two can radically improve a consultant's effectiveness in a system.

Table 3. Wants Hierarchy and Environmental-Quality Phases

	Theme of Phase	Ascendant Want	Secondary Wants
I.	Punitive	To survive	To be secure, to punish and be punished, to be moral and to impose morality, to fight, to withdraw
II.	Autocratic	To give and gain power	To control, to be controlled, to maintain order, to gain status, to obey, to rebel, to have authority, to evaluate
III.	Benevolent	To protect and to be protected	To help, to teach, to parent, to be cared for, to rescue, to be dependent, to give and to receive warmth
IV.	Advisory	To understand and to be understood	To consult, to give and to receive advice, to be rational, to be aware of order, to gain wisdom
V.	Participative	To join and to be joined	To collaborate, to encourage involvement, to persuade, to influence, to be a member, to be included, to include others
VI.	Emergent	To be in community	To be part of a whole, to touch, to be aware, to be self-determining, to be close
VII.	Organic	To feel and to express feelings	To gain sensory gratification, to create self, to gain new experience, to be impulsive and spontaneous
VIII.	Holistic	To be whole	To find roots, to create a free will, to have voluntary control over all bodily functions, to expand self
IX.	Transcendent	To transcend	To be without ego, to be without need, to be born anew, to move into new areas of being and awareness
X.	Cosmic	To join the universal all	To transcend self, to be without want, to transcend the need for separateness

Table 4. Release of New Energy into Life Flow

Environmental Phase		Primary Energy Released	Secondary Energies Released
0.	Chaos	Fear	Anger, dread, primitive emotions, flight
I.	Punitive	Hostility	Retaliation, jealousy, guilt, need to punish and be punished, moralizing, rebellion
II.	Autocratic	Power	Obedience, sense of responsibility, status, sense of authority, need for order
III.	Benevolent	Nurturing	Love, warmth, caring, parental feelings, obligation
IV.	Advisory	Perspective	Vision, sense of relationship, cognitive focus, scientific views
V.	Participative	Consensuality	Loyalty, collaboration, persuasion, need to influence, need to belong, membership feelings
VI.	Emergent	Involvement in community	Feeling of freedom, cooperation, sharing, broader base of perception and emotionality
VII.	Organic	Intuition	Empathy, heightened awareness, impulsiveness, spontaneity, sense of self
VIII.	Holistic	Unconscious and preconscious	Creativity, primitive fears, rootedness, expansion of self
IX.	Transcendent	Altered states	Unity of self, freedom from needs, nonsensory sources, and ego
X.	Cosmic	Universal and nirvanic	Ecstasy, out-of-body perspective, freedom from wants, transcendence of self, entry into infinite

Table 5. Alternative Styles of Life Management

Key Characteristics	External Intervention	Environmental Design
Locus of initiation of change	External to person or other human system	Internal to person or other human system
Direction of focus	Usually micro focus	Usually macro focus
Management required	Requires skilled professional or technical manager or consultant	Low or minimal need for professional manager of process
Resistance level	High induced resistance	Low or negligible induced resistance
Diagnostic model	Medical model, with intervention and treatment geared to specific diagnosis	Emergent model, with program usually unrelated to specific diagnosis
Specificity of focus on outcomes	Highly specific focus on selected outcomes	General focus on unselected, emergent outcomes
Basic skills required	Diagnostic, remedial, interventive, and evaluative	Empathic, nurturing, creative, or other nonskill aspects of personal behavior
Predictability	Highly predictable when performed by skilled professional	Highly unpredictable and emergent outcomes
Trust level	Based on low trust of natural, uncontrolled, or self-determined environment	Based on high trust of person or system to develop from intrinsic factors
Level of differentiation of theory	Highly sophisticated and differentiated theory usually required or useful	Theory need not be sophisticated or differentiated
Focus of responsibility	Responsibility usually built into intervener, who is external to system	Responsibility built into the person or system itself, rather than in external agent

External intervention occurs when someone outside the system attempts to intervene in an organizational or intrapersonal system by doing something designed to influence, improve, change, guide, teach, or correct the system in some way: a trainer comments on the process during a conflict in a training group; a consultant designs a program to change the system; a father rewards a child for being polite to a visitor; a minister gives an opinion in a way designed to change the character of a church member; a manager intrudes at a critical inspection point to improve the quality of the assembly-line product; or a teacher points out an error in a classroom exercise. In each case, a skilled interventionist has taken a significant step with the intention of improving the performance or life quality of the person or the system. An external intervention is presumed to be most effective when it is (a) aimed at a specific behavior, (b) performed in a skillful and sensitive manner, (c) part of a theoretically sound overall intervention program designed for long-range significance, (d) geared to an in-depth diagnosis and not to superficial symptoms, (e) molecular in focus, and (f) performed in an ethical and responsible manner. The external-intervention approach is essentially based on several assumptions that involve low trust and high fear in the person or client system.

The *environmental-design approach* assumes that a consultant can look *with* the person at his or her environment and plan ways to change that environment that will lead to personal satisfaction or improved performance. Or those in a social system can look at their environment to see if performance can be improved by collaboratively changing that environment. The environmental-design approach assumes that persons or institutions can determine their own lives, improve their own environments, make critical choices, learn their own skills, solve their own problems (i.e., live) in surprisingly effective ways.

ADVANTAGES OF THE ENVIRONMENTAL-DESIGN APPROACH

The advantages of using the environmental-design approach in organization development include the following:

1. A single diagnostic framework for examining all organizations;
2. A basis for a longitudinal analysis of organization development;
3. A single variable, trust level, as the key catalytic and leverage variable in all human systems, directly related to significant outcome measures of organizational effectiveness;
4. High face validity, appealing to innovative executives and OD specialists who are looking for something of immediate use in the organizational setting, as well as to theorists and visionaries who prefer more global and futuristic approaches;
5. A broad enough basis for application in any setting;
6. A needed synergy of the NTL, process-oriented approaches to OD with the growth-center, personal-growth approaches.

Environmental-quality analysis is a useful framework for any OD effort, regardless of its empirical or theory-based orientation.

REFERENCES

Gibb, J. R. *Trust: A new view of personal and organizational development.* Los Angeles: Guild of Tutors Press, 1978.

Gibb, J. R. The TORI community experience as an organizational change intervention. In W. W. Burke (Ed.), *Contemporary organizational development.* Washington, DC: NTL Institute for Applied Behavioral Science, 1972.

Likert, R., & Likert, J. G. *New ways of managing conflict.* New York: McGraw-Hill, 1976.

10

OD's Research Base: How To Expand and Utilize It

Donald C. King, John J. Sherwood, and Michael R. Manning

Recent reviews of the OD literature by Kahn (1974), Friedlander and Brown (1974), Beer (1976), Strauss (1976), and Alderfer (1976, 1977) have all voiced a plea for more research. While there is no question that this call is valid, the purpose of this paper is not to join in the cry for more OD research. Such exhortations seldom address in any clear, specific fashion the thorny conceptual, methodological, and operational problems in the conduct of OD research.

OD practitioners typically have neither the time, priorities, nor support to conduct significant research. Those in the academic world whose primary forte is research too often are content to comment on the sorry state of affairs in the area, while using noninnovative methodologies to study safe, peripheral problems.

In this chapter, we will first summarize why research has not played a more vital role in the field of organization development. Then we will discuss four methodologies that can broaden and enhance the contributions of research to the field.

It should be obvious, thus far, that we intend for research people to benefit from this paper; but we want to emphasize that our objective is also to be useful to the *consumers* of research—those consultants, managers, and other practitioners who read the OD literature and evaluate the impact of research on their profession. It is as important that the consumer of research know how much confidence to place in research evidence as it is for the researcher to be aware of rigorous methodologies. We propose that the criteria by which consumers can evalute research and the criteria by which researchers guide their studies are the same.

THE CURRENT STATUS OF OD RESEARCH

To assess the impact of research on organization development, the authors conducted a survey at the OD '78 Conference on Current Theory and Practice in Organization Development in San Francisco, March 16-17, 1978. Participants in the survey were sixty-six professionals who attended a presentation on OD's research base (ten academicians, eighteen internal OD consultants, seven external consultants, and thirty-one individuals from the general areas of human-resource management). The survey was a self-reporting questionnaire, containing six statements about OD research, using seven-point Likert scales ranging from "strongly disagree" to "strongly agree." In addition, respondents were asked to cite research studies that have had a significant impact on the field of OD. On four of the six statements in the questionnaire, the sixty-six conference participants responded with substantial agreement. They indicated that they: (a) have strong concern for the status of OD research, (b) read the OD research literature, (c) are dissatisfied with the quality of research in OD, and (d) find their work in organizations influenced by OD research. The remaining two statements did not receive the consensus of the respondents. The statement "OD is a research-based science" resulted in a bimodal response pattern with half the participants in agreement and the other half disagreeing. The final statement, "I perform OD research," also resulted in a bimodal response pattern; half the group reported that they perform OD research and the other half did not.

The second part of the questionnaire asked conference participants to cite research studies that have had significant impact on the field of organization development. Of the sixty-six participants surveyed, twenty-three (35 percent) *could not* cite a single study that has influenced OD. Ten participants (15 percent) could name but one study, while only thirty-three participants (50 percent) were able to indicate two or more studies. Ninety-seven different studies were included in the total of 155 studies cited. Only seventeen studies received more than one citation. Table 1 indicates the studies receiving the greatest number of citations.

Although the results of this survey may be limited by the fact that only a small sample (N=66) was surveyed and that participants preselected themselves into the data-collection procedure (by first choosing to attend the OD '78 Conference and then by taking part in the presentation of OD's research base), we feel justified in making two assumptions about the current status of OD research.

First, even though the OD practitioners and researchers characterized themselves as reading the OD research literature, being concerned with the status of OD research, and being influenced in their work by OD research, many of the respondents were unable to cite significant OD studies that have influenced their practice. This incongruity was disturbing not only to us but also to a number of conference participants. One participant commented, "The fact that I cannot think of others (research studies) bothers me! I'm not sure why." We too are bothered by the fact that it is so easy to say that OD is influenced by research, yet people become hard pressed to provide evidence in support of this claim. We question whether OD research has had more than a minimal impact on the practice of OD.

Second, the number of different research studies cited (ninety-seven) shows that research relevant to the OD process is being performed and communicated to practitioners. Yet, what appears to be significant to one practitioner apparently does not hold the same value for another. Only seventeen studies received more than one citation. Although Likert's System 4 theory of management received the greatest number of citations, only 13.6 percent of the participants surveyed believe that this research has made a significant impact on the field of OD. It appears that everyone (who can cite studies) has a favorite study, and there is little agreement on what research provides the foundation for developmental work in organizations. Reports on OD research appears to be an unorganized and fragmented literature, having disperse appeal to practitioners and providing little, if any, structure for the strategies employed in planned-change efforts. There simply is no central body of OD research that is recognized by those performing OD activities.

The field of OD is not now but *must become* a research-based science. This is probably the greatest issue confronting the field. It is not merely a question of whether we *should* perform research or not, but a critical demand that we *must!* Kahn states, "Ideas and personal impressions need desperately to be tested by collision with facts. The mill of science grinds only when hypotheses and data are in continuous and abrasive contact" (1974, p. 489).

Table 1. Studies That Have Had a Significant Impact on OD (N=66)

Studies	Number of Citations	Percent of Group Citing the Same Study
R. Likert: System 4 Management	9	13.6
R. Blake & J. Mouton: Managerial Grid	5	7.5
General Foods: Topeka Studies	4	6
K. Lewin: Field Theory	4	6
F. Hertzberg: Motivation	4	6

FORCES DETERMINING THE ROLE OF OD RESEARCH

A number of forces prevent OD practitioners from utilizing their knowledge of research to develop a research-based practice. After reviewing the literature and discussing this issue with conference participants, we have identified six salient forces that determine the role of research in OD. These forces must be addressed before research can become a vital part of organizational change.

OD should be viewed as a science, not merely as an art. A fundamental question is whether OD activities lend themselves to scientific investigation or whether they are merely a creative art that is applied to organizations. We consider the technology of OD to be a science; those who perceive OD only as an art restrict their options significantly. Through the use of rational approaches that are available through scientific investigation, we can accurately evaluate our work as well as maintain the creative approach that is equally important.

OD should clarify its impact on organizations and establish support in the scientific community. Practitioners at the OD '78 Conference expressed relatively little concern about the need for "scientific" proof that the intended effect of their intervention be realized by the client organization. Anecdotal proof that OD works appears to be sufficient for most client organizations. Clients either accept the values and methods of planned change or they do not. Therefore, few incentives exist for conducting rigorous experimental designs that can legitimize consulting efforts. Although scientific proof of one's activities may not be a prerequisite for a practitioner to find work, it would seem very short-sighted to negate the long-term effects of research. OD needs to gain the empirical acceptance of the scientific community, in order to avoid becoming a passing fad. The key to the future of OD may be within this scientific community.

Research or scientific achievement should not lag behind practice. OD research has assumed the role of validating current consulting practices. Typically, after a new consulting intervention has been developed and widely used, researchers attempt to evaluate the impact of the new technique. The disadvantage of this approach is that research is not at the "cutting edge" of the field in terms of new discoveries or insights. Friedlander and Brown (1974) have voiced their concern that, as a consequence of this lag, research may be seen as an "irrelevant appendage" to the field.

OD research should have more methodological rigor. If OD is to enhance its position in the scientific community, OD research must be performed according to contemporary scientific standards. The researcher must make objective use of designs and controls that optimize internal and external validity so that results can be accepted with confidence (Campbell & Stanley, 1963; Cook & Campbell, 1976). Friedlander & Brown (1974) have noted that the obtrusive presence of an outsider (researcher) and the often chaotic and uncontrollable environments of organizations complicate and often confound OD research. This adds to the dilemma and confusion in developing rigorous methodologies.

Systematic programs of OD research should be developed. The OD research literature consists largely of isolated, unrelated studies that do not fit together in any common pattern. With very few exceptions (the Tavistock studies conducted by Rice, 1958 and Trist and Bamforth, 1951, and the participation-in-decision-making studies by Coch and French, 1948, and French, Israel, and As, 1960), no OD research has tried to gain support for theories by repeating the same study in a similar or different setting. Kahn (1974) has criticized OD literature for its autobiographical nature and its almost exclusive concentration on the experiences of the trainees and change agents rather than on the wholistic issue of organizational change. "It (OD) is a literature of training episodes and those episodes are often nonorganizational or extraorganizational" (1974, p. 493).

A straightforward language for the communication of concepts should be established. The term "organization development remains scientifically undefined, a convenient label for a variety of activities. In fact, OD is evolving as a system of colloquial terms (e.g., sensing, mirroring, team building, process consultation, third-party intervention, etc.), none of which is precisely defined nor reducible to observable behaviors (Kahn, 1974). Not only is this nebulous language hard to speak but it is even more difficult to write. It is composed largely of jargon, and unless you speak the language of the field, you have little chance of understanding its literature. White and Mitchell (1978) have suggested that OD use a classification system, along the lines of the familiar biological classification system, to specify the logical relationships among elements of the OD process. They have termed this approach the application of "facet theory."

Thile these six items stress the importance of research in the field and provide general guidelines for the planning, conducting, and reporting of research studies, they do not point toward the specific methodologies that hold the greatest promise for advancing knowledge and practice in OD. Equal amounts of time, money, and energy devoted to research can and do produce widely disparate results that depend, in large measure, on the specific research methodology employed.

FOUR METHODOLOGICAL APPROACHES

Four methodological approaches appears to have great potential for (a) longitudinal research designs, (b) identification of moderating variables, (c) field experiments, and (d) innovative use of laboratory studies. It is important that *both* researchers and practitioners share common values regarding the comparative utility of published research. We all know that all research results are not equally reliable and valid. We all recognize that even well-conducted research is very often situation and time specific. *Yet our reactions to a study too often are based on whether the results and conclusions are consistent with our own values and experience rather than on the quality of the study itself.* The following four methodological approaches can increase our confidence in reported results and provide empirical data to support or refute the conventional wisdom of OD consultation. Several of the recent studies that will be cited as examples of the use of a particular methodology have not yet been reported in the OD literature.

Longitudinal Research

Longitudinal research affords great advantage in that the longer we look the more we will see. Benefits exist in allowing the researcher and the consumer of research to observe trends in performance, behaviors, and attitudes over time. Since the impact of an OD intervention usually is not immediately apparent, longitudinal research is clearly a necessary choice for OD researchers.

Pasmore's (1976) study exemplifies the benefits of longitudinal research. In a two-and-one-half-year action-research project that was part of a larger evaluation study, he investigated the effects of three OD interventions. Two of these interventions combined technostructural and human-process approaches (sociotechnical system/survey feedback and job redesign/survey feedback), while the other intervention used only a human-process approach (survey feedback). The research setting was a production facility of a large, national, food-processing corporation. Pasmore utilized a quasi-experimental design involving two units of the production facility over three time periods. The first time period provided a baseline survey measure, and the three OD interventions were implemented in the next two time periods. Data were collected from two hundred individuals through three surveys, company records, and on-site observations by the author. Results of the study indicated that: (a) the combined interventions (sociotechnical system/survey) feedback and the job redesign/survey feedback) performed similarly in improving employees' attitudes and their perceptions about their jobs; (b) both combined interventions reduced the number of employees required to operate the production system; (c) only the sociotechnical-system/survey-feedback intervention resulted in significant improvements in productivity; and (d) both of the combined interventions yielded more positive effects on employee attitudes than did survey-feedback interventions alone.

Through the use of a longitudinal design, Pasmore was able to examine the effects of combined intervention styles as well as to measure several dependent variables over three time periods. Also, he was able to make first-hand clinical observations over a two-and-one-half-year period. The extended length of this study significantly increases its potential contribution to our understanding of organizational change.

Tolchinsky (1978) is presently conducting an eighteen-month longitudinal study in a Department of Defense military installation. His study concentrates on the differing effects of three survey-feedback interventions: the traditional "waterfall" method, data handback, and a "bottoms-up" approach. The study utilizes a modified time-series design with work groups at random across treatment and control conditions. Performance data are collected on a daily schedule, and attitudinal data are obtained in four time intervals. The longitudinal nature of this design allows Tolchinsky to observe the impact of the different survey-feedback approaches over an extended period of time.

Other studies have utilized longitudinal designs to great benefit. Seashore and Bowers (1970) revisited the Weldon Company in 1969, four and one-half years after OD programs were ended. The same instruments that had been used in 1962 and 1964 were used to obtain data in 1969. Comparative results among data in 1962, 1964, and 1969 indicated that after the two-year change program, Weldon had not reverted to its pre-1962 status. The 1969 results indicated that Weldon was continuing to progress toward organizational goals that had been set by the OD interventions four and one-half to six and one-half years earlier. Using this longitudinal design, the researchers were able to conclude that a "lock-in" effect of goals from the OD intervention had been realized. Also, it seemed highly unlikely that "Hawthorne effects" could explain the results of the 1962-1964 OD program, since consultants were used quite minimally after 1964. Bowers (1973) collected data from 14,000 respondents in twenty-three organizations in which different OD interventions were used. Research in each organization extended over a period of one to five years (most organizations participated for two years) and allowed as many as five measurements to be taken. Barnes and Greiner (in Blake et al., 1964) measured the effects of a Managerial Grid program in a large company. Performance data over a three-year period indicated a sizeable increase in employee productivity that enabled the company to realize several million dollars of controllable cost savings and profit increase. Attitudinal measures showed improved relationships in a shift toward 9,9 scores on the Managerial Grid. Alderfer and Brown (1975), in a five-year study of a boarding school, were able to specify many aspects of organizational consulting as well as performance and satisfaction measures in the client organization that were enhanced by the study's length. Members of the Tavistock Institute (Rice, 1958; Trist & Bamforth, 1951) have used longitudinal studies to great advantage in exploring sociotechnical interventions in the coal-mining industry and in an Indian textile plant.

One may ask just what our definition of "longitudinal" is. A precise answer is beyond the scope of this paper. Even though Likert and Likert (1976) have expressed some estimates of the time dimensions required for effects in organizational work to be realized fully, we are still unprepared to define the time span of "longitudinal." Our proposal is that researchers scrutinize this question whenever they are planning a field study and that consumers of research question the time length of studies they read. In our opinion, the appropriate length of a study will differ with the situation, depending on factors such as the type of intervention to be implemented, the people involved, the tasks, and the interdependence among groups.

Besides being expensive and requiring a great deal of the researcher's time, longitudinal research has another possible disadvantage: problems of controlling extraneous variation. When studies extend over greater lengths of time, not only do they allow us to "see" more, but they allow for more rival explanations (history, maturation, mortality, etc.) for any observed change. Use of Campbell's (1969) time-series designs and Campbell and Stanley's (1963) quasi-experimental designs can help to minimize these threats to validity.

Although longitudinal research is not easily performed, we believe that the results obtained from the studies cited here are indications of the worth of longitudinal designs. Conducting more studies of this nature will help us deal with the complexities that arise throughout the process of organizational change. Longitudinal studies that are designed to minimize extraneous variation and provide timely measurement for dependent variables can definitely add to the research base of OD.

Identification of Moderating Variables

Researchers and consumers of OD research need to be aware of potential moderating variables and their effects. It is too simple to assume that independent variables link together in a simple and straightforward fashion. We live in a world of multiple causation, and our research must take this fact into account. The added identification and measurement of potential moderating variables in our hypothesized linkage between independent and dependent variables can help deal with this complex situation. Although the literature contains some semantic confusion concerning the use of the term "moderator variable" (MacCorquodale & Meehl, 1948; Saunders, 1956; Zedeck, 1971), it is generally agreed that a moderating variable is a construct that varies systematically with the relationship between two variables, thereby moderating the predictive power of these variables.

For example, when designing research to examine the causal relationship between a specific OD intervention and changes in productivity and attitudes, the researcher may simultaneously hypothesize and measure the existence of variables that will moderate the effect of the OD intervention on any changes in productivity or attitudes. Expectations, leadership styles, length of the intervention, personality orientation of the key manager, or style of the consultant may all be potential moderating variables that need to be examined. This added information increases understanding of relationships that are reported.

It is quite plausible that expectations moderate the relationships between interventions and outcomes. In a twelve-month study conducted at four clothing-manufacturing plants, King (1974) focused on managerial expectations in two job-enlargement and two job-rotation interventions. In one of each of the job-enlargement and job-rotation interventions, managers were told that they could expect the intervention to result in increased productivity, while the managers of the other two organizations were told that the interventions would improve industrial relations but would not change previous output levels. The study showed that the managers who were led to expect higher productivity as a result of the interventions increased their plant output during the experimental period. Although this study suffers from certain methodological problems, the experiments emphasize the power of expectations.

Recently, Lloyd (1977) conducted a one-year action-research project in a Department of Defense military installation. He employed a modified Solomon-4 design with work groups that were randomized across treatment and control conditions to investigate the differential effects of two styles of survey feedback. The first model employed the traditional survey-feedback process; participating supervisors were given the survey data reported by their subordinates and received no training in what the data meant or in how to feed back the data. The second model instituted much tighter controls and guidance; extensive training in analysis of the data and how to feed these data back to subordinates was provided for the supervisors. A structure was imposed to ensure that data were shared with subordinates. Lloyd was interested in the effects of the two models on various performance and attitudinal data. He also identified and measured seven potential moderating variables: education, feedback from supervisors and co-workers, motivation for work, autonomy, communication patterns, peer cohesion, leadership style, and individual growth-need strength. Results indicated that the extent to which employees receive clear information about their performance from supervisors and co-workers moderated the effect of the survey feedback on individual job satisfaction. Communication patterns and the quality and quantity of an employee's communication with his or her supervisors were shown to moderate the effect of survey feedback on the dependent measures of job satisfaction and feedback from supervisors and co-workers. Other results suggested that when their supervisors were trained in using survey feedback, employees' perceptions of their productivity increased significantly.

Lloyd's use of moderating variables strengthens our ability to understand the effect of his survey-feedback manipulations. The identification of communication patterns and feedback from supervisors and co-workers as moderating variables is important to researchers and practitioners in developing potent OD designs.

Nemiroff (1975) conducted a study in a medium-sized food-processing plant and identified two moderating variables: bureaucratic orientation and higher-order-need strength. The study hypothesized that task effectiveness and human fulfillment were contingent on congruent "fits" between individual, task/job design, and organizational-structure variables. Bureaucratic orientation was conceptualized as the degree of formalization and authoritarianism that an individual desired. Individuals rating high in bureaucratic orientation were characterized as accepting of authority, preferring to have specific rules and guidelines to follow, preferring impersonalized work relationship, and exhibiting high needs for organizational and in-group identification. The higher-order-need-strength variable is associated with the upper levels of Maslow's need hierarchy: esteem, recognition, and self-realization. The study showed that bureaucratic orientation moderates the relationship between organizational structure and human fulfillment. Likewise, the relationship between task/job design and human fulfillment was shown to be moderated by an individual's higher-order-need strength.

Social desirability has been shown to be an intervening variable by Golembiewski and Munzenrider (1975). Using Likert's Profile of Organizational Characteristics and the Crowne-Marlowe Social Desirability Scale, they found that salespersons offering the highest System-4 ratings of their organization also had the highest social desirability scores.

More research similar to that conducted by Lloyd (1977), Nemiroff (1975), King (1974), and Golembiewski and Munzenrider (1975) is greatly needed. One of the ways in which we are better able to understand the OD process and further expand its research base is through the identification of moderating variables.

Field Experiments

As has been mentioned previously, one of the recurring themes throughout the OD literature is that OD research needs to be more methodologically rigorous. In our opinion, one way to confront the rigor issue is by the use of experimental designs in the field. Experimental designs permit greater confidence in establishing any differences between experimental conditions.

A field experiment is characterized as ". . . a theoretically oriented research project in which the experimenter manipulates an independent variable in some real social setting in order to test some hypothesis" (French, 1953). True field experiments employ the use of control groups and randomize subjects throughout all conditions. Randomization affords the researcher great advantage in terms of internal validity (Cook & Campbell, 1976), while the use of ongoing intact organizations as research settings enhances the validity of the experiment.

True field experiments that promote internal and external validity should be used whenever possible. Since conditions beyond the control of the OD researcher often preclude meeting the requirements of true experiments, quasi-experimental designs may be substituted, with suitable cautions about each design's threats to validity (Campbell & Stanley, 1963; Cook & Campbell, 1976). In fact, it is possible to create "patched-up" quasi-experimental designs in which the particular threats to internal validity are determined and control after control is used until as many threats as possible have been ruled out (Cook & Campbell, 1976).

Probably the most cited research study that employed a quasi-experimental design is the Coch and French (1948) study of the Harwood Manufacturing Company. They used three conditions to examine the effects of participation on change: no participation, participation through representation, and total participation. Results showed significantly higher productivity with greater participation. The frequent references to this classic study as one of the few existing examples of a field experiment demonstrates the lack of such major studies in the last thirty years.

In a study to evaluate the effectiveness of internal consulting efforts in the military, Adams (1977) developed a design that focuses on the traditional "waterfall" survey-feedback intervention. Since a complete random assignment of treatments was not feasible, the researcher utilized a quasi-experimental, three-group, pre-post test design. Subjects in the two experimental groups received a survey-feedback intervention from the internal consultants, while a control group received no treatment, and a "placebo" group experienced workshops on race relations and drug and alcohol abuse. Data confirmed that as a result of the survey-feedback manipulations, the experimental groups showed significant improvement in one of three work categories comprising organizational efficiency. Intergroup relations improved in all but one of the work units within the two experimental groups; however, no statistically significant improvements were observed when compared to control and placebo groups. Satisfaction also increased (although not significantly) for the majority of the work units receiving the survey feedback. Inconclusive results were observed concerning the degree to which immediate supervisors provide support and interest in subordinates' problems. One experimental group indicated significant improvement in this area while the other experimental group did not.

The strength of Adams' design rests on three principles. First, unlike the majority of field experiments, a pilot study was performed by the researcher. This allowed Adams to pretest and validate his survey instrument, to gain some knowledge of how organizational members perceived survey feedback as an organizational-effectiveness intervention, and to avoid numerous problems in his actual research. Second, the use of a placebo treatment allows the researcher to control any Hawthorne effect or the alternative hypothesis that any difference between groups is simply a function of the consultant's presence or the convening of group meetings. Third, the consultant and researcher roles were separate, thereby controlling any experimenter-expectancy effects.

To study the effects of a team-development intervention on work-group performance, Woodman (1978) has worked with sixty-eight three-person surveying groups from a land-survey course. All students were randomly assigned to surveying groups, with these groups randomized throughout the experimental treatments. The experiment employed a "posttest-only control group" true experimental design (Campbell & Stanley, 1963) with an additional placebo control condition added to test for possible Hawthorne effects. The research showed that group members receiving the team-development intervention perceived their groups as being more effective and reported higher levels of participation and involvement than did members who did not experience the intervention. These results were statistically significant. Groups in the team-development condition expressed greater satisfaction with their performance and their group and expressed greater agreement on group goals than did the controls, although these differences were not statistically significant. No performance differences, in terms of grades, were observed.

This "quasi-laboratory" research setting is unique in that it retains the majority of the control available in true laboratory settings, while at the same time it provides a realistic environment with established work groups composed of individuals who are truly involved and committed to the group's performance of the task. This study's generalizability is enhanced because ad hoc groups were not utilized. Aside from providing a realistic and controlled environment, the study's large sample size (twenty-three groups in each of the experimental and placebo conditions and twenty-two groups in the control condition) affords sufficient statistical power for treatment-group comparisons.

In Lloyd's (1977) previously cited study, the use of a modified Solomon-4 group design allowed Lloyd to control four of Campbell and Stanley's (1963) threats to internal validity: mortality, instrumentation, statistical regression, and selection. The randomization of work groups added further strength to this design. Tolchinsky's (1978) time-series quasi-experimental design also utilizes the principle of randomization.

Alderfer (1977) cites a study by Coughlan and Cooke (1974) that examined a collective decision-making intervention in public elementary schools. The study utilized a modified four-group design, randomly assigning twenty-four schools from five school districts to the four experimental and control conditions. Experimental, in contrast to control, groups indicated greater use of the collective processes and more positive changes in work attitudes.

These field experiments are indicative of the great potential of rigorous experimental designs. Utilization of these or similar methods creates confidence in the observed results. But the implementation of research of this kind is not without its costs or trade-offs.

Lloyd (1977) has critiqued the use of a rigorous experimental design in field research. He has cited critical issues regarding methods of randomization, experimental manipulation, and the utilization of control groups in his survey-feedback study.

Although randomization negates the issue of preselection and enhances the use of statistical computations that are generalizable, *it may create artifacts that are not found in nonrandomized studies*. To randomize subjects in a waterfall survey-feedback intervention, as Lloyd has done, one cannot involve entire vertical segments of an organization, but must use chance to select work groups into the experimental and control conditions demanded by a randomized design. This method allows for the possibility that a supervisor who has many subordinates—some of whom are participants (control or various treatment groups) or nonparticipants in the experiment—may relate differently to subordinates in various classifications. *Experimental manipulations may create demand characteristics.* An environment in which subjects from different treatments are aware of the differences existing between work groups may allow them to gain insight into the variations of the experiment and to determine the independent variables. The use of control groups allows researchers to control for threats to internal validity (Campbell & Stanley, 1963), *yet this may create an ethical dilemma.* Control groups that are subject to obtrusive pre- and posttest measurements develop expectations, from hearing and observing the activities of other treatment groups, that by design cannot be fulfilled in the control situation.

As Lloyd (1977) and others have shown, these three issues can be dealt with in the field, but not without a great expenditure of time and effort by the researcher. It is our conclusion that even though field experiments are difficult to perform, their increased use by OD researchers is necessary to provide the groundwork for a research-based science.

Innovative Use of the Laboratory

Probably the most underemployed technique available to the OD researcher is the use of laboratory methodology. If used in creative ways, laboratory studies can be very useful to the OD researcher, particularly in the control of extraneous variables, which usually is impossible in field settings.

The laboratory's major strengths are threefold (Kerlinger, 1973). First, the laboratory allows situational control. The experimenter can isolate the research situation from any extraneous influences that might affect the dependent variables. Second, the laboratory affords an operational strength; that is, the experimenter can implement random assignment and manipulate one or more independent variables. Third, laboratory research is precise with respect to the source of variance. A high degree of accuracy and definition can be achieved in measurements by using precise instruments, resulting in less error variance and in higher reliability.

A major criticism of laboratory research is that results obtained from the laboratory cannot be generalized to describe the real world because of the artificiality that characterizes this method (Kerlinger, 1973). Fromkin and Streufert (1976) have proposed convincing arguments supporting the use of laboratory research and have shown that many of the criticisms of the laboratory also apply to field settings. If the researcher pays careful attention to the artifacts distinguished by Rosenthal and Rosnow (1969) (i.e., demand characteristics, evaluation apprehension, and experimenter expectancy) and employs Fromkin and Streufert's "boundary variables" to help bridge the gap between laboratory data and organizational applications, the researcher can greatly enhance the generalizability of results. For these reasons, we support the pursuit of rigorous OD research in the laboratory.

Lipshitz (1976) developed an innovative laboratory design to study the impact of consultant prestige and process interventions on group performance and group cohesiveness. He utilized a $2 \times 2 + 2$ design (consultant prestige times intervention style plus control groups). Subjects were led to believe that the consultant was of either high or low prestige. High-prestige consultants were introduced as faculty members with considerable consulting experience while low-prestige consultants were presented as first-year graduate students with no consulting experience. The prestige factor was crossed with type of intervention style—instrumental process analysis or interpersonal process analysis. The instrumental-process-analysis intervention utilized a role-negotiation approach that clarified the expectations that team members held for each other in their working relations and adjusted role behaviors and expectations. The interpersonal-process-analysis intervention employed an image exchange that focused the attention of team members on how they were perceived by others, allowing the parties involved in the exchange to correct misperceptions that they felt existed in their images. The last two conditions were control conditions. One control required that groups perform the process interventions without the aid or presence of a consultant. In the other control condition, there was no intervention *or* consultant, and the groups performed their tasks. Subjects were composed of sixty three-person teams whose common task was a simulation that employed strategic organizational properties.

Results of Lipshitz's study indicate that:

1. Teams utilizing process analysis, with or without a consultant, improved more in their work process and cohesiveness;
2. Teams utilizing consultants were not significantly different from teams performing the tasks on their own;
3. There were no differences because of consultant prestige;
4. Teams with instrumental-process-analysis interventions had greater improvements in work processes and performance, while interpersonal-process-analysis interventions contributed to higher cohesiveness; and
5. No consistent patterns resulted from the interaction of prestige and style of intervention.

This study models important characteristics for researchers and consumers of OD research. First, the study did not attempt to build a "metatypical" organization but instead employed an important laboratory principle of choosing a number of variables that are significant in organizations (task interdependence, incompatibility of objectives, conflict, choices to be made between quality and quantity of production, and uncertainty) and manipulated these factors in the simulation. Second, this study clearly demonstrates the fact that OD issues can be examined in the laboratory. And third, the laboratory provides an environment in which variables inherent to the OD process can be examined, which cannot be done in the field. For example, the manipulation of high- and low-prestige consultants would be difficult to perform ethically in a work organization, but it is very worthy of investigation.

Two other studies from the literature show the usefulness of the laboratory to OD research. Robey (1974) conducted a job-enrichment experiment in the laboratory that indicated that individual differences mediate individuals' behavior and attitudinal responses to enriched jobs. Hand, Estafen, and Sims (1975) tested the effects of data survey and feedback in the laboratory; pre-post measurements showed a difference in satisfaction between experimental and control groups, but no performance differences.

OD has an available methodology of laboratory experimentation that may be of greater value than is realized. Weick (1965) and Fromkin and Streufert (1976) have advised organizational researchers to "go back to the lab!" Similarly, we would like to suggest the same strategy to the OD researcher, not as an end in itself, but as a piece of the puzzle that should be utilized. The potential of the laboratory is great for the field of OD; it may provide a method that can help OD research pioneer the development of new techniques. This could help close the gap between research and practice and also enhance OD's research base.

SUMMARY

At this time, it is crucial that OD establish itself as a research-based science. To do so, the cooperation of both the researcher and the practitioner is needed. Researchers must know and utilize methodological designs that optimally enhance OD's research base; practitioners or consumers of research must be aware of these designs and be able to recognize and evaluate studies on the merit of their contribution to a research base. We have discussed four methodologies that can promote OD's research base: (a) *longitudinal research*, the collection of data over a sufficient time period, with appropriate measurement intervals; (b) *identification of moderating variables*, a demonstration of the linkages of variables in a realistic manner; (c) *field experiments*, the exercise of control and determination, with some certainty of whether our interventions are useful; and (d) *laboratory experiments*, which provide the greatest scientific control and which can be utilized whenever research topics do not lend themselves to the field. By utilizing these four approaches, the researcher and practitioner can make major contributions to the development of OD's research base.

REFERENCES

Adams, J. An evaluation of organization effectiveness: A longitudinal investigation of the effects of survey feedback as an action research intervention on unit efficiency, employee affective response, intergroup relations and supervisory consideration in the U.S. Army. Unpublished doctoral dissertation, Krannert Graduate School of Management, Purdue University, 1977.

Alderfer, C. P. Organization development. *Annual Review of Psychology*, 1977, *28*, 197-223.

Alderfer, C. P. Change processes in organizations. In M. D. Dunnette (Ed.), *Handbook of industrial and organizational psychology*. Chicago: Rand McNally, 1976.

Alderfer, C. P., & Brown, L. D. *Learning from changing: Organizational diagnosis and development*. Beverly Hills: Sage, 1975.

Beer, M. The technology of organization development. In M. D. Dunnette (Ed.), *Handbook of industrial and organizational psychology*. Chicago: Rand McNally, 1976.

Blake, R. R., Mouton, J. S., Barnes, L. B., & Greiner, L. E. Breakthrough in organization development. *Harvard Business Review*, 1964, *42*, 133-155.

Bowers, D. G. OD techniques and their results in 23 organizations: The Michigan ICL study. *Journal of Applied Behavioral Science*, 1973, *9*, 21-43.

Campbell, D. T. Reforms as experiments. *American Psychologist*, 1969, *24*, 409-449.

Campbell, D. T., & Stanley, J. C. *Experimental and quasi-experimental designs for research*. Chicago: Rand McNally, 1963.

Coch, L., & French, J. R. P., Jr. Overcoming resistance to change. *Human Relations*, 1948, *1*, 512-532.

Cook, R. D., & Campbell, D. T. The design and conduct of quasi-experiments and true experiments in field settings. In M. D. Dunnette (Ed.), *Handbook of industrial and organizational psychology*. Chicago: Rand McNally, 1976.

Coughlan, R. J., & Cooke, R. A. *The structural development of educational organizations*. Ann Arbor, MI: Institute for Social Research, 1974.

French, J. R. P., Jr. Experiments in field settings. In L. Festinger & D. Katz (Eds.), *Research methods in the behavioral sciences*. New York: Holt, Rinehart and Winston, 1953.

French, J. R. P., Jr., Israel, J., & As, D. An experiment on participation in a Norwegian factory. *Human Relations*, 1960, *13*, 3-19.

Friedlander, F., & Brown, L. D. Organization development. *Annual Review of Psychology*, 1974, *25*, 313-341.

Fromkin, H. L., & Streufert, S. Laboratory experimentation. In M. D. Dunnette (Ed.), *Handbook of industrial and organizational psychology*. Chicago: Rand McNally, 1976.

Golembiewski, R. T., & Munzenrider, R. Social desirability as an interviewing variable in interpreting OD effects. *Journal of Applied Behavioral Science*, 1975, *11*, 317-332.

Hand, H. H., Estafen, B. D., & Sims, H. P. How effective is data survey and feedback as a technique of organization development? *Journal of Applied Behavioral Science*, 1975, *11*, 333-347.

Kahn, R. L. Organizational development: Some problems and proposals. *Journal of Applied Behavioral Science*, 1974, *10*, 485-502.

Kerlinger, F. N. *Foundations of behavioral research* (2nd ed.). New York: Holt, Rinehart and Winston, 1973.

King, S. A. Expectation effects in organizational change. *Administrative Science Quarterly*, 1974, *19*, 221-230.

Likert, R., & Likert, J. G. *New ways of managing conflict*. New York: McGraw-Hill, 1976.

Lipshitz, R. The effectiveness of third party process interventions into simulated organizations as a function of the consultant's prestige and style of intervention. Unpublished doctoral dissertation, Krannert Graduate School of Management, Purdue University, 1976.

Lloyd, R. F. Introducing model II survey feedback: A longitudinal investigation of the effects of traditional survey feedback and a proposed feedback style on job attributes, employee affective reactions and organizational performance measures. Unpublished doctoral dissertation, Krannert Graduate School of Management, Purdue University, 1977.

MacCorquodale, K., & Meehl, P. E. On a distinction between hypothetical constructs and intervening variables. *Psychological Review*, 1948, *55*, 95-107.

Nemiroff, P. M. The impact of individual, task and organization structure variables on task effectiveness and human fulfillment at a continuous automated-flow production site: A contingency approach. Unpublished doctoral dissertation, Krannert Graduate School of Management, Purdue University, 1975.

Pasmore, W. A. Understanding organizational change: A longitudinal investigation of the effects of sociotechnical system, job redesign, and survey feedback interventions on organizational task accomplishment and human fulfillment. Unpublished doctoral dissertation, Krannert Graduate School of Management, Purdue University, 1976.

Rice, A. K. *Productivity and social organization: The Ahmedabad experiment*. London: Tavistock, 1958.

Robey, D. Task design, work values, and worker response: Experimental test. *Organizational Behavior and Human Performance*, 1974, *12*, 264-273.

Rosenthal, R., & Rosnow, R. L. *Artifact in behavioral research*. New York: Academic Press, 1969.

Saunders, D. R. Moderator variables in prediction. *Educational and Psychological Measurement*, 1956, *16*, 209-222.

Seashore, S. E., & Bowers, D. G. The durability of organizational change. *American Psychologist*, March 1970, *25*(3), 227-233.

Strauss, G. Organizational development. In R. Dublin (Ed.), *Handbook of work, organization, and society*. Chicago: Rand McNally, 1976.

Tolchinsky, P. D. The effects of survey feedback interventions on employee attitudes, expectations, and performance: A longitudinal field study. Unpublished doctoral dissertation, Krannert Graduate School of Management, Purdue University, 1978.

Trist, E. L., & Bamforth, K. W. Some social and psychological consequences of the longwall method of coal getting. *Human Relations*, 1951, *4*, 3-38.

Weick, K. E. Laboratory experimentation with organizations. In J. G. March (Ed.), *Handbook of organizations*. Chicago: Rand McNally, 1965.

White, S. E., & Mitchell, T. R. Organization development: A review of research content and research design. In W. L. French, C. H. Bell, Jr., & R. A. Zawacki (Eds.), *Organization development: Theory, practice, and research*. Dallas, TX: Business Publications, 1978.

Woodman, R. W. Effects of team development intervention: A field experiment. Unpublished doctoral dissertation, Krannert Graduate School of Management, Purdue University, 1978.

Zedeck, S. Problems with the use of moderator variables. *Psychological Bulletin*, 1971, *76*, 295-310.

11

OD in Schools: The State of the Art

Michael Fullan and Matthew Miles

INTRODUCTION

Organization Development (OD) in schools and school districts has greatly expanded from little or no activity fifteen years ago to an apparent flurry over the past five years. Yet, despite the number of articles and books about OD work in schools, we really do not know the answers to some basic questions.

1. What is the extent of OD work in school districts across Canada and the United States?
2. How many OD consultants are active in education? What is their background and the nature of their activities?
3. What are the conditions or factors associated with sustained or successful OD efforts compared to less successful ones?
4. What policy and strategic implications derive from a thorough assessment of where OD is and where it is going?

With these questions as a focus, and with the National Institute of Education support, we undertook a state-of-the art study of OD in schools and school districts. There were four major components of the larger study (Miles, Fullan, & Taylor, 1978).

1. A review of reviews of OD studies.
2. An empirical analysis of the number of OD *consultants* working in schools and the nature of their work.
3. An identification and analysis of *school districts* in which sustained OD work was going on.
4. Three mini case studies of OD programs in different districts.

In this article we concentrate on items 2 and 3. Our analysis is an assessment of the state of the art of OD in schools in terms of the extent and nature of work of

Based on a study funded by the National Institute of Education, Contract No. 400-77-0052. Gib Taylor made substantial contributions to the gathering of data and to writing sections of the larger report. Our thanks also to Richard Schmuck for his valuable suggestions and to Joan May for her administrative assistance.

OD consultants in education ($N=357$ in the final sample) and the extent, nature, and impact of sustained OD programs in school districts ($N=76$). In assessing school-district programs we identified "sustained" OD efforts as:

> A sustained attempt at system self-study and improvement over a period of at least eighteen months, focusing on change in organizational procedures, norms, or structures using behavioral science concepts.

Excluded from our definition were activities of an individual or short-term nature, for example, in-service training of individuals (one-time workshops for teachers, principals, etc.) that did not aim directly at system or subunit improvement.

THE CONTEXT AND HISTORY OF OD IN EDUCATION

Most people tend to treat schools as a taken-for-granted part of the social background. Schools do an effective job of keeping children safely off the streets and out of the labor market. So—except for an occasional indignant article in the newspapers or magazines, or the inconvenience we experience when teachers strike—we go about our business, expecting that schools will continue to be kept, and that our children will emerge from them with reasonable amounts of literacy, computation skills, and useful information.

Yet schools are a pervasive institution in developed societies. All of us must spend at least ten—usually twelve or thirteen—years of our young lives in them. On any given weekday in 1976 in the United States, about 45,000,000 students (nearly 90 percent of all children aged 5-17) were in public elementary and secondary schools, and 5,000,000 more were in 18,000 nonpublic schools. There are about 16,000 public school districts, with 89,000 school buildings, employing 2.6 million adults. Put another way, about 17 percent of *all* public employees are teachers and school administrators. In the United States, about seventy-five billion dollars was spent in 1976 on elementary and secondary schooling; this was 5.8 percent of GNP (U.S. Dept. of HEW, 1977). So the scale is substantial.

Schools, of course, are organizations as well as subsystems of organizations called school districts. They presumably are subject to the ills for which OD is a potential cure, have money to pay for professional intervention efforts, and might be able to accomplish their missions with more effectiveness as a result. It is likely, however, that proportionally fewer schools than other nonprofit agencies or profit-making organizations are using OD.

Although schools are organizations, they do have special properties that make them interesting and effect efforts at facilitative intervention.

1. There is *goal diffuseness*: the organization's mission usually is stated abstractly, with output measurement a difficult matter (Miles, 1967; Miles & Schmuck, 1971), partly because of the long time-line involved.
2. *Technical capability* is often suboptimal; the knowledge base underlying educational practice is relatively weak, and/or not well diffused to practitioners (Sieber, 1968).
3. There are typically *coordination* problems; schools and school districts tend to be low-interdependent, "loosely-coupled" systems (Bidwell, 1965; Weick, 1976) in which goals do not connect well with means, and

in which accountability is low and autonomy high. As Miles (1977) points out, such a feature is not necessarily to be deplored: loosely coupled systems tend to be more flexible and adaptive, less a prey to environmental threat, less vulnerable to incompetence, and more innovative than are more tightly coordinated systems.

4. Schools have *boundary-management* problems; the skin of the organization seems unbearably thin, over-permeable to the dissatisfied stakeholders. (Parents feel free to complain and exert pressure on teachers, but does a motorist ever get into an oil refinery to second-guess the way someone is running a catalytic cracker?)

5. An associated reality is that schools (at least public schools) are "domesticated," owned by their environments, and are *noncompetitive* for resources (Carlson, 1965). Survival is guaranteed, and as Pincus (1974) has suggested, the incentives for innovation are thus feeble.

6. Schools form a *constrained, decentralized* system. Although in the United States there are 16,000 districts and 125,000 separate buildings, each nominally autonomous, there are many national constraints exerted by standardized testing, a national textbook market, various accreditation and certification requirements, and a variety of legislation (Miles, 1977).

We might expect, then, that schools might seek assistance with problems generated by one or more of these properties, for example, help with goal setting, coordination, or environmental buffering, or—less optimistically for OD's future in schools—avoid seeking help *because* of these very properties (if goals are diffuse and survival is guaranteed, why aim for self-renewal?) Our study was in part aimed at assessing which alternative is more empirically frequent.

Some History

OD in schools, like OD itself, is only about two decades old. The first activity that might reasonably be labelled OD (as contrasted with human relations training of individuals) is probably the work at China Lake by Buchanan and others in 1954. The Esso developments in the late 1950s were the first in-company work with any momentum. As in industrial settings, T-group work within schools began as early as the mid-50s, but the first OD project as such in schools was that in 1963 (Miles, Project on Organization Development in Schools) at Columbia. Subsequent projects and centers that had a strong effect on the development of educational OD were the USOE-financed COPED project (1964), the sustained program at the Center for Advanced Study in Educational Administration at the University of Oregon (1968 onward), the briefer efforts of the Educational Change Team (University of Michigan 1967-70), and the Program in Humanistic Education (SUNY Albany, 1969-73). For more historic detail, the reader is referred to Miles and Schmuck (1971).

NTL began the first systematic training program for OD practitioners in 1965; the OD Network has grown from about 375 members in 1970 to 1,131 presently. OD in education, as might be expected from the chronology above, has developed more slowly. By 1971 Schmuck and Miles located 187 practitioners who said they had carried out OD work lasting a year or more with schools, but they could not find more than a handful of school districts in which an actual institutionalized OD capability existed. Blumberg (1976) pointed out that only one-half of 1 percent of the 1,131 members of the OD Network in 1974 listed public school districts as their affiliation.

Blumberg went on to predict that diffusion of OD to any substantial extent among schools was unlikely because of such features as the interpersonal orientation of school administrators, the individually oriented style of staff-development programs, the lack of "hard data" on educational OD outcomes, and current economic constraints. Derr (1976) went further, claiming that properties of schools such as lack of performance indicators, guaranteed survival, noncollaborative stance of employees, and "civil-service mentality" were basically incongruent with OD concepts. These assertions can be countered, and were, by Miles (1976) who suggested that OD might well diffuse broadly in schools, *if* more school administrators than at present had a direct, personal exposure to OD interventions, if financial and organizational incentives were more vigorous, if a critical mass of practitioner advocates began to develop, and if more coherent documentation and evaluation data became available.

In any case, although the general OD literature has included a dozen reports or so each year of OD work with schools, almost nothing is known about how widely OD is actually diffusing in schools or about what the effects of OD are when given a serious try in the special sort of animal that school districts are claimed to be. Hence this study.

OD CONSULTANTS

We identified an initial sample of 1,012 OD consultants and practitioners. This list was compiled from regional and national OD Network lists, state departments or offices of education, associations of administrators, and OD researchers and practitioners. We used basic lists, snowball sampling, and cross-referencing. We are confident that this list constitutes the most fully identified sample available of those who are purportedly involved in OD in education.

The final sample (based on returns) is somewhat complicated. The total sample included all those who were *potentially or thought to be* involved or knowledgeable about OD in education. As it turned out—and as we expected—some people were not actually active in OD, or were active in industry but not in education, or were active in higher education but not in school districts. Others were sources for nominating others rather than OD consultants themselves. The breakdown of the returns is as follows:

Questionnaires mailed	1,012
Returns by those not involved in OD in education	225
Subtotal	787
Returns of those involved	357

Two hundred twenty-five respondents sent back the questionnaire and stated that they were not involved in OD in school districts. There are no doubt many more people who were not involved but did not respond at all. In any case, at least the 225 should be deleted from the original sample. Thus, the percentage return is approximately 45 percent (357/787). The final sample of 357 persons represents known, active OD consultants in school systems.[1] Of the 430 respondents who did not respond, we suspect that many of them—at least half—were not directly involved in OD work.[2] There were no doubt others who were involved in OD in industry and business but not in education and, thus, did not respond. We did, however, receive higher rates of return from people on lists based on known OD consultants than from the more general lists. All in all, we believe that we ended up with the most comprehensive sample of OD consultants and practitioners in education that has hitherto existed.

The basic information we collected from OD consultants included job title, base of work, sex, geographical region of work, type of formal and informal training, type and amount of OD work in school districts (including time span, problems addressed, approaches used), and knowledge or nominations of school districts involved in sustained OD. It also should be noted that we did not restrict the report of OD activities by consultants to sustained OD efforts (a minimum of eighteen months). We asked them to report on OD activities in education regardless of the duration.

Twenty-one percent (76) of the sample were professors (associate, assistant, etc.) in education or other disciplines; 20.7 percent (N=74) were directors, managers of a department or special project; 11 percent (N=38) were superintendents or assistant superintendents; 10 percent (N=37) were consultants (within school districts and external); 8 percent (N=27) were school principals; and 5 percent (N=17) were teachers. Five percent (N=16) were Ministry or state officials, and a further 5 percent were presidents or vice presidents of OD consulting companies. The remaining 13 percent came from groups under 5 percent (deans or associate deans, executive secretaries of school districts, etc.).

The work places of these consultants further clarify their roles. There are two large groups: 35 percent (123) are based in school districts, and 26 percent (91) work from university settings. Eleven percent (39) are based in state or provincial departments, and 9 percent are free-lance. There are very few consultants in business companies (aside from the free-lance consultants already mentioned). In examining the remainder of the data, we also report relevant cross-tabular analysis

---

[1]Actually a small percentage (7 percent) are not consultants but are people who were knowledgeable (e.g., school superintendents) about sustained OD in school districts and nominated such districts.

[2]We erred on the side of being overly inclusive. Some of our lists contained large numbers of people who had "attended" an OD conference, and other lists, such as the list of public information officers for each state and the list of the American Association of School Administrators, were used as sources for nominating others. We know that many of these people were not involved in OD work, but they were potential sources of information about other consultants and about possible OD districts.

of activities by work base. In particular, we are interested in determining if there are any differences between OD consultants who are internal employees of school districts and those who work from a university or external base.

The sample was predominantly male (84 percent). Twenty-three percent (82) of the respondents were from Canada, and only twelve consultants in Canada were from outside Ontario. In the U.S., 21 percent (74) of the total sample were from the Midwest, 18 percent (63) were from New England and the Eastern Metro region (New York, New Jersey), 9 percent (32) were from the Mid-Atlantic region (Pennsylvania, Virginia, etc.), 8 percent (29) were from the Northwest, 8 percent (28) were from the Southwest, and approximately 5 percent (18) were from each of two regions: Plains, (Dakotas, etc.) and Mountain (Montana, etc.). In short, the sample was diversified in terms of geographical distribution. When we compared the regional distribution by work base, we found a similar pattern with one startling exception. Of those who worked for school districts, 44 percent were in Ontario, Canada, while only 5 percent of those in universities were in Ontario. There are in fact very few university-based OD consultants in Canada—a total of six respondents from the eighty-two in Canada. Also, as we will see in the school-district data, much of the work done in Canada (again, mainly Ontario) tends to be individualistically or personnel-development oriented rather than organizational or system oriented.

About 88 percent of the sample had received some formal training, which we defined as either a university program or workshop or conference training. We attempted to distinguish between some of the major types of training. A large minority, 39 percent (131), had university training (usually a Ph.D.). A substantial percentage of respondents had received NTL training (33 percent—18 percent of the university-trained people just mentioned and 15 percent who had no university training in OD), and 38 percent had received their training through workshops and conferences. The remaining 8 percent had received no training whatsoever. Thus, university training and/or NTL training accounted for the formal training of 55 percent of the total sample. On the other hand, 45 percent of our sample of OD consultants in education had received only conference or workshop training.

At least two implications of this are worth considering. First, the large proportion of consultants who have received little direct training in OD probably reflects the lack of widespread availability over the past ten years of university and other more sustained training programs. It was beyond the scope of our study to assess the extent of such programs currently available. Second, it is clear that almost half our sample are doing OD in schools without much formal training. This may be related to the diffuseness and ambiguity of what OD in education really is (see Fullan, 1975). It also may mean that there are many effective OD consultants in education who have learned their trade on the job and through selected workshops. As is shown in the school district data, some of these people have other full-time jobs in school districts. They may not be identified as OD consultants in professional associations, but may in fact reflect a much larger number of OD consultants in education than was previously suspected in the OD literature.

Further data on nonformal educational experiences tend to confirm the interpretation that a great deal of OD knowledge and skill is learned on the job. Running workshops, doing consulting, working with other OD consultants, reading and doing OD on the job were frequently mentioned activities by virtually all the respondents in the sample.

We again compared work base by type of training for school-district and university-based consultants. Not surprisingly, consultants working in and for school districts did not have as much formal training as university-based consultants. If we compare the three most intensive training categories—university training (excluding NTL), NTL (no university training), and NTL (with university), we found that university-based people were more likely to have had formal OD training, even those who took NTL training but did not have previous university training in OD.

We also were interested in finding out the amount of OD work that had been carried out since 1970. Seven percent (N=24) stated that they had never done any OD work at all. This portion of our sample were respondents who were knowledgable about major OD efforts but not directly involved themselves (e.g., state information officers, superintendents). A further 7 percent (N=25) indicated that they had not done any OD work with school districts (i.e., their OD work was in higher education or in business organizations). A total of 43 percent (N=153) of the sample had worked in only one school district, 18 percent had worked with two districts, 11 percent with three, and 14 percent with four or more districts. Stated another way, 75 percent of the sample had worked in two or fewer school districts, and 25 percent had worked in three or more different districts. As might be expected, those in university settings reported working in many more districts than did those in school districts.

The respondents listed a total of 611 school districts in which they had worked (although some of these represent different consultants working in the same district). It is interesting to compare the starting dates for the OD projects by year from 1967 to 1977 for both the consultant sample and the school-district sample. There were no substantial differences between school-district and university consultants within the consultant sample concerning starting dates.

While there was only a modicum of growth from 1967 to 1973, a substantial increase in OD starts is evident in 1974 and 1975 for both consultants[3] and school districts. In all, 60 percent of the consultant-reported starts and 52 percent of the district-reported starts were 1974 or later. In any case, to keep perspective, we must remember that our sample of seventy-six districts covers something like one-half to 1 percent of all school districts in the United States and Canada.

We attempted to find out the typical subunits or levels in the school districts with which we worked. It was difficult to obtain valid information because respondents tended to work with a variety of subunits or worked with one level in

---

[3]The higher number of starts in 1970 for the consultant data reflects the fact that this was the earliest date on which we asked for information. Several respondents reported activities that had commenced in 1968, 1969 and carried over into the 1970s. All of these were coded as 1970 for the starting year, thus inflating that figure.

one case and another level in another case. We were forced to leave 30 percent of the sample uncoded. We did find that high percentages worked with a school faculty (26 percent of the total sample) or with several schools (a further 19 percent). Others worked with administrative groups: superintendent plus principals (7 percent), central office staff (7 percent), principals (4 percent). About 9 percent claimed they worked with the total system. There were only five cases (2 percent) in which parents and/or students were the primary focus. School-district and university-based consultants did not differ in the subunits with which they worked.

Information was also gathered about time span (length of the project) and number of contact days within the time span. We were surprised to find that almost half the sample (48 percent) claimed that they had worked more than one year in the school district in which they had carried out OD. In fact, 13 percent stated that they had worked four years or more in a given district. On the other hand, a total of 28 percent indicated that they worked from a few weeks up to six months. The remaining 24 percent indicated that the typical work span for them was seven to twelve months. Somewhat surprisingly, university-based consultants worked just as long within a school district when they worked on an OD project.

We asked respondents to state in their own words the kind of problems to which the OD efforts were addressed. We developed codes from these according to whether the problems were related to:

1. Macro-structural issues (e.g., reorganization, changing the structure);
2. Organizational functioning (either task oriented—goal setting, problem solving, etc.—or socio-emotionally oriented—climate, communication, etc.);
3. Organizational outputs (productivity);
4. Educational internal issues (e.g., curriculum, teaching);
5. External issues (school/community relations, finances);
6. Personnel issues (staff development);
7. Subsystem issues (team building);
8. Student issues (achievement, learning atmosphere).

Of the problems mentioned first, 25 percent were in the organizational task-oriented domain (problem solving was mentioned most), 14 percent related to socio-emotional issues (mostly communication). Seventeen percent concerned individual staff or leadership development, and a further 10 percent concerned team development. Nine percent of the cases involved curriculum/teaching or other types of internal educational issues. Only 8 percent of the problems concerned structural change, and only 5 percent or eighteen instances involved student effects; of these, eleven of the eighteen cases concerned race relations. There were no differences between school-district and university-based consultants in relation to the types of problems they addressed.

Thus, OD undertaken by the consultants in our sample tends to be directed either to organizational problem solving and communication or to staff/leadership development. It might well be that only the former is directed at the organization while staff/leadership training focuses on individuals. Furthermore, only a minimal amount of attention is paid to structural issues or student effects.

The range of OD approaches used by the consultants further clarifies the nature of their activity. We asked them to indicate how much they had used the eight approaches in Table 1 (taken from Schmuck & Miles, 1971). We also included an "other" category, but it was rarely used.

Table 1. Respondent's Use of Approaches to OD

	Not Used At All	Used Once or More
1. Training (direct teaching)	25%	76%
2. Process consultation	28%	72%
3. Confrontation	44%	56%
4. Data feedback	32%	68%
5. Problem solving (meetings)	26%	74%
6. Plan making	32%	68%
7. Establishment of OD task force	51%	49%
8. Techno-structural activity	62%	38%

It can be seen that five approaches are used relatively frequently: training, process consultation, data feedback, problem solving, and plan making. Confrontation, OD task force, and structural approaches are used much less frequently, although it may be significant that 38 percent mention some attempt at structural change, 49 percent refer to using an OD task force, and 56 percent mention a confrontation approach. These data may be slightly inflated, since some people responded "we use all eight," but the relative emphases are probably accurate. Comparisons between school-district and university-based consultants revealed only one difference: university consultants were more likely to use data gathering and feedback (81 percent) than were district consultants (64 percent).

It will be recalled that in addition to gathering information on their activities, we also utilized the consultants as sources of information about school districts in which they had been involved or knew about and in which sustained (minimum of eighteen months duration) OD programs had been undertaken. A program could have started anytime since 1964. We reasoned that our sample of consultants would be more knowledgeable about possible districts than any other group. We did not know how many districts would be nominated, but we expected that a relatively small number—twenty-five to thirty-five—of districts would be involved in OD programs lasting over eighteen months. In fact, we received 390 nominations from 62 percent of our sample. We ended up with a final refined sample of seventy-six school districts—a much larger number of districts carrying out sustained OD programs than we (or anyone else we contacted) had realized were in existence. Moreover, it provided us with the opportunity to carry out a detailed large-scale analysis of the nature of OD programs and their impact on school districts—an aspect of the study to which we now turn.

SCHOOL-DISTRICT SAMPLE

The school-district analysis represents the most central part of our study, because it allows us to examine a large number of cases in which OD really has been attempted in a serious or sustained way. There has not been a complete analysis of the data, but there are some clear patterns in the findings thus far. These findings are presented in the following four subsections: characteristics of our sampling and final sample, an overview of the nature of the OD programs in the districts, issues concerning the operation of the program, and the outcomes or impact of the programs on the districts.

Characteristics of the Sampling and the Sample

We mailed a twelve-page questionnaire to the sample of 390 school districts that had been nominated by one or more consultants in the previous sample. We provided a definition of OD and asked specifically whether such a program had been operating for at least an eighteen-month period in the period since 1964. If the answer was yes, we requested that the remainder of the questionnaire be filled out; it asked for considerable detail on the characteristics of the program and its activities, how it got started, how it was supported financially, the impact of the program, and its future in the district.

After one mail reminder and a phone call, we received a return of 136 responses (34 percent) from districts. Of these, eighty-seven or 64 percent said that sustained OD efforts as defined had happened; the remaining forty-nine (36 percent) said that such activities had not occurred or were not sustained. We further refined the sample of eighty-seven by deleting nonpublic schools and, in two cases, two higher-education institutions. The final refined sample on which we base our analysis in this section consists of seventy-six school districts in Canada and the United States in which sustained OD programs had been carried out. Phone calls were made to districts in order to verify ambiguous data or to gather more specific information on particular aspects of the program.

The reasons for nonresponses are not clear. We suspect that there were a variety of reasons that OD work had not been carried out for a minimum of eighteen months or that the school district did not consider itself to have an OD program. Undoubtedly, some respondents were too busy to spend the time gathering the detailed information we requested. We are currently comparing the characteristics of the school districts in our nonrespondent category with those who indicated that they did not have an OD program that lasted eighteen months and with our final refined sample, to determine if there are any major differences (see Miles, Fullan, & Taylor, 1978). We have no direct way of knowing what proportion of actual OD efforts our final sample represents. It certainly is not complete. On the other hand, it represents a large number of OD efforts in districts with a wide range of characteristics, and for the first time (as far as we know) provides the opportunity to do a quantitative analysis of the nature of OD programs and their impact in school districts.

The main characteristics of a sample of seventy-six districts can now be summarized. A majority (59 percent) of the respondents were local school-district administrators, (superintendents, assistant superintendents, principals, directors of instruction); staff personnel accounted for 14 percent, and internal OD specialists or coordinators for 9 percent. Teachers (3 percent) and others (department and unit heads) accounted for the rest (16 percent). In one case the respondent was external to the district (a state official).

Seventy-six percent of the districts were in the United States, with the remainder in Canada (Manitoba, Ontario, Quebec, and Saskatchewan). The regional spread was wide; only in the Midwest were there as many as 20 percent in a single region.

The settings were also diverse: 38 percent were suburban districts, long considered more likely to innovate, but 41 percent were urban or metropolitan, and 21 percent towns or villages. Perhaps the most striking property of the settings is that they over represent larger districts. For example, only 12.5 percent of our U.S. districts had 1,000 pupils or fewer, while 26 percent of all U.S. districts are this small. On the other end, although only 1.2 percent of U.S. districts have over 25,000 pupils, 19.5 percent of our U.S. sample districts were this large. One might conclude that larger districts are more likely to (a) have problems of coordination, communication, etc., and (b) have the resources to pay for OD. In fact, although larger size did *not* correlate with more dollars directly in our study, we did note that 55 percent said that their expenditures were at the 75th percentile or better for their states, 34 percent said they were about average, and only 11 percent said they were at the 25th percentile or lower. So we have a bias toward above-average district wealth.

However, the districts in the sample were clearly not restricted in the social-class backgrounds of populations served. The median district had 15 percent upper-middle-class parents, 35 percent white-collar, 30 percent blue-collar, and 15 percent semiskilled or unskilled parents. When we characterized districts as to their overall socio-economic balance, we found that 34 percent had a predominantly middle-class (or upper-middle-class) composition, and 61 percent were predominantly blue-collar or working class; 5 percent had no single class level predominating. So, if anything, sustained OD seems more frequent in districts with strong working-class representation. (Again, these are self-reported data.)

Overview of the Nature of the OD Programs

The length of OD work in these seventy-six districts ranged from one and one-half years (our bottom-end definition) to ten years, with a median at three. We conclude that once an OD effort gets past the eighteen-month investment, it tends to be sustained. (In fact, as we shall see, 88 percent of our sample said OD was continuing at the moment, and 78 percent predicted institutionalized continuation.)

The targets of attention tended to be "several schools" (22 percent), "total system" (18 percent), or "multi-level" (17 percent). It was rare for the work to be limited to a single school (4 percent) or only administrators—the superintendent plus principals (12 percent) or the central office alone (3 percent). The total number of persons involved in the seventy-six districts ranged from nine to over 3,000; the median number involved was in the 300-700 range.

We examined the respondents' accounts of their work carefully, noted what sorts of consultants they were using, the materials they cited, and the way they characterized the overall strategy used. Not surprisingly, given our general definition, when districts are asked about "sustained efforts at system self-study and improvement," there are many different varieties, as Table 2 indicates. We might note that the approaches, when arrayed in the order noted in Table 2 (roughly,

---

Table 2. General Approach of OD in the School Districts*

	Districts N	%
Indeterminate (workshops, meetings, etc., but approach not clearly defined)	5	6.6
Personnel development (emphasis on skills, personal growth, etc.)	14	18.4
Desegregation (racial attitudes, behavior)	2	2.6
Curriculum change (specific projects or comprehensive)	5	6.6
Accountability (systematic assessment and planning, often state-specified)	8	10.5
MBO or PPBS (as central feature)**	9	11.8
Comprehensive school improvement model (IGE, CKF, NASE)	6	7.9
"Classical" OD***	27	35.5

*Analysis and classification of the primary focus or approach of the program as described by the district.

**MBO stands for "Management by Objectives," and PPBS for "Program Planning and Budgeting System." Each is a systematically developed program for goal setting, planning, and performance review. Altogether, 26 percent of our districts said there was some linkage between the OD program and MBO work; 11 percent said the same for PPBS; 5 percent had both. In 28 percent of districts the linkage to MBO, PPBS, or other system-oriented approaches was direct, and there were another 16 percent in which such programs existed but were weakly linked or not at all. The 11.8 percent figure above refers only to those districts in which MBO or PPBS were central.

***Districts classified as having "classical" OD programs ordinarily reported much attention to issues such as system-level communication, problem solving, norms, group functioning, and, generally, the human side of the organization; the consultants they used often were those mentioned in Schmuck and Miles (1971); the materials usually were drawn from the general OD literature. Not a few mentioned Schmuck and Runkel (1972).

from an indeterminate, person-centered approach to more system-oriented, classical approaches), had no meaningful relationship to the size, wealth, socio-economic status or setting of the district, to the costliness of the OD effort, to the proportion of system staff involved, or to numbers of inside or outside change agents used.

However, "classical" OD was more likely to start with structural-change problems, and more system-oriented approaches (like those toward the end of the list) were more likely to be used in districts in which a good deal of other change was going on and likely to go on longer. But except for these differences, the approaches did not look very different in terms of general contextual and input features.

At a more specific level, we asked districts to describe the OD activities that had gone on, using a check list originally developed by Schmuck and Miles (1971). The data appear in Table 3.

This table can be compared with Table 1. As with the consultant data, we note that the most frequently used technologies are training, data feedback, problem solving, plan making, and process consultation. But the districts emphasize plan making much more (84 percent compared with only 61 percent of consultants), as well as problem solving (75 percent versus 65 percent) and data feedback (70 percent versus 61 percent). School districts, like consultants, use the other three approaches less frequently. Confrontation is used by 54 percent of districts and 49 percent of consultants. OD task forces appear in 51 percent of districts, and are mentioned by 42 percent of consultants. The least typical approach, technostructural activity, is reported by 37 percent of districts and 32 percent of consultants. The fact that district figures are usually higher than those for consultants is probably because districts typically described a number of activities over several years, while the typical consultant thought primarily of his or her own practice, which characteristically does not include all eight approaches.

Table 3. Percentage Use of the Eight Approaches to OD

	Not Used at All	Used Once or More
1. Training (direct teaching)	26%	74%
2. Process consultation	38%	62%
3. Confrontation	46%	54%
4. Data feedback	30%	70%
5. Problem solving (meetings)	25%	75%
6. Plan making	16%	84%
7. Establishment of OD task force	49%	51%
8. Techno-structural activity	62%	32%

In general, we note that the OD efforts reported clearly transcend training and have a strong instrumental (plan making, problem solving) emphasis. But we also note that only about half say that OD-managing task forces are in place, and that only about a third brought about structural change.

These activities were aided by external and/or internal consultants in all districts. The number of external consultants involved ranged from one to 187, with the median number being three. The time spent by the most salient external consultant ranged from two to 990 days, with the median being fifteen days. If we remember that the median effort time is three years, we can conclude that the usual external practitioner resricts interventions considerably to workshops, offsite sessions, and the like.

The picture for internal change agents is considerably different. In the districts, the median number of system members involved as facilitators, trainers, consultants, etc. was twelve. So districts were relying quite heavily on internal talent. When asked how much time the most salient inside change agent had put in on the program, forty-three districts answered. The range was from five to 1,000 days, with a median of 200 days—more than a dozen times the investment put in by the median outsider. Another finding of substantial interest is that inside change agents tended to be line managers: 81 percent of the districts involved central-office administrators as inside change agents, as did 73 percent for principals. Of other involved, 58 percent mentioned teachers, and 56 percent central-office specialists. Only 33 percent and 15 percent respectively mentioned parents and students. When asked about the two most salient inside change agents in the program, 30 percent of districts indicated superintendents or assistant superintendents, and 27 percent said principals. Only 18 percent of districts mentioned persons identified specifically as "internal consultants" as being most salient.

We might comment on the question of inside-OD-practitioner training and affiliation with professional organizations. We noted with some interest that the main way the most salient insider got involved was through being hired or assigned to do the work, either alone or as assistant to another change agent (40 percent). Secondarily, he or she was the prime mover (18 percent), i.e., initiated the project. The main formal training received was through university auspices (27 percent), followed by workshops and courses (25 percent). However, 29 percent had no formal training at all. The most frequent *informal* training for inside change agents was "on the job" experience as an educational (*not* as an OD) specialist (15 percent); in contrast, only 6 percent learned by doing OD on the job. But the great bulk of the insiders (62 percent) had no *informal* training, such as the above, or parallel work with other OD consultants, or teaching courses or workshops. Finally, we noted that three quarters (75 percent) of the insiders had no affiliation with outside professional groups; only 9 percent, or 5 people, were said to be members of the OD Network. Thus, the picture is one of active, sustained work by insiders with little formal or informal preparation for what they are doing, and little sense of external colleagueship. We suspect that many of these people are not known as OD practitioners outside their immediate districts. This finding may account for the skepticism expressed (Blumberg, 1976) about the extent of OD diffusion: OD efforts in schools may be simply less visible to externally based consultants.

There are two major implications of these findings. First, evidently there are many internal OD practitioners who are in *line* positions. Much of the literature refers to internal, OD cadres in *staff* positions (Schmuck et al., 1977). This raises an important question for future research on OD concerning the advantages and disadvantages (e.g., in terms of impact) of having OD work integrated as a line responsibility versus having it operate in a service or supportive role. One of our three case studies (Miles, Fullan, & Taylor, 1978) provides evidence of the effectiveness of OD organized on a line-authority basis, but more research is needed before drawing even tentative conclusions. Secondly, it appears that there is much "hidden" OD work in school districts, which neither contributes to the theory and practice of OD beyond the district nor benefits from association with others doing similar work.

This pattern also raises questions about the nature of OD training: about the effectiveness of on-the-job training supplemented by reading and workshops, compared to more intensive external training; and whether the loose or individualistic approaches to OD can contribute to the further development of OD technology in education, or whether they add to the confusion over what OD is. These questions cannot be answered in this study.

Operating Issues in the OD Programs

Our questionnaire asked for information on many different aspects of the program. First, we were interested in the initial problems for which OD was seen as a potential solution. The most frequently mentioned issues were communication (25 percent), reorganization/redesign (11 percent), goals and goal setting (10 percent), and decision making (8 percent). Only 5 percent mentioned student issues. When start issues were aggregated into more general areas, we found that 32 percent mentioned task-oriented organizational issues such as problem solving and coordination, 21 percent were concerned with educational output (goal setting, effectiveness), and another 25 percent with internal educational issues such as curriculum, classroom climate, programs, and finance. A total of 41 percent mentioned socio-emotional issues (communication, trust). Other areas included structural issues (18 percent mentioned items such as reorganization or consolidation), external educational issues such as school-community relations (13 percent), personnel issues (10 percent), and the functioning of subsystems such as teams (4 percent). Perhaps the most interesting finding here is the emphasis on task-oriented, goal-oriented items, and the educational-programmatic context. Though socio-emotional starting problems were frequently mentioned, it seems as though the problem is basically one of "getting the job done." Educational goals may be diffuse, but that does not hinder the districts in our sample from being concerned about them.

We also asked about the conditions that made it possible for OD to begin. Here the responses focused heavily on the behavior of top management: 41 percent mentioned the commitment or support of existing top management or board, and 21 percent mentioned initiative taken by a *new* top manager. Twenty-one percent also acknowledged the presence of a grant or other extra funds, 21 percent cited a problematic or changing situation of some sort, and 18

percent mentioned outside-group initiative or support. Twelve percent mentioned the initiative of an internal change agent (but only 7 percent mentioned an
external consultant), and 7 percent said a study or survey had provided start
conditions. (These percentages total more than one hundred because some
respondents mentioned two conditions.) We see here a good deal of support for
the idea that OD diffusion in education really depends on the superintendent as
gatekeeper.

The questionnaire asked respondents to divide the OD work in their districts
into phases and to characterize the work in each phase. The resulting accounts
rapidly become rather idiosyncratic, with the number of phases ranging from two
in some districts to six in others, and with descriptions such as "testing the water,"
"writing the curriculum," and "political reorganization." Nonetheless, it may be
useful to look at what was going on in the first two phases. First phases varied in
length from one to eighty-four months, with a median of eight months. The most
frequently mentioned problems dealt with during the first phase were communication (22 percent), planning (19 percent), goal setting (27 percent), and problem
solving (16 percent). Table 4 shows the aggregated results for the problems
mentioned according to Phase I and Phase II: the figures are percentages of
districts mentioning one or more issues in that category. Table 4 also shows the
percentages of districts mentioning one or more desirable *outcomes* in each general
category as well—both expected and unexpected outcomes.

We note that task and output orientation increased or was maintained during
the early phases, with decreasing emphasis on socio-emotional issues as such. The
increase in personnel issues (which included such items as performance review,
staff development, and hiring) suggests that many projects included a training
component as soon as things were reasonably launched. Similarly, subsystem
functioning received more attention.

Although Table 4 does not show it, little direct attention was paid at the start
(5 percent) and early phases (2 percent) to student issues *as such* (their attitudes,
functioning, etc). We conclude from this that OD's early stages involve the adults
of the system, who focus on organizational task issues. "Student" issues are
considered only at the more general level of output and program, with a secondary
(indeed decreasing) emphasis on the classical problems of trust, openness, morale,
etc. However, socio-emotional *outcomes*—both expected, and, quite strikingly,
*un*expected (positive)—are indeed quite prominent. We shall have more to say
about this later. We should also note here that, in relation to *initial problem*,
organizational-level outcomes (task and socio-emotional) are well achieved, but
matters involving educational issues (program, curriculum, etc.) either external
or internal, are achieved by a somewhat smaller percentage than those initially
mentioning them. This lends some, but not strong, weight to the criticism
that OD tends to be process-oriented rather than focused on the content of
primary tasks.

We also were curious about what it took to support the enterprise. We already
have identified the presence of many internal change agents. We also found that
only 26 percent of the districts said they had an actual cadre of OD specialists or
trainers within the district (more support for the idea that line managers are doing

the work). However, 55 percent of districts provided released time for administrators and teachers; 51 percent mentioned an OD planning or steering group, and 48 percent a district-level coordinator. Building-level OD coordinators were much less frequent (19 percent).

Table 4. Initial Problems, Those Worked On During Early Phases of OD Effort, and Achieved Outcomes

	Initial Problem	Phase One	Phase Two	Achieved Outcomes (Expected)	Achieved Outcomes (Unexpected)
Task-oriented	32%	41%	30%	37%	5%
Output	21%	28%	22%	20%	8%
Educational issues (internal)	25%	12%	20%	14%	8%
Socio-emotional	41%	28%	15%	47%	28%
Structural	18%	5%	4%	13%	1%
Educational issues (external)	13%	4%	3%	4%	9%
Personnel	10%	12%	21%	18%	12%
Subsystem functioning	4%	5%	13%	4%	0%

The most frequently used materials were printed: reprints from books or journals (70 percent mentioned these), questionnaires (69 percent), training manuals or handbooks (63 percent), and forms for simulations, games, and exercises (60 percent). Even such familiar items as films (45 percent), transparencies (45 percent), audiotapes (21 percent) and slide-tape presentations (25 percent) are used by a minority. When districts were asked to mention the most crucial or essential materials by name, the winners proved to be training manuals (25 percent), with other modes trailing far behind.

The question of how much OD really costs any organization is not easy to answer. The financial resources provided for the OD effort as a whole varied wildly in this sample: one district said it got by with $600, while another spent $1,550,000. Even when these figures are adjusted to an annual cost, the range is still very substantial (from $200 to over $750,000). Over the whole sample, the *median* amount spent was only $5-10,000—less than half of one teacher's salary. Median amounts for various subcategories were $5,000 for released time and substitutes, $1,000 for materials, $1,000 for travel, zero for new internal salaried positions (although 32 percent of the sample spent $14,000 or more on this), and $3,000 for external consultants. Some districts spent nothing at all in a given category, while others seemed incredibly lavish ($100,000 for materials, $500,000 for released time, $250,000 for travel, $250,000 for new positions, and $500,000 for external consultants were all reported in one district or another). Annual costs do seem to make a difference in overall impact, as we will see in the next subsection, but do not necessarily cause people to favor OD efforts and are *negatively* related to how institutionalized the program becomes.

Outcomes and Their Explanations

We were naturally concerned to develop a general measure of the success of OD programs, both to see what these programs appear to have accomplished for their users and to provide a dependent measure against which we could run explanatory variables. The initial criteria of OD "success" generated were:

1. *Impact* on the district as a system (including impact on students).
2. Positive *attitudes* toward OD, especially those that bear on whether it should be used in schools more generally.
3. *Institutionalization* or durability of the OD effort.

A successful OD effort is one that makes a difference locally, has become "built in," and has partisans who have positive, even evangelistic attitudes that will encourage wider diffusion of the effort to other districts. Although these are self-reported indicators of success, we did find variations. We also used open-ended questions to develop measure of impact based on *specific* descriptions of changes.

We will summarize a good deal of analysis to say that it does not seem wise to combine the three above criteria into a single measure; they are only moderately correlated with each other, and the factors that explain their occurrence also vary a good deal. The discussion that follows gives a *descriptive* account only of how the districts fared in their outcomes. For a more detailed and technical analysis of these data, see Miles, Fullan, and Taylor (1978).

Impact (Expected). When we asked respondents to describe what good consequences had occurred of an *expected* sort, the most frequent mentions were of improved communication (20 percent). Other specific expected positive outcomes were planning (8 percent), decision making (10 percent), improved relationships (8 percent), productivity (8 percent), new educational programs (8 percent), commitment to change (6 percent). If we use our aggregated categories for the diverse outcomes described, we end up with an interesting finding: 47 percent mention socio-emotional improvements in organizational functioning, and 37 percent task-oriented ones. This suggests support for the view that successful OD tends to induce a cultural shift (in social processes) along with task-oriented results.

Other frequent categories included organizational output improvement (20 percent), internal educational issues (14 percent), personnel issues (18 percent), and structural changes (13 percent). As was seen earlier, direct changes in students rarely are mentioned here (4 percent).

We also were interested in *why* these changes were seen to have occurred.

Although many districts (30 percent) gave credit to background conditions such as capable staff, dollar investment, and administrative support, the dominant explanation (50 percent) is given in terms of socio-emotional aspects of the OD process itself, such as participation, more open communication, commitment, humane atmosphere, and the like. Another 14 percent mentioned more general properties of OD, such as feedback, capable consultants, and so on. The other major cluster, quite naturally, stresses results (21 percent): "we planned it that way," "the change effort caused it," "good vehicle for problem solving." Task-focused aspects of OD, such as "clearer role expectations," and "better management system," were invoked by only 7 percent of districts in explaining good outcomes, even though the OD process often seemed to have been launched with task-oriented hopes and rhetoric.

Impact (Unexpected). To a researcher, *un*anticipated good consequences are always of interest; 59 percent of our sample mentioned such changes when asked. The most frequent unexpected gains were spin-off or extension to new participants (16 percent), improved communication (14 percent), and increased acceptance of change (11 percent). For our aggregated categories, we note with interest that 28 percent mentioned unexpected socio-emotional outcomes in organizational functioning, as contrasted with 5 percent mentioning task-related ones. This is quite congruent with the findings mentioned above. Another 17 percent mentioned various unexpected gains related to educational issues, most notably, improved school-community relations. We also found 12 percent mentioning personnel issues, and 8 percent output issues.

Impact (Undesirable). Our next question focused on whether there had been undesirable or negative consequences of the effort. Although we seemed to be dealing with a population of satisfied users, it turned out that 72 percent could point to at least one negative outcome, a finding that increases the plausibility of the remainder of our data. Negative results were *not* more frequent among districts where high impact was reported (the "churning-of-the-system" hypothesis); nor were they more frequent where low impact was reported (the "a-little-OD-is-a-dangerous-thing" hypothesis). Rather, they simply seem to be routinely reported accompaniments of OD work. We did note that negative changes were reported by 83 percent of the districts with the most dissemination-prone attitudes toward OD; only 67 percent of the districts without such attitudes did so. This suggests that people who think OD is a good idea and worth disseminating are more likely to mention its negative aspects as well as its benefits.

The results were scattered; 15 percent each mentioned resistance, refusal to participate, and feelings of fear or threat; 13 percent mentioned general negativism toward OD activities; and 11 percent mentioned overload or too-heavy time commitments required. When these are classified more generally, it appears that 66 percent mentioned direct negative consequences of the *program* (such as feelings of threat or work overload) and 60 percent mentioned *attitudes* toward the program (such as lack of interest, criticism of "games," or outside helpers). Only 6 percent mentioned program failure as a negative outcome, and 7 percent mentioned program ineptness.

The explanations for these bad outcomes centered mostly on poor communication (20 percent), followed by resistance, fears (18 percent), worry about being too personal (14 percent), lack of commitment (14 percent), and resistance to new ideas (12 percent). Only 10 percent mentioned poor planning or implementation issues; it appears that explanations center mostly on the behavior of negativists rather than on the advocates of OD.

Impact on Students. Since schools are supposed to exist for students, we thought we should ask explicitly whether the OD program had direct (or even indirect) effects on students, in or out of the classroom. Interestingly enough, 70 percent said that such effects had occurred; 18 percent were unsure or said it was too early to tell, and 12 percent left the item blank. Of the fifty-three districts who mentioned student effects, 6 percent said they were only indirect and another 17 percent did not specify the sorts of student change noted. Over half (53 percent) mentioned various "soft" effects, notably improved learning atmosphere, improved relationships, and attitudes; only 13 percent mentioned gains in achievement scores. If we take a skeptical stance, note that for only 37 percent of all districts were specified "soft" student effects mentioned, and achievement gains were noted in only 9 percent.

The specific explanations for student effects were extremely scattered, and only half the respondents offered them. For example, 49 percent mentioned various pedagogical reasons, such as the fact that the program focused directly on improvement in classroom programs; 28 percent credited socio-emotional aspects of the OD program, and 10 percent the task side. Twenty-three percent felt that good results of the program generally had induced classroom changes, and another 15 percent commented on good program activities. Only 13 percent mentioned background conditions. The moral seems to be that OD is reported to change student experience—at least on soft variables—*if* it is well executed and has a clear linkage to the classroom. However, this was the case only in a minority of the districts in our sample, and only on the basis of self-reports.

Impact on Other Change Efforts. The OD programs in our study were not occurring in a vacuum; 39 percent of the districts said that multiple instructional innovations were taking place, another 49 percent mentioned one or two such changes, and only 12 percent failed to mention any other instructional innovations. Thirty-five percent of districts were attempting to cope with some form of mandated change during the time of the OD program (e.g., desegregation, bilingual programs), and 46 percent mentioned concurrent changes in key personnel, including replacement of top management, expansion, cutbacks, and reorganization.

When asked about the pace of educational change efforts occurring concurrently with the OD program, 61 percent said it was faster than usual, 30 percent about the same, and only 9 percent said it was slower. On the question of whether the OD effort contributed to this, the findings were quite clear: 63 percent said the OD program had directly caused a few (30 percent) or many (33 percent) other change efforts to take place. Another 28 percent said the OD work had had a supporting or sustaining function; only 9 percent said OD was irrelevant to other change efforts; and *no* respondent said OD had slowed down or blocked other change efforts. So at least from the district viewpoint, OD tends to stimulate other educational change efforts, in addition to the direct effects we already have noted.

Additional evidence for the change-causing effects of OD appears in the forty-six districts in which the pace of change had been faster during the OD period. Eighty percent said OD had caused a few or many changes. In the twenty-three districts in which the pace of change had been about the same, 38 percent saw OD as causing change; and in the seven districts in which change had been slower, only 28 percent thought OD had caused change. The gamma between these two variables is .69—a strong relationship.

Similarly, for nine districts in which no *instructional innovations* had been reported, OD was seen as causing many changes by only 22 percent; for thirty-five districts in which one or two innovations were mentioned, 31 percent said OD had caused change; and in twenty-one districts with even more instructional change, 43 percent said OD had caused change.

Districts in which *mandated change* was occurring did not differentially mention OD as causing change, as might be expected; such changes were a context, not a result.

Finally, looking at *personnel* changes, the picture was uncertain. While OD effects were seen as causing a few or many changes in 66 percent of the thirty-six districts that had *no* personnel changes, the figure for the thirty-six districts that mentioned personnel changes was 57 percent. OD seems to have figured causally in the nine districts that mentioned reorganizations (78 percent of these saw OD as "causing change"), but otherwise there seemed little connection. We suspect that personnel shifts are the context for and precipitate OD work (e.g., during expansion or when a new manager arrives) as often as OD affects organizational personnel changes (e.g., resignations, firings).

Positive Attitudes. The second criterion of success concerned whether districts currently held a positive attitude toward the OD program and the dissemination of OD to other school districts. When asked if they would have done anything differently, only 51 percent said yes. The most frequent after-the-fact wish was that the program had gone more slowly (21 percent), then came the need for better commitment from the top (16 percent), and better planning and preparation (21 percent). Others included more use of outside consultants (10 percent), better involvement of parents (10 percent), and the need for better evaluation (10 percent). The flavor of the first three items indicates that OD may well have been launched a bit precipitously.

When we asked our respondents whether they thought that OD should be used more widely in this country's schools, 64 percent said they definitely thought so, 26 percent said "yes, probably," 7 percent were not sure, and 3 percent passed. No one expressed doubt or definite disapproval.

Districts in which attitudes toward OD seem positive might be expected to do some proselytizing, a behavior that bears on whether OD will diffuse more widely. We found that of our districts 60 percent had explained their OD programs at conferences or workshops, 40 percent had sent consultants to other districts, 37 percent had visited other districts to explain their work, 37 percent had sent out reports or materials, and 29 percent had written articles on their OD experiences. These represent proactive dissemination efforts. We also found that 74 percent had had informal contacts with people from other districts, and 51 percent reported that others visited them. So while dissemination efforts are not widespread across our districts, a moderate amount of diffusion effort seems to be occurring.

Institutionalization. The final measure of success referred to whether OD was going to continue in the district. As of the spring of 1977, 88 percent said that it was still going on. The primary explanations for continuance were the good results obtained (23 percent), the commitment and hard work of participants (15 percent), and the support of top management (14 percent).

When respondents were asked to predict the future of OD in their districts, 8 percent said it would not continue (or was already terminated) and 14 percent were uncertain. Another 24 percent said that OD would continue, but with some qualifications (go more slowly, or on a contingent basis, or unevenly); 38 percent said it would continue (but gave no qualifications); and 16 percent said it would continue, expand, and be further institutionalized. The gross figure is that 78 percent of districts predicted continuation.

Factors Correlated with Outcome Measures

In order to analyze factors that account for different degrees of success, we developed indices using the questions just described to measure the three criteria. We then ran three step-wise multiple regressions on a total of forty-seven predictor variables, one regression for each outcome variable.

Impact. The best predictors of impact were scale of effort and technical support. Length of program ($r=.36$), use of federal funds ($r=.24$), number of outside consultants ($r=.37$), and expenditures for materials ($r=.22$) were correlated positively with impact. *Task* orientation ($r=.29$), efforts with a *structure* ($r=.17$), and *system* focus ($r=.31$) were correlated with impact, but *personnel-development* approaches ($r=.16$), i.e., approaches that focus more on individual staff and leadership development as distinct from more system-oriented programs, were negatively correlated with impact. OD support mechanisms internal to the district also were important, particularly the presence of an OD steering group ($r=.22$) and the number of inside OD consultants ($r=.28$).

Attitudes Toward Dissemination of OD. As with impact, scale of effort and technical support for the OD program are associated with positive attitudes; length of program ($r=.34$), expenditures for materials ($r=.37$), presence of a district OD coordinator ($r=.31$), and number of outside consultants ($r=.16$) are correlated with attitudes toward diffusion.

Structural emphasis ($r=.12$) and especially task orientation ($r=.25$) continue to be important. The major new variable is focus on educational issues.

Positive attitudes about the usefulness of OD and the tendency to proselytize are more likely when the initial emphasis of the program (the problem for which OD was to be the solution) is on educational matters internal to the school district (r=.23). Users of OD are more likely to want to disseminate it to other districts when it is clear that the OD program has been of strong educational use.

Institutionalization. The most important finding in terms of whether or not the program has or will continue in the district is that large-scale programs are *less* likely to become institutionalized. Those with larger annual costs (r=.12), more contact with outside consultants (r=.28), and expenditures for new positions (r=.14) have negative relationships to institutionalization. Further, the amount of federal funds involved is correlated slightly negatively to institutionalization (r=.12). Further analysis revealed that districts receiving *some* federal money did as well as districts receiving no federal money, but districts in which the *majority* of funds came from federal sources were less likely to continue the program—a finding that is familiar from other studies of educational-change implementation.

Second, there is a clear indication that structural (r=.18) and system-oriented approaches (r=.21) are associated with institutionalization, but personnel development (r=.13) is again a counter indicator.

Summary. Impact, positive attitudes, and continuance of OD programs are more likely to occur when the OD approach is task oriented and has a structural, system-oriented focus (not a personnel-development one); impact and attitudes are more positive when the scale of effort and technical support are large, although larger size interferes with the likelihood of institutionalization. Overall, it seems that OD programs are more successful if they are of moderate size, focused on educational issues, and characterized by a task-oriented, structural, system-changing approach with technical support through the use of internal OD consultants and OD materials.

United States/Canada Outcome Differences

A final analysis involved differences in the three outcome measures in Canada and the United States. Canadian school districts with sustained OD programs are much less likely than U.S. school districts to have high impact, high attitude, or high institutionalization: 68 percent of the U.S. cases have high impact compared to 20 percent of the Canadian cases; 57 percent of the U.S. cases have high attitude compared to 35 percent of the Canadian cases; and 80 percent of the U.S. cases have high institutionalization compared to 70 percent of the Canadian cases. We also calculated the general OD approaches (refer to Table 2) for the Canadian and U.S. cases. Fifty percent of the Canadian cases were characterized as "personnel development" or "workshop" compared to only 16 percent of the American cases. In short, Canadian school districts (fourteen of the twenty were in Ontario) were much more likely to have individualistic rather than system-oriented approaches to OD, which accounts for the comparatively low impact on outcomes and attitudes in the district. We can only speculate on the reasons for this difference, but one major factor is apparent. OD in education has diffused to Canada (primarily from the U.S.) without a corresponding development of the *infrastructure* necessary to support systematic or comprehensive OD efforts. For example, there were very few OD consultants in Canada who had training in OD outside the school district and even fewer university-based consultants who were available for direct OD work or for training others. It appears that at this time the more superficial, individualistic (personnel- rather than system-oriented) aspects of OD have been diffused without the more fundamental and comprehensive components of OD. We wonder whether what we have called "classical OD" can be understood under these conditions and whether partial diffusion does more harm than good in terms of the evaluation it may receive from would-be users.

CONCLUSIONS

Our data analyses still are not complete, but some conclusions and implications seem possible at this point.

Success Probabilities. Judging from this self-selected population of educational OD users, if a school district starts OD and continues it for at least eighteen months, the chances are a good deal better than even that there will be impact on the district, both generally and in terms of the stimulation of instructional change (and, to some degree, impact on students). It is also typical for such OD users to believe that OD should be more widely used in their country's schools and to make proactive dissemination efforts. Finally, the chances are nearly eight in ten that OD programs, once launched and continued for a year and a half, will continue. Our three indicators of "success," however, are not strongly correlated.

OD's Diffusion Rate in Schools. The data lend weight to the idea that direct dissemination efforts from top managers who have themselves been centrally involved will make the most difference, along with the presence of capable inside change agents and helpful supporting materials. If the Canadian data are any indication, it also may mean that staff- or leadership-development training is the easiest or most likely aspect of OD to diffuse and the least likely to have an impact.

Training and Professional Affiliations for Inside Change Agents. Most insiders in our sample received little formal or informal training, and few had outside affiliations. The fact that program satisfaction was as high as it was under these conditions in our sample suggests the possibility that diffusion would proceed more rapidly if internal OD practitioners became more professionalized.

Reasonable Direct-Cost Expectations. Although it is possible to spend large amounts of money (which gets somewhat more impact, causes proselytizing, and reduces institutionalization), the median district spent *under* $10,000 a year; even those at the 75th percentile spent under $25,000. This is fully comparable to amounts typically spent on in-service training programs—most of which are seen as a waste of time by teachers. If we accept the testimony of our respondents, the benefits obtained for costs of OD are quite substantial—again, depending on the nature of the OD program established. In any case, a large amount of money is not necessary (and may be detrimental to institutionalization) to establish a sustained OD program in a school district.

Major Limitations to the Data. First, the analysis is based on self-reports of individual respondents providing information on behalf of the school district. We still do not know the realistic assessment of OD by teachers, students, and other administrators in those school districts, although we did take considerable care to build measures on specific accounts of the program. Second, we still do not have a complete mapping of the universe of OD school districts because our seventy-six school districts represent an unknown proportion of the total, albeit a much larger one than was previously known and analyzed. Third, a major question remains about what OD is. Are personnel development and curriculum change true examples of OD? What are the different forms of OD in practice? We chose to provide a general definition in order to incorporate a variety of approaches to organization development in our sample. More clarification and analysis is needed for the purpose of defining and classifying the major characteristics of OD in terms of a set of criteria that sort out questions of assumptions, objectives, and the nature and activities of OD programs (see Miles, Fullan, & Taylor, 1978, for a discussion of these issues).

The Diffusion of OD. There are a very large number of practicing OD consultants in education, and a large number (although proportionately small) of school districts have established, sustained OD programs. These districts are of various sizes, are regionally spread, and are based in a variety of socio-economic and urban/rural settings. It does seem probable that OD is diffusable to school districts and has diffused to a larger extent than we and others had realized.

The question of whether it is a good thing for schools is much more difficult to answer. Those who have given it a try generally say yes. It does appear that it makes life better for the adults—and about half the time for the students—in those districts in our sample. There seems no reason why larger probabilities of student impact—including change in learning outcomes—could not be achieved if OD programs were designed that way. The innovation-encouraging nature of OD programs is a further point in their favor. The negative outcomes noted do not seem substantial enough to sap the commitment and optimism of our respondents. So, we conclude that OD *can* be beneficial to schools. Whether it is or not seems to depend a great deal on the attitude and support of top administration, the establishment of strong internal OD consultants (possibly in line positions), the selective use of external consultants, and a deliberate, explicit approach that combines task, structural, and socio-emotional focuses in a system-oriented framework.

REFERENCES

Bidwell, C. The school as a formal organization. In J. G. March (Ed.), *Handbook of organizations*. Chicago: Rand McNally, 1965.

Blumberg, A. OD's future in schools—Or is there one? *Education and Urban Society*, 1976, 8, 213-226.

Carlson, R. O. Barriers to change in public schools. In R. O. Carlson et al., *Change processes in public schools*. Eugene, OR: CASEA, University of Oregon, 1965.

Derr, C. G. Schools and organizational development: Applications and prospects. *Education and Urban Society*, 1976, 8(2).

Fullan, M. An overview and critique of OD in schools (Open University Course E283, Management of Education). Milton Keynes, United Kingdom: Open University Press, 1975.

Miles, M. B. Some properties of schools as social systems. In G. Watson (Ed.), *Change in school systems*. La Jolla, CA: NTL/Learning Resources Corporation, 1967.

Miles, M. B., & Schmuck, R. A. Improving schools through organization development: An overview. In R. A. Schmuck & M. B. Miles (Eds.), *Organization development in schools*. La Jolla, CA: University Associates, 1971.

Miles, M. B. *Planning and implementing new schools: A general framework*. New York: Center for Policy Research, 1977.

Miles, M. B. Diffusing OD in schools: A critique. *Education and Urban Society*, 1976, 8(2), 242-254.

Miles, M. B., Fullan, M., & Taylor, G. *OD in schools: The state of the art*. Final report to the National Institute of Education, Washington, D.C., Contract No. 400-77-0052, 1978.

Pincus, J. Incentives for innovation in public schools. *Review of Educational Research*, 1974, 44(1), 113-144.

Sieber, S. D. Organizational influences on innovative roles. In T. L. Eidell & J. M. Kitchel (Eds.), *Knowledge production and utilization in educational administration*. Eugene, OR: CASEA, University of Oregon, 1968.

Schmuck, R., & Runkel, P. *Handbook of organizational development in schools*. Palo Alto, CA: Mayfield, 1972.

Schmuck, R., Runkel, P., Arends, J., & Arends, R. *The second handbook of organization development in schools*. Palo Alto, CA: Mayfield, 1977.

United States Department of Health, Education and Welfare, *Digest of Educational Statistics*, Washington, D.C., 1977.

Weick, K. Educational organizations as loosely coupled systems. *Administrative Science Quarterly*, 1976, 21, 1-19.

Section III:
NEW INTERVENTIONS IN ORGANIZATION DEVELOPMENT

OVERVIEW

One of the primary ways in which to insure the long-term survival of an organization development effort in a single organization is to infuse the process with new interventions from time to time. This involves an obvious risk, however. Since OD is often accused of being just another fad, the use of some of the latest techniques can exacerbate the perception of "gimmickry." But providing new techniques and methods can have two significant advantages. First, new technology can help to solve change problems that have appeared to be without solution—it can sometimes provide a breakthrough. Second, in an ongoing OD effort, activities need to be repeated, for different groups as well as for the same group over time. Team building is not a one-time affair. Data collection by means of a questionnaire usually needs to be done more than once. For the OD practitioner, these activities can become repetitive, boring chores. Mitchell (1977) has highlighted this problem by explaining what he calls "consultant burnout." So a new technology that will accomplish the same objective as an old technology can be a source of renewed energy.

The chapters in this section cover interventions that are new but that also build on previous work. The OD Readiness Check List developed by Pfeiffer and Jones (Chapter 12) is new, but the concept on which it is based is at least twenty years old. Lippitt, Watson, and Westley (1958), in their now-classic book, delineated the fundamental steps in a planned change effort. These steps have become what is equivalent to the eleven commandments of OD. First, thou shalt define the change problem. Second, thou shalt assess the system's potential and readiness for change. Now enter Pfeiffer and Jones. They have developed a check list of fifteen dimensions to be used in organizational assessment. Their check list can save the OD practitioner a lot of frustration and can provide a more solid basis for the decision to initiate OD.

Another intervention that builds on past work, in this case on a significant amount of research, is a diagnostic tool based on the concept of organizational climate. The climate survey explained by Litwin, Humphrey, and Wilson (Chapter 13) has been developed empirically from the original work of Litwin and Stringer (1968). Thus, organizational climate is defined by and derived from perceptual data collected from many people in different organizations over time. Moreover, climate provides a conceptual framework or cognitive map for organizational change. The primary dimensions of this climate system are performance (clarity, commitment, standards) and development (responsibility, recognition, teamwork). A given manager would receive feedback on each of these dimensions from the climate questionnaire. In addition to the value of the diagnostic tool itself, Litwin, Humphrey, and Wilson also provide an alternative to the much-used—and one of the few diagnostic survey instruments up to now—Profile of Organizational Characteristics developed by Likert (1967).

Dyer and Daniels (Chapter 14) also use a diagnostic questionnaire (Dyer, 1977) in their OD work, but what is new is their use of an audiotape that substitutes for the actual presence of the consultant. Dyer and Daniels discuss the pros and cons of this kind of intervention and provide a systematic methodology for consulting by tape.

Hersey, Blanchard, and Hambleton (Chapter 15) also build on their previous work. They have now developed a maturity scale to be used in conjunction with their situational-leadership system of instruments. In their chapter, they show how the instruments can be used in an MBO process in which the leader and subordinate contract for an appropriate leadership style to accomplish their objectives most effectively.

The kind of developmental work evidenced in this section helps to assure OD's stability and progress while simultaneously avoiding the pitfall of doing what is different just because it is new.

REFERENCES

Dyer, W. G. Management profiling: A disparity model for developing motivation for change. In W. W. Burke (Ed.), *Current issues and strategies in organization development*. New York: Human Sciences Press, 1977.

Lippitt, R., Watson, J., & Westley, B. *Dynamics of planned change*. New York: Harcourt Brace Jovanovich, 1958.

Litwin, G. H., & Stringer, R. A. *Motivation and organizational climate*. Boston: Division of Research, Graduate School of Business Administration, Harvard University, 1968.

Mitchell, M. D. Consultant burnout. In J. E. Jones & J. W. Pfeiffer (Eds.), *The 1977 annual handbook for group facilitators*. La Jolla, CA: University Associates, 1977.

12

OD Readiness

J. William Pfeiffer and John E. Jones

An intriguing parallel exists between the concept of organization development (OD) "readiness" and the developmental trait of "reading readiness." Once an individual child is ready to read, it is somewhat immaterial which teaching method is used. Conversely, when a child is not ready to learn to read, all strategies are relatively unsuccessful in teaching that child how to read. In an analogous way, once an organizational system has the necessary prerequisites, change is likely to take place regardless of which methodology is applied. Conversely, the most sophisticated techniques employed by the most competent and experienced consultants and managers are doomed to failure when the organization itself is unready to undertake a project of planned change.

ENTRY CONSIDERATIONS

There are four major OD entry strategies: working from the top down, intervening at "crunch" points, working with "bellwether" groups, and conducting training. Each of these approaches has both its disadvantages and its advantages; however, in the context of OD readiness, these considerations take on a significance different from that which is commonly attributed to them.

"Top-Down" Strategy

When possible, the best strategy is to begin OD efforts by conducting assessment, diagnosis, and team-development activities with top management. The change agents can legitimize themselves, support for the OD effort can be garnered, and the top group can demonstrate that it is willing to subject itself to the process. It is important to recognize, however, that a top-down strategy can also create problems. Managers at lower levels often become resistant to change originated by the senior executive group. An additional, potential drawback of this strategy is that the change agents can be seen as pawns of the executive group.

Originally published in J. W. Pfeiffer and J. E. Jones (Eds.), *The 1978 Annual Handbook for Group Facilitators*. La Jolla, CA: University Associates, 1978.

Crisis Intervention

Intervening when the organization is experiencing some significant difficulty is often an attractive entry approach. Considerable energy can be focused on change efforts when system relief is felt to be needed within a part of the organization that is experiencing stress. This approach is a common marketing strategy on the part of both internal and external OD practitioners. The potential disadvantages of intervening in crisis situations include the tendency to foster a dependency on external help and the likelihood that OD will be seen as a short-term problem solution rather than as long-range systemic planning for change. A return to "normal" organizational conditions can be interpreted as an OD success, and the precipitating factors may not be confronted.

Dealing with Successful Groups

Often OD can proceed best when there is little or no stress in the organizational unit that is contemplating open-system planning. Change agents can be used to focus on problematic issues in successful parts of an organization. Here the problem-solving methods most common in OD, which are essentially cognitive in emphasis, can be utilized to good advantage. Because there is no excessive overload of emotion, persons involved in the problem situation can approach its amelioration more calmly and rationally. The disadvantage of this entry strategy is that persons in such situations are not likely to seek assistance. Sometimes managers in successful parts of the organization are reluctant to experiment with structure, communication, and participation. Since it often happens in OD efforts that things get worse before they get better, managers may resist opening up situations in which productivity is satisfactory.

Training

Management development as a pre-OD intervention is one of the best strategies. If there is any doubt that the organization is ready for large-scale problem solving, it is almost always advisable to do training first. It makes little or no sense to attempt to use OD methods on a reluctant client. It is often more advisable to concentrate efforts on training for individual managers, supervisors, and leaders, rather than on consulting services for management groups, departments, and divisions.

Training provides a foundation of skills, experience, and concepts on which OD programs later can be based. Training also legitimizes internal and external OD consultants. The consultant can find many opportunities in training to work with individual managers and supervisors on applications of their learning to the actual situations in which they find themselves.

READINESS INDICATORS

In an article entitled "A Current Assessment of OD: What It Is and Why It Often Fails" (Pfeiffer & Jones, 1976), we indicated some of the reasons why a particular

OD intervention might be unsuccessful. These include (a) unrealistic expectations, (b) inadequate support, (c) failure to follow through, (d) ineffective use of consultants, (e) management resistance, (f) size of the organization, (g) unwillingness to model behavior, and (h) inadequate skills.

If the right questions could be asked in a brief interview or survey-feedback instrument, it would be possible to determine whether or not an organization had reached the stage of readiness to undertake an OD intervention. A number of variables seem to offer the most promise. Franklin (1976) contrasted organizations with successful and unsuccessful OD efforts along eight dimensions: (a) the organization's environment, (b) the organization itself, (c) initial contact for the OD project, (d) formal entry procedures and commitment, (e) data-gathering activities, (f) characteristics of the internal change agents, (g) characteristics of the external change agents, and (h) exit procedures. The results of the study indicated no single dimension that was essential or sufficient to distinguish between successful and unsuccessful OD interventions; however, three general areas did serve to differentiate the OD efforts:

1. *The stability of the organization.* Organizations that are more open to and involved in adjusting to change are more likely to be successful in OD efforts than those that are more stable or oriented toward the status quo.
2. *Interests and commitment to the OD effort.* More specific interests and greater commitment to the OD project, as well as strong support from top management, are associated with successful change.
3. *Characteristics of the internal change agents.* Internal change agents involved in successful interventions possess assessment-prescriptive skills and are more carefully selected and receive less change-agent training prior to the OD effort than internal change agents involved in unsuccessful OD interventions.

Stated more comprehensively, the traits identified by Franklin seem to indicate that organizations that are oriented toward and committed to planned change are more amenable to OD interventions from internal change agents who are not preconditioned toward ready-made answers. Since OD necessitates a large-scale involvement of people in identifying and solving problems in open ways, change-oriented systems are most likely to have the culture necessary for organizational experimentation and self-scrutiny. These conclusions are a helpful jumping-off point for exploring the indicators that reveal organizations that are ready to deal with the change implied in undertaking an OD program. The following fifteen indicators in three broad areas have been extrapolated from our experience and are used as the basis of the OD Readiness Check List that appears at the end of this discussion.

General Considerations

Size. The size of an organization is one of the key indicators of the potential success of OD (Pfeiffer & Jones, 1976). It is worth reiterating the point: much of the technology of OD simply does not apply to large organizations. A useful question about organizational size is the following: is the organization manageable, that is, is it within the span of control of a single individual and within the realm of intervention by one or two internal change agents, with assistance by external specialists?

We contend that it is exceedingly difficult to use "traditional" OD techniques in a coordinated way to produce meaningful changes in organizations exceeding about five hundred people. Larger systems require different types of interventions and, in OD terms, can be dealt with only through subsystems. It may be that the only practical approach is OD within parts of the system. In fact, in large-scale organizations, subunit OD is, in our judgment, the best of the alternatives available to the consultant.

Growth Rate. Those organizations that are declining in size, experiencing a slow rate of growth, or growing very rapidly are less likely to be ready for OD than those organizations that are growing at a moderately rapid rate. Organizations that are growing very rapidly may have little or no energy available for OD interventions; relatively static organizations may be reluctant to tamper with the status quo; organizations that are declining in growth may want quick cures rather than long-term planned change.

Crisis. An organization in which there is visible evidence of crisis that is perceived by a variety of people at various levels is quite likely to be ready for OD. Organizations that are experiencing significant stress tend to be receptive to intervention; however, they are also likely to become dependent on consultants rather than to develop self-renewing planning. Crisis necessitates change, and OD potentially facilitates participative solutions that can result in shared commitment to action.

Macroeconomics. The economic situation in which the organization functions must, of course, be considered. The Vietnam war had a great deal of impact on a number of organizations, as did the more recent oil embargo. The consultant must judge whether the macroeconomic factors are such that success in the OD intervention can be foreseen and the intervention can, in fact, be afforded.

OD History. Does the organization have a history of OD interventions? Experience indicates that when the history of the organization is *too* laden with OD interventions, the latest one becomes simply the project of the year, and people tend to lose interest in the effort. Given an organizational history of several OD attempts, it is very difficult to make an intervention that will have an impact on the organization—particularly when OD efforts have been controversial, unsuccessful, or only partially successful in the past. In that case, the change agent may be regarded as guilty by association. Low expectations resulting from previous OD interventions frequently limit the effectiveness of new efforts.

Culture. Is the culture of the organization viable, permeable, and supportive of radical change? Very frequently, the other indicators of OD readiness are positive, but commitment to the status quo in the organization may be very strong. The culture of the organization may present such a formidable block that it is virtually impossible to discuss the changes necessary for carrying out a successful OD program. Bureaucratic, heavily unionized, and ritualistic organizations are likely to be closed, nontrusting systems that do not invest heavily in efficiency and effectiveness.

Resources

Time Commitment. Is the time commitment of the organization or of the managers of the organization adequate to allow for the development of a meaningful OD intervention? Another way to look at this point is whether the organization is committed to all the meetings necessary in OD. Since OD programs progress primarily through myriad meetings, it is important for the organization to be aware of the depth of its commitment to the process. Organizations take a long time to become the way they are, and a reasonable expectation of the time it takes to initiate and stabilize planned change is at least three years of concentrated work.

Money. Is the organization able to afford the cost involved in an OD effort, both indirectly in time taken away from work and directly in fees for external and internal consultants? Is the management ready to invest sufficient money in the project?

Access to People. Within the initial concept of the OD intervention, is access freely allowed to all people in the organization? If limitations are imposed and individuals at particular levels of an organization cannot be reached, an organization is clearly signalling its lack of readiness. OD programs are doomed to failure if particular key executives put themselves above the process. Ironically, internal OD consultants often do not have access to high-level managers, clearly reducing the impact of the OD program.

Labor Contract Limitations. This variable considers the limits placed on the intervention by the members of management who are responsible for negotiating labor agreements. If the limits of worker participation are too restrictive, the OD effort is severely hampered simply by the inability of the change agents to obtain a mandate broad enough to deal with the problems that are relatively certain to be identified.

Structural Flexibility. It sometimes becomes apparent during an OD project that structural changes need to be made. Does the organization have the capacity to reshuffle managers and departments and change reporting procedures, communication patterns, and reward systems?

People Variables

Interpersonal Skills. It is important to consider whether there are adequate interpersonal skills in the organization to deal with OD change. Very frequently, the other criteria for readiness will be apparent, but the necessary skills are absent. The methods of OD are essentially verbal, and they require communication skills. If the personnel in the organization are deficient in their ability to express themselves, to listen, and to respond creatively and productively in the ideas of others, then the discussions and meetings required in an OD program are likely to be ineffective.

Management Development. To what degree do managers understand and incorporate applications of behavioral science principles in their work? If managers are poorly educated and have underdeveloped interpersonal skills, OD meetings can be futile at best and explosive at worst. An ongoing management development program can provide a "floor" for organization problem solving and unfreeze individual managers for interpersonal feedback processes.

Flexibility at the Top. It is necessary that those people who are in positions of power in the organization be sufficiently flexible to open themselves to influence from below. Although it may not be necessary to *begin* the OD effort at the top, it clearly is critical that top executives be knowledgeable about and supportive of the program and willing to open up the system. One or two key executives who are personally and/or organizationally rigid can often preclude the success of an OD intervention.

Internal Change Agents. We believe that the best OD staffing consists of an interplay among managers, internal change agents, and external consultants. The major motivation of the outside consultants should be to autonomize managers so that they take responsibility for conducting the organization's ongoing developmental efforts. Without people in the organization who are familiar with experiential methods, consulting, change strategy, and training methods, the organization becomes dependent on external sources of help.

CONCLUSION

If it is determined that an organization does not have the requisite OD readiness, what strategy is open to the consultant? The most frequent answer is training as a readiness-inducing strategy within organizations. Some of the indicators previously discussed, such as size, rate of growth, and macroeconomics, are beyond the effect of training. Other important criterion variables, however, are amenable to a meaningful education program. It is possible that the conceptual and personal skills that are requisites of OD readiness can be taught in a variety of formal and informal organizational training programs.

If, however, the organization cannot be affected meaningfully by OD technology, the consultant should be willing to walk away. A consultant's continued history of failure in OD projects with organizations for which it is clear that OD interventions are unlikely to be successful makes it difficult for other consultants to work with clients. We consider such persistent opportunism to be unethical (Pfeiffer & Jones, 1977). The individual practitioner should examine the indicators for the given organization. If those indicators do not predict success, and if they cannot be dealt with in a training education model, the consultant should be direct and simply say that the culture is too strong to augur for the success of change, or that the sense of complacence in the organization is too high for commitment to change, or that the internal history of the organization is such that a new project will not be taken seriously. To undertake an OD effort in the face of predicted failure is unwise—both for the particular consultant and for other professionals in the field.

OD READINESS CHECK LIST

The brief instrument that follows summarizes the chief indicators of OD readiness, weighting each indicator according to its relative criticalness. The check list may be used as the basis for a subjective assessment of an organization to determine the degree to which that system is likely to support an OD effort. This assessment can be made by a group, ideally consisting of key managers, internal change agents, and external consultants. OD practitioners also can use the instrument to analyze their own histories of failures, successes, and decisions not to initiate OD interventions.

REFERENCES

Franklin, J. L. Characteristics of successful and unsuccessful organization development. *The Journal of Applied Behavioral Science*, 1976, *11*(4), 471-492.

Pfeiffer, J. W., & Jones, J. E. A current assessment of OD: What it is and why it often fails. In J. W. Pfeiffer & J. E. Jones (Eds.), *The 1976 annual handbook for group facilitators*. La Jolla, CA: University Associates, 1976.

Pfeiffer, J. W., & Jones, J. E. Ethical considerations in consulting. In J. E. Jones & J. W. Pfeiffer (Eds.), *The 1977 annual handbook for group facilitators*. La Jolla, CA: University Associates, 1977.

OD READINESS CHECK LIST

J. William Pfeiffer and John E. Jones

This instrument summarizes the chief indicators of OD readiness and assigns each indicator a weight according to its relative degree of criticalness. The following interpretations of scoring can be helpful to consultants: a score of less than 50 would suggest training, small-scale projects, and crisis interventions; 50-70 would indicate management development and pre-OD activities; 70 and higher would indicate that the consultant test the willingness of the organization to commit itself to planned change.

Instructions: Using the following check list, indicate the degree to which each of the fifteen dimensions is a concern to you with regard to the organization's readiness for OD. Circle the number under the appropriate heading for each factor. Each dimension has been scaled according to its relative importance in predicting the organization's receptivity to OD interventions. Total the scores for an overall OD readiness index.

General Considerations	No Concern	Mild Concern	Moderate Concern	Significant Concern	Critical Concern
1. Size	4	3	2	1	0
2. Growth Rate	4	3	2	1	0
3. Crisis (potential positive or negative influence)	4	3	2	1	0
4. Macroeconomics	4	3	2	1	0
5. OD History	4	3	2	1	0
6. Culture	4	3	2	1	0
Resources					
7. Time Commitment	8	6	4	2	0
8. Money	8	6	4	2	0
9. Access to People	8	6	4	2	0
10. Labor Contract Limitations	8	6	4	2	0
11. Structural Flexibility	8	6	4	2	0
People Variables					
12. Interpersonal Skills	12	9	6	3	0
13. Management Development	12	9	6	3	0
14. Flexibility at the Top	12	9	6	3	0
15. Internal Change Agents	12	9	6	3	0

Total Readiness Score

13

Organizational Climate: A Proven Tool for Improving Performance

George H. Litwin, John W. Humphrey, and Thomas B. Wilson

PART I: ORGANIZATIONAL CLIMATE IS A SYSTEM

The effect of climate on our activities and on our relations with each other is obvious; we organize much of our lives around the next day's weather forecast for the simple reason that the climate determines what activities are possible and what behavior is reasonable.

Just as we receive clues about what activities and behavior are appropriate from the physical climate, so, too, do we receive clues about what to say, how hard to work, and how to act from the climate of the organization in which we work. When people refer to an organization as "a fun place to work," "tightly knit," or "a big bureaucracy," they are referring to and giving us clues about that organization's climate. Although organizational climate might appear to be an intangible quality, it does have a very real effect on the people who live and work in the organization. Research has demonstrated that climate dramatically affects not only the people but also the performance and growth of the organization.

Climate Affects Performance

If you think about an organization with which you are familiar, you can probably describe its climate and at least some of the factors that contribute to that climate. Your description of the climate is influenced by the structure of the organization, the actions of its management, the attitudes of its workers, and your own experience.

Technically stated, climate is a set of measurable properties of a given environment, based on the collective perceptions of the people who live and work in that environment, and demonstrated to influence their motivation and behavior. Simply stated, climate is a way of measuring people's perceptions of what it is like to work in a given environment. We know from decades of research that motivational states affect behavior and organizational performance. Organizational climate describes a set of conditions that arouse or inhibit various motivational states. By changing the climate, the manager is able to effect change in employee motivation and, in turn, impact performance.

Though we often find that managers are skeptical about the importance of climate, they usually are convinced when we describe the results of climate-research studies that have shown that the climates of various organizations differ dramatically and that these differences are predictive of a company's health, performance, and growth. Our research further indicates that conventional measures of organizational performance, such as profitability and return on investment, are lagging indicators of actual organizational achievements. That is, these indicators show the results of individual actions long after they occurred. Climate, on the other hand, is a short-term indicator of organizational performance, for it measures current activities and their ultimate impact on bottom-line performance.

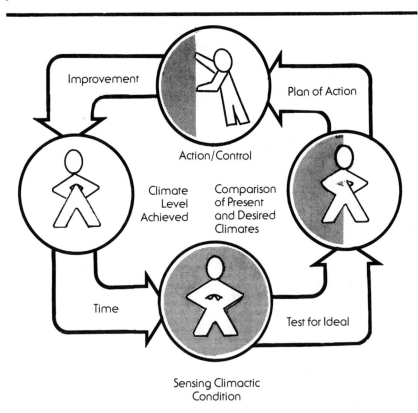

Improvement

Plan of Action

Action/Control

Climate Level Achieved

Comparison of Present and Desired Climates

Time

Test for Ideal

Sensing Climactic Condition

Figure 1. How Climate Can Be Controlled

Climate Can Be Controlled

Climate itself not only generates behavior, it is created by behavior. Climate is created by the actions of managers and the reactions of workers.

If we extend the weather/climate metaphor, we can understand the basic process through which climate can be controlled. When we feel discomfort in our home, we are sensing a climate condition. We cannot see or touch the cause of the discomfort. In checking the thermostat for the room temperature, we consider the present temperature and we imagine what climate would be achieved at some desired level. Then we take action to adjust the temperature. Figure 1 illustrates this process.

If we apply this process to an organization, we can see how the climate system can be used to continuously assess and control climate to impact short- and long-term performance. Controlling climate becomes a holistic process, based on climate feedback, to provide managers with guidance in achieving organizational health and productivity. Controlling climate in an organization involves:

1. Use of a questionnaire (instrument) to sense climate conditions in the organization or work group.
2. Managerial action to determine the climate conditions and supporting systems required for high performance.
3. Analysis of primary factors or determinants causing the current conditions; development of plans to alter these underlying causes if necessary (the climate-system model allows us to attack causes rather than deal with symptoms).
4. Tracking specific actions to change climate conditions, including improvements in management systems, development of management skills and practices, and building of team norms and values.
5. Periodic assessment to allow adjustments and to ensure continuous monitoring of the condition and capability of the organization.

Overview of the Organizational-Climate System

We think of organizational climate as a system composed of interrelated parts. A change in one part of this system impacts all the others. Figure 2 represents the organizational-climate system demonstrating these interrelationships. We believe that an understanding of how this system works is critical to influencing organizational climate.

Figure 2 may be read like a flow chart. The arrows represent the relation of determinants (independent variables such as management systems) to results (dependent variables such as motivation arousal). These elements affect each other and are influenced by the overall environment. For simplicity, this figure identifies only the most significant elements of the total system.

The three major sections of the organizational-climate system shown in Figure 2 are:

1. *Determinants:* the three forces affecting organizational climate: management systems, individual manager practices, and norms and values of the work group (the three boxes at the top).

2. *Climate profile:* the set of six statistically validated measures describing the present climate in the organization (center of chart).
3. *Effects or consequences:* the three primary results of organizational climate: motivation arousal, employee health and retention, and organizational performance and development (the three boxes below the climate profile).

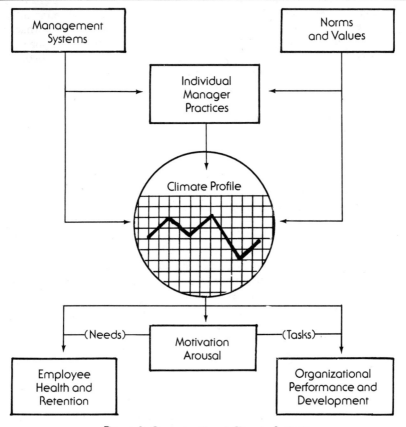

Figure 2. Organizational-Climate System

Climate Profile: The Elements of Climate

Climate is a conceptual tool for understanding the dynamics of an organization. Since organizations are social creatures, i.e., involve the interactions of people, we find behavioral expressions more relevant than financial or physical ones. Though there is controversy among social scientists concerning what elements should be included in a discussion of climate, our research has led to the statistical validation of six dimensions described below and shown in Figure 3.

The six dimensions of climate are *clarity, commitment, standards, responsibility, recognition,* and *teamwork.* We do not argue that these are the only dimensions or that they are merely industry-specific measures. Rather, we believe that they are valid and useful for research across industrial and organizational lines. This research has allowed development and validation of the climate-systems model described in this paper, which is a powerful tool for analysis and action planning.

Clarity involves the individual's degree of understanding of an organization's goals and policies and the extent to which he or she understands the requirements of his or her job. High clarity exists when each individual knows exactly what his or her job entails and has a thorough understanding of organizational goals and policies. For clarity to exist, work must be carefully planned and organized, and information should flow smoothly through communication channels.

Commitment is the expression of continuing dedication to goal achievement. Commitment is developed through a mutual process of setting goals and standards and through regular reviews to determine how performance compares with previously set goals and standards.

Standards means the emphasis that management places on high standards of performance and the degree to which pressure is exerted on employees to improve performance. High standards are developed, for example, by management's evidence of personal commitment to goals.

Responsibility is the degree to which employees feel personally responsible for their work. High levels of responsibility exist when individuals are expected to solve problems and make decisions on their own. Individual initiative is encouraged, and judgment is trusted.

Recognition involves the feeling that people are recognized and rewarded for doing good work. Good performance is rewarded more often than poor performance is criticized. Rewards are clearly related to excellence of performance. Nonmonetary rewards are used.

Teamwork involves the feeling of belonging to an organization; it is characterized by cohesion, mutual warmth and support, trust, and pride. In a work setting in which teamwork is strong, employees and management trust and respect each other, and people back each other up when things "get tough."

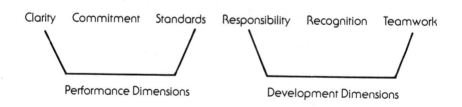

Figure 3. The Six Dimensions of Climate

In working with our clients, we use a questionnaire to measure the climate of an organization. It is a fourth-generation climate questionnaire, refined from the instruments developed by Litwin and Stringer in 1967 and 1968. During the last ten years, we have been able to establish national norms from which to interpret and tabulate the responses to the questionnaire. The result is a climate profile—a computerized report that analyzes the questionnaire responses against national industry norms. The climate profile graphically depicts the organization's climate scores and the forces influencing climate. It is used as a feedback device to help managers identify and improve the conditions that are necessary for sustained top performance.

Effects of Climate

Motivational Arousal is a direct result of the organization's climate (see Figure 2). It is the creation of particular psychological states that predispose an individual to behave in certain ways. For example, a highly effective sales group of a large insurance firm had a climate that facilitated achievement motivation and elicited achievement-oriented behavior. The sales people were concerned with their personal successes and the overall success of their team. Their "dollar performance" reflected these conditions.

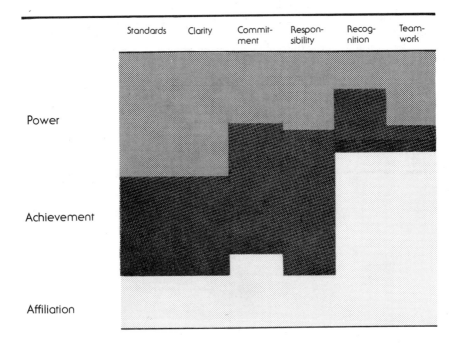

Figure 4. How Climate Affects Motivational Arousal

Understanding the motivational effects of climate is vital, because these effects operate on a day-to-day basis. Climate creates expectations; expectations arouse and reinforce certain kinds of motivation while inhibiting others. The combination of aroused motivation and the skills of individual workers, plus the effectiveness of the team, result in productive behavior. The desired balance between various motivational states is dependent on the purpose and nature of the organizational tasks. Hence, motivation that is appropriate to the task at hand will result in high performance, whereas inappropriate motivation may negatively affect performance.

Figure 4 describes the effects of organizational climate on motivation arousal. The data are based on original research done by Litwin and Stringer in 1968, but have been reanalyzed and reinterpreted to fit within the climate-systems framework. The figure shows the effect of each climate dimension on the primary social motivations: power, achievement, and affiliation. Standards and clarity are strong stimulants of power motivation, leading to concern with maintaining or increasing control. Commitment and responsibility are strong stimulants of achievement motivation, developing a concern with excellence and goal achievement. Recognition and teamwork strongly stimulate affiliative motivation, causing concern with the quality of human relationships and with feelings of trust, mutuality, and teamwork among organizational members.

Employee health and retention and short-term performance are affected by various climate conditions as well. Research in several corporations suggests that health and retention are affected by levels of job stress. Our own research indicates that dimensions such as standards and clarity tend to induce high stress, while dimensions such as teamwork and recognition tend to result in lower stress. A very similar pattern affects employee retention. A low-stress climate, characterized by high levels of teamwork and recognition, leads to very high employee retention. Organizations in the same industry that are high in standards and clarity and lower in recognition and teamwork show patterns of lower retention and higher turnover at all levels.

We have studied organizational performance under a variety of conditions in six different industries. Although a number of industry-specific factors have been indicated, it is possible to organize the data around several major findings. One is the kind of climate that is required to achieve *short-term performance* results. The studies show a strong pattern between certain climate dimensions and performance measures that extend over a short time period (ninety days or less). Thus, it is possible to describe the kind of climate conditions that are necessary to achieve short-term, monthly, and quarterly targets.

Figure 5 summarizes the effects of climate on employee health and short-term performance. Data for these findings result from more than fifteen years of research on climate and its effects. There is an inverse relationship shown—the climate conditions that influence short-term performance most directly affect employee health and retention least positively. This finding appears to cross industry lines; that is, the job structures and management pressure that most directly generate short-term productivity result in stress that creates a higher incidence of health problems and employee turnover.

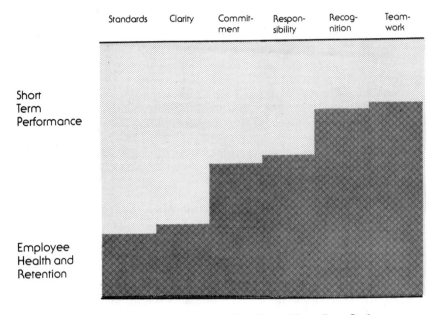

Figure 5. How Climate Affects Employee Health and Short-Term Performance

Determinants of Climate

Based on our research findings, the most significant force affecting organizational climate is the leader or manager. His or her actions and approach to the job of managing have a strong effect on the beliefs and expectations of the work group. In Figure 2 we referred to this force as "individual manager practices." By "practices" we mean the specific actions and behavior of the manager, rather than general observations about his or her "management style." This behavior includes a wide range of factors: the extent to which the manager rewards innovation, conducts team meetings, and provides informal feedback; the honesty of communication during discussions of individual performance; the method of decision making; and many others.

We also have found that specific combinations of management practices affect each of the six climate dimensions. Subsequently, we have developed and statistically validated a specific equation or formula to predict the effect of these practices on the unit's climate. Our most important finding is that this combination of specific management practices is the most effective single predictor of climate in an organization or work group.

Management systems are the policies, procedures, and structures developed by organizations to handle expected operational requirements. Management systems have less of an effect on climate than do individual manager practices, but they do impact organizational life. We measure individual management systems in terms of their perceived value in contributing to the work unit's overall objectives.

We measure the formal systems, i.e., policies and procedures that are endemic to all organizations, and study their impact on the firm's climate. These include mission, strategic plans, organizational structure, operational plans, budgets, information systems, compensation, appraisals, recruitment and selection, promotion and placement, and manpower plans.

Norms and values are the patterns of behavior considered to be acceptable within an organization. Norms and values have a significant influence on the climate of a work group. Such norms include the way employees dress, the manner in which employees support or compete with each other, and the accepted response to authority, conflict, pressure, and rules. Norms are a function of expectations, culture, and rewards. There are many ways of measuring these norms. We examine the way that people would like their work place to be and investigate the traditions, history, and culture of the firm.

Figure 6 summarizes the results of our studies of six different industries. This information is based on a statistical analysis of the Forum's data base. The figure explains which determinants are most influential in affecting each climate dimension. The dimensions on the left—standards and clarity—are those most strongly affected by management systems and least affected by norms and values. The dimensions on the right—responsibility and teamwork—are those least affected by management systems and most strongly impacted by norms and values.

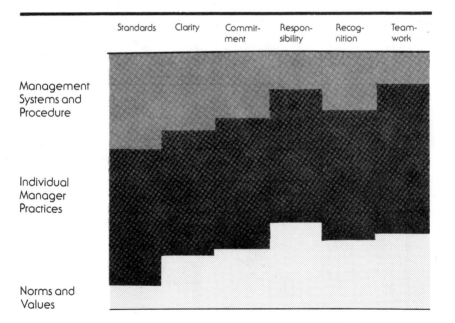

Figure 6. Determinants of Climate

This organizational-climate system can help managers or the internal consultant determine where to begin a program of change, once the desired climate change is established. For example, in our work with a large broadcasting company, the climate analysis showed that change was needed in three areas: commitment, standards, and teamwork. These areas are those most dramatically affected by management practices. Therefore, we began a program to develop managers through recruiting, training, and coaching. Specific practices known to be related to standards and commitment were introduced in these training and coaching sessions.

Further, the data showed that management systems and procedures did not support improvement in the areas of standards and commitment. To change this negative effect, the missions and goals of the various radio and television stations were examined. New mission statements were written, defining systems and procedures more carefully and in ways that supported individual commitment

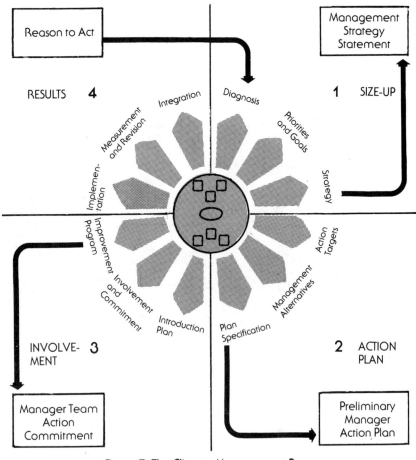

Figure 7. The Climate-Management Process

through a required process of mutual goal setting and periodic reviews of department and station achievements.

To improve teamwork, norms and values had to be affected throughout the organization. A series of departmental and interdepartmental team meetings was organized within individual stations. The result of these directed actions was a series of strong performance improvements in management and sales.

Managers and executives must become aware of the total work environment and become more sensitive to every determinant of climate. And all of us, as organizational members, must become more conscious of the climates we inhabit and create. By becoming more aware of the climate and working to improve it, we can make career and work situations more satisfying, enjoyable, and productive for ourselves, for those with whom we work, and for the organization as a whole.

PART II: APPLYING THE CLIMATE-MANAGEMENT PROCESS

The climate-management process is a series of steps and tools that are used to apply the concepts and principles—the *energy*—of the organizational-climate system to assist a manager in recognizing and then working effectively on specific problems and opportunities. It was first developed by The Forum in 1970 and has since been refined through The Forum's work with thousands of managers in major United States corporations. As can be seen in Figure 7, the climate-management process involves four steps: the size-up, the action plan, the involvement, and the results.

We will review these four steps in detail through a case study of a sample company, Delta Corporation—a company that provides software-systems design and consulting services to major national banks. We will see how Delta effectively used the climate management process to improve the organization's climate and, therefore, its performance, in specific and measurable ways.

As a first step, Delta's chief executive participated in The Forum's organization and management audit (OMA), a program designed to help managers manage climate effectively. He and his employees completed the Climate and Practices Questionnaire, describing their working environment (climate) and practices that could be improved (management strengths and weaknesses).

Questionnaire results were returned to the chief executive in the form of an organizational status report (OSR) after being processed through The Forum's computer. The results of this report are shown in Figure 8.

With the questionnaire results in hand, Delta's chief executive and his officers were ready to begin the first step of the climate-management process.

Step 1: The Size-Up

Managers have a great deal of difficulty in defining their situations and developing a planned management approach that is appropriate to their personalities and the requirements of their work units. They especially have difficulty sensing and assessing how effective their approach really is, since they usually receive feedback from indirect sources. It is difficult to relate random information to the situation as a whole and to determine what could be done differently to improve performance.

But if actions are implemented without careful prior assessment and planning, the results can be disastrous. The manager's first step in the climate-management process—the size-up—is all important. The size-up includes three steps: (a) developing a diagnosis, (b) setting priorities and goals, and (c) forming a strategy.

The size-up begins even before the organizational status report is received (Figure 8). Before the questionnaire results were returned, Delta's chief executive made management judgments in order to establish what climate was required to achieve optimal performance, taking into account the needs and values of the people in his organization and the current operational situation. His "required climate" featured commitment and standards (both at the 85 percentile), responsibility (at the 80 percentile), and slightly less focus on clarity, recognition, and teamwork, (all at the 70 percentile). Additionally, he focused more on short-term performance issues than on long-term team development. The "required climate" provided him with a basis for comparison with results from the completed questionnaires.

The executive compared his required climate with the questionnaire results, completed the size-up phase, and summarized his findings in a written management-strategy statement. Following are excerpts from the management-strategy statement developed by Delta Corporation.

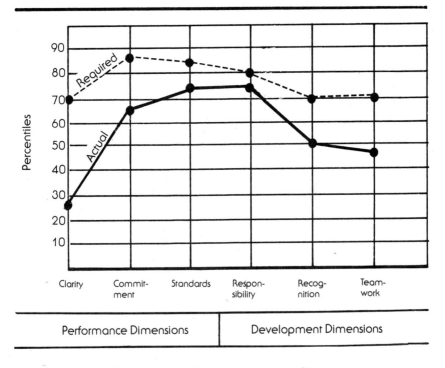

Figure 8. Delta's Required and Actual Climate

Developing a Diagnosis. Overall health (C+) is inadequate to support unit requirements, and expected health (B−) indicates no substantial improvement. There are serious difficulties with clarity, recognition, and teamwork, evidenced by the following kinds of problems: poor communication among key staff members, long and unproductive meetings, and misdirected effort. Clarity and recognition seem to be chronically depressed and probably have been for at least the past two years.

Performance is being sustained by strengths in commitment, standards, and responsibility—dimensions which provide strong motivation for superior levels of achievement. Still, the company as a whole is underperforming, and if the situation does not improve, we anticipate negative reactions from clients during the next several months. The problem, though serious, can and should be corrected within a six-month period.

The diagnosis accurately reflects existing strengths as well as weaknesses. Organizational strengths are important factors that should be considered in any change strategy, since they maintain the company's capacity to perform.

Setting Priorities and Goals. The chief executive called a meeting of his senior executives and their key managers. He explained the questionnaire and the size-up process. Each of them then went through the climate-management process; they developed a required climate, then worked jointly on a size-up. The "team action plan" that resulted was similar to the one developed by the chief executive, but was different in some important aspects.

The senior officers recognized the specific nature of their problems and isolated several factors on which to work. They established clarity, teamwork, and recognition as the priority dimensions and incorporated their findings in their own strategy statements.

Clarity needs the most effort, with a six-month goal to bring it to the 50 percentile level. Teamwork is the second priority, with a goal of 60 percentile. Recognition is the third, with a goal of 60 percentile. In addition, commitment, standards, and responsibility should be maintained within 5 percent of their present levels.

The overall goal, within this six-month planning period, is a climate health of B+. Primary opportunities for improvement include a dedication to management goal setting and planning and the willingness of company members to participate. In view of the need for strong integration of efforts, the sales and management meetings already scheduled represent an opportunity to discuss and effect change.

We should plan to examine our own management practices (and those of the team), such as planning activities, productivity of staff meetings, and personal day-to-day interactions. We should plan how to deal with the obstacles we already face, such as heavy individual and unit travel schedules that make regular meetings difficult, a tendency toward general under-organization, and increasing revenue pressures—all of which will require a diversion of attention and energy to immediate short-term concerns.

Forming a Strategy. Delta's size-up showed difficult, demanding circumstances, offset by some strengths, requiring immediate and continuous action to prevent long-term negative results.

The climate survey results evident in the organizational status report forced the officers to reexamine the adequacy of the planning framework, the organizational integrating devices, and the productivity of staff meetings. They also had to look more closely at the nature and quality of their management practices and judge honestly how these had contributed to the low levels of clarity, recognition, and teamwork.

Delta's strategy included both short-term and long-term goals. The officers agreed, however, that a plan based on the size-up would help them to avoid the problem-focused management that lowers the chances of reaching long-term goals.

Step 2: Action Plan

After sizing up a situation, the management team must determine what actions to take. This presents two problems: the first lies in discovering and choosing among the array of available alternatives; and the second involves difficulties in fore-seeing potential results of the alternatives.

Most managers believe that their choices are limited, but they will find an almost limitless number of possible approaches to any given situation. Just as marketing product managers experiment with their "marketing mix"—tuning up methods of advertising, pricing, and distribution to find the combination that ensures the product's success—so can team managers examine the variables involved to achieve the most appropriate mix of solutions. Variations in what managers do day-to-day in informal interactions, mixed with changes in the information they have and the way they share it, or with the system they use to measure performance, combine to provide almost limitless, creative, managerial resources.

If the manager has a framework in which to examine the alternatives, he or she can determine the particular mix that is best for both the situation and the individual. Using the size-up, the manager can judge the relative impact of various management mixes. Through the action plan, the second step, he or she can test the mixes, tune them, track them, and make the necessary changes.

The three steps in the action plan are: (a) developing action targets, (b) examining management alternatives, and (c) forming a plan specification. This phase culminates in the preliminary manager action plan—termed "preliminary" because it needs to be tested with team members in the involvement phase. The purpose of this preliminary plan is to help managers identify those specific management practices that they should focus on to improve climate, based on the results of the size-up.

Developing Action Targets. Delta's officers examined the specific management practices connected with each of their priority climate dimensions (clarity, teamwork, recognition) and determined which offered the greatest opportunity for influencing the company's climate. They selectd four practices on which to concentrate. They chose those practices that were most closely related to their priority dimensions of recognition and teamwork, thereby offering the greatest opportunity for involvement and subsequently, improvement of company climate. The four practices were:

1. Recognizing good performance more often than criticizing poor performance.

2. Being supportive and helpful in daily contact with subordinates.
3. Conducting team meetings to increase trust and respect among team members.
4. Building friendly relationships, as opposed to being cool and aloof.

The management team also focused on two other practices that did not impact the priority dimensions directly, but related to issues identified in the size-up. These two practices were:

1. Relating the reward system to performance excellence rather than to other factors.
2. Expecting subordinates to find and correct errors or problems on their own.

Examining Management Alternatives and Forming a Plan Specification. After choosing action targets, Delta proceeded to develop management alternatives to those targets. The team charted each of the practices they had selected to identify opportunities for improvement in coaching, formal and informal meeting interaction, and organizational structure and systems. For example, Delta's chief executive and his senior vice president discussed and analyzed the practice of "recognizing good performance more than criticizing poor performance." They discussed goals and the improbability of reaching those goals because of day-to-day pressures, and developed alternatives when they were indicated.

During the last phase of the action plan, plan specification, the managers selected a plan from the alternatives developed. For example, the officers began to use feedback on an informal basis, in coaching and in regularly scheduled meetings. They also extended the scale on their performance appraisal system from 100 to 150, to recognize outstanding performance. They had created an excellent plan, but still did not recognize all the practices that they could implement personally. They were, therefore, ready for the next step: involvement.

Step 3: Involvement

A challenge of paramount importance for the manager is that of involving his or her people in the management of the organization. Mutual planning and goal setting, team building, and team involvement have become part of the management lexicon. Most managers agree that people pursue plans more aggressively when they have been involved in the decision process, but there is less agreement on the best way to achieve that involvement.

The failure of management to productively involve subordinates is more often a failure of "how" rather than "why"—a failure of tools rather than of intent. In the involvement step, the manager learns to take advantage of the experiences, feelings, and judgments of his or her subordinates, allowing the manager to share responsibility with team members while retaining accountability.

The involvement step includes: (a) plan introduction, (b) gaining involvement and commitment, and (c) defining a formal improvement program.

Plan Introduction/Gaining Involvement and Commitment. This phase is designed to involve the manager's key people, resulting in a total team plan. The phase can be initiated at an earlier point in the process, as it was at Delta. The chief executive and his senior officers discussed many of the issues and identified priority dimensions.

When the chief executive involved his key people in the climate-management process, they found that its principles and methods were effective. Later, in the involvement phase, they discovered things they had not suspected until meeting with the wider team.

The management team examined the team action plan to determine what decisions could be made to produce immediate results. They realized, among other things, that clarity was lowered significantly by the physical separation of unit members on two floors of the building.

"The total team's action plan became much broader than my original plan," observed the chief executive. "Through our discussions, I became more in touch with overall operations, and my key people were able to get commitment from *their* managers to a program they believed in and would follow."

Defining a Formal Improvement Program. The formal improvement program included a variety of changes, including.

1. Modifying Delta Corporation's office layout and relocating personnel.
2. Aiding professional growth by scheduling management meetings four times a year (geared to clarity, recognition, and teamwork).
3. Reviewing and extending Delta's five-year plan, creating a more clearly defined sense of purpose.
4. Improving Delta's wage and salary programs.

Step 4: The Results

Management success usually becomes apparent in subtle changes. For example, at the end of a quarter, it is easy to see that branch profitability has increased. In the first two weeks of that quarter, however, it is extremely difficult to recognize and monitor the subtle changes in quality that will result in that profitability. It is also difficult to measure the level of commitment of people in the branch and to determine whether conflicts that previously hindered performance have been resolved, whether corrective actions really have taken hold, whether people have slipped back into old behavior patterns, or whether smiling faces mask frustration and disintegrating plans.

When sailors want to get as much speed from their boats as the wind and sea will allow, they attach "telltales" to their rigging—little pieces of yarn that blow in the wind and indicate turbulence, stall areas, or areas of counterproductive force. By adjusting the sails so that the telltales flow smoothly, sailors can improve the performance of their boats, often resulting in the difference between winning or losing a race.

Telltales can be used by managers on a day-to-day basis to help them determine the effectiveness of their plans and to make the necessary adjustments. Although the climate-management process cannot predict results in the way a television network predicts the winner of an election, it can give the manager early readings and clues concerning the success of a plan.

The three activities involved in the results phase of the climate-management process are: (a) implementation of the plan, (b) progress measurement and plan revision, and (c) plan integration.

Implementation of the Plan. Within two months after the questionnaires were collected, Delta had entered the implementation stage. The process began at the conclusion of the wider management team meeting.

Delta's chief executive enumerated the steps in their improvement program. "We changed the office layout, even took down a few walls to create different spaces. Then we changed the physical location of a number of people in a way that greatly improved communication. We scheduled management meetings and really *did* practice giving positive feedback on a regular basis (it came hard—just remembering details!). We began revisions of our five-year plan and defined our goals and the strategies necessary to achieve those goals. Finally, we hired a consultant to review our wage and salary program."

As the Delta team entered the final stage of their program, they were no longer using the climate-management process as an exercise, but were implementing it as an on-going operational tool.

Progress Measurement and Plan Revision. Delta officers agreed that they would measure progress by participating annually in the climate-management process.

Results from the second organization and management audit showed an overall climate index of B− with an expected climate of B+. Clarity showed strong improvement, and recognition and teamwork levels also increased. The other dimensions remained approximately the same.

"In addition," reported the chief executive, "our operating results, which had been good, improved even further. Business is going extremely well, and our growth plan is still very aggressive. We are back on target and have exceeded our year-end performance goals. Overall, the quality of management has improved substantially. This process really provided our people with an arena in which to manage effectively."

Delta's second climate report is shown graphically in Figure 9. Although the report demonstrated some progress, it also revealed a need for further improvement, suggesting that the company's action plan might need to be revised.

Plan Integration. The final phase of the climate-management process—integration of the process within the organization—occurred automatically as unit members used the process and discovered the changes they could effect as a result.

After a year, Delta's management team found that application of the climate-management process had proved to be successful, and that it had become integrated into the organization's work mechanism. Managers and personnel understood the process and saw that it produced results. They integrated climate language into discussions of everyday situations, and climate dimensions became a basic part of the organization. The climate-management process was used each year; the group completed questionnaires and created written and formalized size-ups, action plans, involvements, and results.

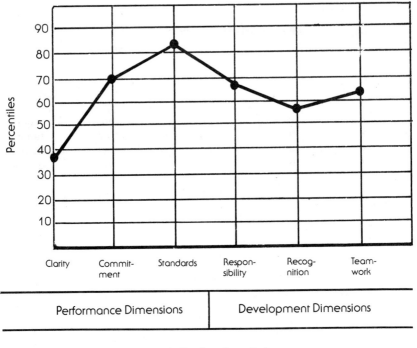

Figure 9. The Results at Delta

PART III: CLIMATE AS AN ORGANIZATION DEVELOPMENT TOOL

For the Practitioner: A Diagnostic Model

The climate system offers the organization development practitioner a diagnostic model, well-founded tools, and technological support to achieve a stronger impact on the organization. It provides managers with important information regarding their work units through feedback on overall organizational climate and individual management practices. It also provides data with which to direct improvement efforts.

Results can be measured over time as they relate to the specific areas of change. Thus, the organization development practitioner can be a valuable asset in helping the manager align specific improvement efforts with overall corporate strategy.

The practitioner becomes a more effective element of organizational improvement. He or she forms a partnership with the key manager, with each party having a specific area of expertise and a defined role. The practitioner achieves greater power and credibility with the client organization, and proven track records can be established. Consequently, the organizational-climate system can be an important intervention tool for the organization development practitioner.

For the Manager: A Systems Model

The organizational-climate system provides the manager with a simple, easy-to-understand, conceptual model that shows how performance is achieved. Not only does the system relate to real-life situations, but it is presented in a logical, flow-chart format that is compatible with the manager's thinking process.

The organizational-climate system does not purport to tell managers how to manage. It does not say that they should be "9/9," "System 4," "participative," "authentic," or whatever. The manager determines the kind of climate required for high performance, receives specific data on where his or her unit stands in relation to the required climate, and chooses from a variety of actions those necessary to achieve this requirement. Hence, the organizational-climate system is objective and free of value judgments.

The organizational-climate system provides the manager with hard data on organizational conditions and his or her own management practices, comparing his or her unit with national norms. Since managers are accustomed to working with objective, quantified information, they can use their own analytical skills to integrate the data and can build a high degree of ownership for change.

In summary, the organizational-climate system offers several unique advantages in the effort to overcome differences of perspective between the individual practitioner and the manager. A partnership can be formed, with each party having a particular area of expertise and role.

For example, through the climate system, the practitioner and manager could assess climate and identify weak areas. They could develop a specific plan and implement a series of action steps based on a clear understanding of those needs.

The organizational-climate system, or climate-management process, has been applied in many industries, among them service, financial, manufacturing, and research organizations. Although the theory and fundamental principles are based on complex behavioral sciences, the terms have been translated into a manager's day-to-day vernacular. Furthermore, the practices and systems are specific, descriptive statements, not complex generalizations. Ultimately, the organizational-climate system has provided organization development practitioners and managers alike with sound concepts and tools for achieving better bottom-line performance and organizational health.

14

Consulting by Tape (Consultatape): A New Method for Using Outside Resources on Internal Management and Organizational Problems

William G. Dyer and Philip B. Daniels

The spread of organization development (OD) into contemporary organizational activity in the past was influenced strongly by the joint utilization of external and internal consultants working together on problems and issues in the organization. This trend has continued, although as many organizations have developed their own internal capabilities by creating an OD or training staff or department, there has been a tendency to use fewer external consultants. The rationale for cutting back on the use of the external consultant generally has been:

1. The external consultant is usually expensive.
2. The external consultant often is not available on a regular, ongoing basis.
3. There is a tendency to become dependent on the external consultant. He or she "calls the shots" in the development of the OD or training activities.
4. When the external consultant is present, management often looks to the external person—not the internal person—as the source of power; this gradually reduces the effectiveness of the internal person.

We have been experimenting with a procedure by which we can diminish the negative aspects of the outside consultant while maintaining the desirability of bringing new, "outside" approaches to internal problems.

THE IDEAS: CONSULTING BY TAPE

The use of the cassette tape as a training aid has been a popular innovation in the last decade. Complete tape-assisted training packages dealing with a variety of training issues have been developed. These programs are all "canned"; that is, the materials are preprepared and the assumption is made that the tape covers all that the users need. Besides these packaged programs, there is an increasing number of tapes available whereby one can listen to an authority expound his or her particular area of expertise. But again the assumption is made that what is presented is what is needed to deal with a particular manager's or organization's problems.

The question we asked ourselves is whether it is possible to use the tape recorder as a vehicle for achieving the advantages of the external consultant while also making the consultation relevant to a particular manager's or organization's problems. We began experimenting with a consultation tape utilizing a standard, data-based management-development procedure we had already developed. The result is what we now call the Consultatape Method of management consulting.

The data-based procedure already developed consisted of:

1. administering an anonymous profile questionnaire to the manager's associates at work;
2. using a computer to summarize the multiple-choice data and having a secretary type the written comments;
3. presenting feedback to the manager in the context of a management-development seminar; and
4. helping that manager to interpret the feedback and create goals and plans for his or her own improvement.

The profile questionnaires used in that process were designed around Likert's (1967) four systems or styles of management. Each of the thirty-six multiple-choice items in the questionnaire contains options that correspond with one of the systems or styles of management. The person filling out the questionnaire is asked to respond two ways to each item: (a) in terms of how he or she feels the manager is actually behaving, and (b) in terms of how the manager "ought" to behave if he or she is to be fully effective in the job situation. The respondent is also asked to make written recommendations to the manager, indicating what he or she might do to become more effective.

There are four different versions of the basic profile instrument: one to be filled out by the manager's subordinates, one by the manager's peers, one by the manager's superior, and one by the manager in question. All four versions of the questionnaire deal with the same issues; the response options on particular items are parallel, with only minor differences to make each option appropriate for each of the four respondents (see Dyer, 1977).

The computer program presents feedback in terms of the systems or styles of management the manager seems (to others) to be employing. The computer also can do some analysis of the data. Based on the "actual" versus the "ought to" ratings, the computer calculates a disparity and then prints out goal statements for those areas of performance in which the manager is least effective.

All written comments are typed, and in some cases summarized, for the manager. The problem of deriving goals from written comments is left largely to the manager when the feedback is given in a workshop setting. The trainers who are conducting the workshop give some help to participating managers, so they are not strictly on their own with the complex feedback.

In addition to the four instruments used in management development, there are others dealing with organization analysis; these are the basis for developing an organization improvement program (Dyer, 1975). We have been using these instruments for years as part of our management training and organization development strategies. We felt that we might be able to make this process available to other managers who could not attend the workshop or seminar where this process was used. By utilizing the Consultatape process, the internal consultant is able to serve a liaison function to get the process going with individual managers, and then take over a more active consultation and follow-through role that is necessary once the basic feedback process is in operation.

Management Development

When a manager or training and development person identifies a manager who needs help with his or her management performance, it may be helpful to have an outside person work with the manager who is in need of development, particularly if:

1. No one in the organization has the relationship base to work with the manager;
2. The manager is reluctant to deal with inside people;
3. There is a need for objectivity and power from the outside;
4. There are differences of opinion about the change needed, and an outside view is appropriate; or
5. A particular expertise is lacking inside the organization, resulting in the need for an outside resource.

In our current program, data-gathering instruments are sent to the client manager either directly or through an internal training and development person. These instruments are distributed and completed by subordinates, peers, and supervisors. The collected, completed instruments are then sent to the outside consultant. Usually the consultant would have the following data bank on each manager:

1. Six to eight instruments dealing with the manager's style as seen by subordinates. This covers such areas as goal setting, decision making, communications, motivation, interaction-influence, control, and leadership.
2. Four to six instruments completed by peers or colleagues.
3. One or two instruments filled out by supervisors.
4. A self-assessment instrument completed by the manager.

Each instrument includes a set of open-ended questions to elicit comments and suggestions from the respondent. It is from this instrument data base that the outside consultant begins a consultation process with the client-manager.

Organizational Improvement

Organizational problems may also be identified in a fashion similar to the management data. A manager or internal OD person who sees a problem in the organization or one of its subdivisions distributes to the employees instruments designed to discover their perceptions of the problems that exist and their recommendations for changes. The instruments cover a wide range of organizational areas: climate, goals, teamwork, development, management, conflict, stress, rewards, motivation, etc. In addition to structured questions, there are also several open-ended questions to elicit comments. These instruments are completed and sent to the external consultant; they provide the data base for the subsequent consultation process.

THE METHODOLOGY

When the outside consultant receives the instruments, he or she goes through the following steps:

Review of Data. All available data from the instruments are read and analyzed, and major themes are identified. This is predominantly a context analysis.

Computer Printout. The quantifiable data are put through a computer process, and a detailed summary is given in a printout. The printout shows how people evaluate the manager and how they think the manager should function to be more effective. The areas of greatest disparity between how the manager is seen and how he or she should function to be effective are then identified. This allows the consultant to identify areas of weakness and strength. The printout also compares the manager with national norms for managers. For organizational data, areas of strength and weakness are also shown, and the organization is compared with norms for other organizations.

Developing Recommendations for Change. Using both the written comments and the computer printout, the consultant now provides a set of recommendations to the manager or organization in order to plan a change program based on the data. It is important that the consultant identify themes and patterns in responses and not react to isolated comments. The client is also asked via tape to review all of the data and to identify his or her own areas for change. Then the client and consultant compare their recommendations.

Preparing the Tape. With all the data and the set of recommendations available, the consultant is now prepared to construct the tape. Since all the data will be sent to the client, the consultant first has to explain the meaning of the data. The first part of the tape is a common or "canned" segment that describes the data base and theory used in the data analysis. This follows a short introduction in which the consultant talks directly to the client and describes what will be included in the total tape.

The consultant then reviews each segment of the data. All data sheets are numbered; the client is referred to each numbered sheet and is "walked through" the data by the consultant. Periodically the client is asked to stop the tape and do some personal analysis. After the client has looked at all the data, he or she is asked again to spend some time thinking about the data and doing an individual analysis before he or she begins to do any action planning.

In the next segment of the tape the consultant gives an analysis of the data and asks the client to compare his or her own analysis with that of the consultant.

Following the analysis and diagnostic phase, the consultant asks the client to complete a change-planning form and do some actual planning for change. The process of building a change plan is described on the tape. The consultant gives some suggestions for action, but the building of the plan is the function of the client. (See Appendix I for a copy of the planning form.)

The client is then asked to send a copy of the change plan to the consultant in preparation for the follow-up activity.

THE FOLLOW-UP

After the change plan has been completed, the client then can negotiate various follow-up activities with the consultant. The client may then call and talk by phone with his consultant (telephone consultation) to review prepared actions or results of actions. At this point correspondence (mail consultation) may also be a useful vehicle. It may be advisable to regather the data via the instruments (follow-up data collection) and have a second look at the data, comparing the first with the second to see if any improvements have been made. Then, if needed, personal consultation visits can be arranged.

THE ROLE OF THE INTERNAL OD SPECIALIST

The outside consultant using the tape process may cooperate with an internal OD person in a useful blending of resources. Assuming that a manager wants an outside resource for himself or his unit but would like some personal, ongoing assistance from the internal specialist, the linkage is as follows:

1. The internal OD specialist (IODS) contacts the external consultant and arranges for the consultation to begin.
2. The IODS sends the consultant any relevant data in addition to the data gathered by the instruments.
3. All tapes and data are sent back to the IODS, who reviews everything and then gives the data back to the manager.
4. The IODS and the manager work together in formulating the change plan.
5. The IODS works with the manager in an ongoing consulting relationship to facilitate the implementation of the change plan.
6. The IODS may contact the outside consultant by phone or mail to obtain any assistance needed.

A FIELD TEST OF CONSULTATAPE

We have now gone through a field-testing period with the Consultatape. Managers have completed the data, sent it to the consultant, received back the tape, and done the action planning. Following are some of the current findings, although more testing is still needed.

Using an Inside OD Person. We have compared reactions of managers who received the tape and did their planning alone with those of managers who went through the data analysis and planning phase with an internal consultant. There is almost unanimous agreement that the help of the internal person facilitates movement through the program. Respondents say they need someone with whom to talk, to get ideas, to check out feelings and reactions, and to get support for formulating the change plan. Those who did not use an inside consultant have suggested that it would be useful (and some did this) to ask someone—a friend, spouse, peer, or superior—to go through the tape with them, read the data, and help develop an action plan.

Personal Nature of the Tape. Respondents have all indicated a preference for a personalized tape. They appreciated the voice calling them by name, talking about the data in a concerned way, giving support and encouragement. There were parts of the tape that were "canned" (theory and method), and these were tolerated, but the personal contact had the most impact.

Stopping the Tape. Within the tape are instructions to stop the tape and do certain individual analyses or thinking. People generally were pleased to know when to stop and to have instructions for personal thinking and planning.

Theoretical Background. The tape includes a section that describes the theory and method for constructing and analyzing the data base. Respondents generally felt that this amount of background was adequate and have not asked for more. It is possible that the managers were so intent on getting into the data that they rushed through the background explanation.

Data-Review Meetings. Initial responses indicated that people wanted more instruction on how to share the data and the change plans with the people with whom they work. This instruction is now being added. Most respondents felt at a loss and uneasy about how to share their planning with others. From much experience, we have found it important to instruct people clearly about what *not* to do with the data they receive. If they try to identify people who are anonymous, if they react in hostile, punishing ways, or if they get very defensive or hurt with their people, the possibility that they can work on a change effort is minimized.

OTHER USES

We have been experimenting with the audiotape as a means of consulting, using instrumented data as the base. There are obviously other ways in which such consulting can be done.

Problem Presentation. If a client were to send to a consultant a detailed presentation of a problem area, the consultant might be able to use this as the base for analysis and recommendations. In any type of consulting, the analysis and recommendations are only as good as the accuracy of the data base.

Process Analysis. Another possibility is for the client to send to the consultant tapes of meetings, interviews, performance reviews, etc., conducted by a manager. The consultant could review this data base and give an analysis of the manager and recommendations for improvement.

Video Tape. It is apparent that consulting could also include the use of video tape or video discs. This may be, in time, a more personal and impactful method by which to gather and respond to data.

Case Studies. There is already a pattern in which one person gathers data and constructs a case study, and others then analyze the case. If the client has been briefed in case construction, a good case might be presented to the consultant for his or her analysis.

VALUE OF THE TAPE CONSULTATION

The process we have described seems to have value for the client. It allows the use of outside consultants at a minimum of expense to the client. (At most, the development of a tape plus the follow-up activities may represent one day of a consultant's time.) Tape consulting tends to reduce the centrality of the outside consultant since the consultant is not physically present. It allows continual follow-up activity at the discretion of the client without requiring a major contract or commitment from the external consultant. Tape consulting also lets the internal OD specialist organize and develop the ongoing internal activities but still use outside help in a limited way.

PROBLEMS OF TAPE CONSULTING

It should be recognized that this new method is not a perfect tool and that certain problems have been experienced. The use of the consultant is limited by the data base available. To the extent that the consultant receives data, he or she is limited in his or her diagnosis and action-taking potential. The client also may want help in areas not available through the data with which the consultant has to work. In addition, there is an impersonality in the relationship that is a negative factor to some consultants and some clients. Some may want or need a closer pattern of interaction, and as a result of the distance between consultant and client, it is sometimes easy for the client to reduce commitment to follow through on action plans. Finally, the client may depend too much on the consultant, even through the tape, and be reluctant to engage in change alone.

REFERENCES

Dyer, W. G. How to teach OD to line managers. *OD Practitioner*, February 1975, 7(1).

Dyer, W. G. Management profiling: A disparity model for developing motivation for change. In W. W. Burke (Ed.), *Current issues and strategies in OD*. New York: Human Science Press, 1977.

Likert, R. *The human organization*. New York: McGraw-Hill, 1967.

APPENDIX: PERSONAL CHANGE PROGRAM

I. Identify the major areas that you plan to improve that are included in your data.

A.

B.

C.

D.

II. (1) For each area above, outline the specific step-by-step actions needed to achieve your planned improvement.

Action	Who Will Be Responsible	When Will You Start	What Person(s) Will Support This Effort
A.			
B.			
C.			
D.			

(2) *Evaluation:* How will you determine whether you have in fact improved in each of the above areas?

A.

B.

C.

D.

III. Does the above action plan meet the following criteria?

_____ 1. There is evidence of need for change.

_____ 2. The significant people of power and influence needed are involved in the change action and will support it.

_____ 3. The people who must implement the change are involved in and/or informed of the change action.

_____ 4. The change plan specifically identifies who is to do what, when.

_____ 5. The plan has specific deadlines, i.e., when change will start and either terminate or become established.

_____ 6. There are clear criteria for evaluating the success of the change action.

_____ 7. The change is supported by policy, procedure, scheduling, and announcement.

_____ 8. You personally have real commitment to achieve the change.

_____ 9. The change plan clearly deals with a problem area and will help you to become more effective.

_____10. Sufficient resources (time, people, money, etc.) have been allocated to achieve the change goal.

15

Contracting for Leadership Style: A Process and Instrumentation for Building Effective Work Relationships

Paul Hersey, Kenneth H. Blanchard, and Ronald K. Hambleton

One of the problems of organization development is that most interventions stress the use of collaborative or interpersonal strategies for change. If most OD consultants and practitioners use these strategies and thus concentrate on the "people variable" in helping organizations, it is clear why there are more OD intervention failures than successes. The same change strategy will be effective in some situations but ineffective in others. There is no "best" strategy that works every time. Effective OD interventions depend on a good diagnosis of the situation and a determination of the approach with the highest probability of success for the particular environment.

The collaborative change strategy so often used tends to be effective in organizations that are in "fairly good" shape; that is, their members have the skills and ability to implement desired change but need someone to help facilitate it. However, most organizations that need OD interventions require more. Because this is true, OD practitioners and change agents must develop their skills in structural, technological change strategies as well as maintain their skills in interpersonal, participative change strategies so that the movement toward "humanizing" organizations can have some hope of success.

Situational leadership and management by objectives (MBO) are described in this chapter in a way that shows both practicing managers and OD consultants exactly when participative and supportive strategies are appropriate and when more directive technological strategies are appropriate. The chapter is divided into three sections: (a) a review of situational leadership and MBO; (b) a description of the development of two instruments to measure maturity; and (c) a discussion of the use of the maturity instruments to facilitate the process of contracting for leadership style.

MANAGEMENT BY OBJECTIVES

The concept of management by objectives (MBO) was introduced by Peter Drucker in the early 1950s. Since its introduction, MBO has grown rapidly in popularity throughout the world. Aided by the work of Odiorne (1965), Humble (1967), and others (Batten, 1966; Miller, 1966; Reddin, 1971), managers in many types of organizational settings (for example, industrial, educational, governmental, and military settings) have been attempting to run their organizations with the MBO process as a basic underlying management concept. Unfortunately, MBO success stories have not occurred as often as anticipated by proponents of MBO or by practitioners who have applied it. Why? It is our contention that there has been a major missing link: contracting for leadership style (Hersey & Blanchard, 1974). In most MBO programs, an effort is made only for managers and their subordinates to reach agreement on performance goals; little attention is given to developing "contracts" between managers and their subordinates regarding the role of managers in helping their subordinates accomplish the negotiated objectives.

As it is practiced in most organizations, management by objectives begins with agreement among the top management on the common goals for the entire organization. At that time, any changes needed in the organization's structure—for example, changes in title, duties, or span of control—are made. Next, each manager and each subordinate independently proposes time-oriented goals for the subordinate's job and the method to be used to evaluate on-the-job performance. The two sets of goals are discussed by the manager and the subordinate, and a set of mutually agreed-on goals and methods is produced. Also, checkpoints are established. These are times when a manager and a subordinate can compare the expected performance goals with what actually has been accomplished; necessary adjustments can be made and inappropriate goals discarded. At the end of the time period, a final mutual review of performance goals and outcomes takes place. If there is a discrepancy between the two, an effort is made to determine reasons for the discrepancy. With the reasons in hand, steps can be taken by a manager to try to improve performance during the next time period. This sets the stage for a determination of goals or objectives for that time period.

The entire cycle of management by objectives is represented in Figure 1.

The Missing Link

The special aspect of MBO, as compared to many other management systems, is that managers and subordinates participate in the establishment of objectives (or performance goals) *and* in the evaluation that takes place in relation to the agreed-on objectives. It has been found that participation in the formulation of objectives tends to make subordinates feel more personal responsibility for their attainment and is thus more effective than having objectives imposed by an authority figure in the organization. The problem with MBO—and a reason why *few* effective implementations occur—is that the role of the manager in helping subordinates accomplish objectives is *not* usually specified.

We believe that MBO can be a more powerful tool for productivity improvement if managers negotiate with their subordinates the leadership styles they will use to help their subordinates meet their objectives. Just as golfers, with the aid of their caddies, select a club depending on the ball's lie on the course, so managers, with the help of their subordinates, should select leadership styles to be used in achieving agreed-on objectives. Situational leadership, developed by Hersey and Blanchard (1969, 1977), should help in this selection.

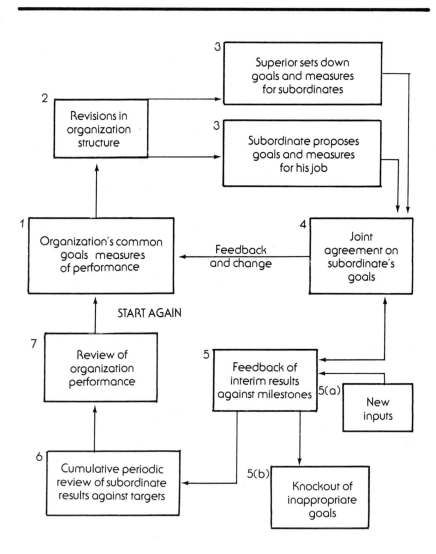

Figure 1. The Cycle of Management by Objectives (Odiorne, 1965)

SITUATIONAL LEADERSHIP

Situational leadership was introduced to help people, whether managers, consultants, administrators, teachers, trainers, or parents (anyone trying to influence the behavior of others) be more effective in their everyday interactions with others. The concept is based on the amount of direction (task behavior) and the amount of socio-emotional support (relationship behavior) a leader must provide, given the situation and "the level of maturity" of a subordinate. The concept can be applied effectively to groups as well as to individuals; however, in this paper, we will discuss its application primarily in relation to a single subordinate.

Task Behavior and Relationship Behavior

The recognition of task behavior and relationship behavior as two critical aspects of a leader's behavior has been an important part of management research over the last several decades. They have been labeled various things, ranging from "autocratic" and "democratic" to "employee-oriented" and "production-oriented."

For some time, it was believed that task and relationship behaviors were either/or styles of leadership and, therefore, could be represented on a single continuum, moving from *very authoritarian* leader behavior (task) at one end to *very participative* leader behavior (relationship) at the other end.

In more recent years, the idea that task and relationship were either/or leadership styles has been dispelled. In particular, extensive leadership studies at Ohio State University (Stogdill & Coons, 1957) questioned this assumption and showed that other assumptions were more reasonable and would lead to more useful theories of leadership.

By spending time actually observing the behavior of leaders in a wide variety of situations, the Ohio State staff found that they could classify most of the activities of leaders into two distinct behavioral categories or dimensions. They named these two dimensions "Initiating Structure" (task behavior) and "Consideration" (relationship behavior). *Task behavior* is the extent to which a leader engages in one-way communication by explaining what each follower is to do as well as when, where, and how tasks are to be accomplished. *Relationship behavior* is the extent to which a leader engages in two-way communication by providing socio-emotional support, "psychological strokes," and facilitating behaviors.

In the leadership studies mentioned, the Ohio State staff found that leadership styles tended to vary considerably. The behavior of some leaders was characterized mainly by directing activities for their followers in terms of task accomplishment, while other leaders concentrated on providing socio-emotional support in terms of personal relationships between themselves and their followers. Still other leader styles were characterized by both high-task and high-relationship behavior. There were even some leaders whose behavior tended to provide little task or relationship for their followers. No dominant style of leadership emerged across a wide range of leaders working in many different settings. Instead, various combinations were evident. The observed patterns of leader behavior can be plotted on two separate axes, as shown in Figure 2.

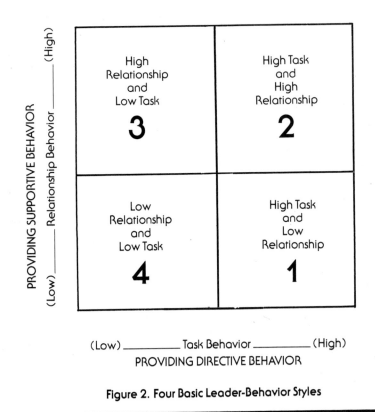

Figure 2. Four Basic Leader-Behavior Styles

Since research in the past several decades (Fiedler, 1967; Hemphill, 1949; Reddin, 1967, 1970) has clearly supported the contention that there is no "best style of leadership," any of the four basic styles shown in Figure 2 may be effective or ineffective. According to Hersey and Blanchard (1977), the effectiveness of a leadership style will depend on the situation in which it is applied.

Situational leadership is based on an interplay among (a) the amount of direction (task behavior) a leader gives, (b) the amount of socio-emotional support (relationship behavior) a leader provides, and (c) the "maturity" level that a follower exhibits on a specific task, function, or objective that the leader is attempting to accomplish through the individual.

The Concept of Maturity

Maturity is defined in situational leadership as the willingness and ability of a person to take responsibility for directing his or her own behavior. *These variables of maturity should be considered only in relation to a specific task to be performed.* That is to say, an individual (or a group) is not mature or immature in any *total* sense. People tend to have different degrees of maturity for specific tasks, functions, or objectives that a leader is attempting to accomplish.

Thus, a sales representative may be very mature in the way he or she approaches sales calls but may not demonstrate the same degree of maturity in developing and writing customer proposals. As a result, it may be quite appropriate for this individual's manager to provide little direction and help on sales-call activities, yet provide a great deal of direction and close supervision over the individual's proposal-writing activity.

When we talk about the maturity of individuals as their willingness (motivation) and ability (competence) to take responsibility for directing their own behavior, we are suggesting that the concept of maturity consists of two dimensions: *psychological maturity* and *job maturity.*

Psychological maturity is related to willingness or motivation to do something. An individual who has high psychological maturity in a particular area of responsibility thinks that responsibility is important and has self-confidence and good feelings about that aspect of his or her job. That person does not need extensive "patting on the back" or encouragement to do things in that area. A comment from a person who is high in psychological maturity relative to one job objective might be: *"I really enjoy that aspect of my job. My boss doesn't have to get after me or provide any encouragement for me to work well in that area."*

Job maturity is related to the ability or competence to do something. An individual who has high job maturity in a particular area of his or her work has the knowledge, ability, and experience to do tasks in that aspect of the job without the need for direction from others. A person high in job maturity perhaps would say: *"My talent really lies in that aspect of my job. I can work on my own in that area without much help from my boss."*

If persons are divided into high and low levels on each dimension for each job objective, four combinations arise that can be used to describe persons:

1. Individuals who are *neither willing nor able* to take responsibility (low on both psychological and job maturity).
2. Individuals who are *willing* but *not able* to take responsibility (high psychological maturity but low job maturity).
3. Individuals who are *able* but *not willing* to take responsibility (high job maturity but low psychological maturity).
4. Individuals who are *both willing and able* to take responsibility (high on both psychological and job maturity).

The highest level of maturity for an individual (in situational leadership terms) would be combination 4; the lowest level would be combination 1.

The Basic Concept

According to situational leadership theory, a leader should provide constant direction and low socio-emotional support for a follower who is low in maturity relative to a particular job objective. As the level of maturity of the follower increases in terms of accomplishing a specific task, the leader should begin to *reduce* task behavior and *increase* relationship behavior. This should be the case until the individual reaches a moderate level of maturity. As the follower moves into an above average level of maturity, it becomes appropriate for the leader to decrease not only task behavior but relationship behavior as well. At this point, the follower is not only mature in terms of the performance of the task but also is psychologically mature. Since the follower can provide his or her own "strokes" and reinforcement, a great deal of socio-emotional support from the leader is no longer necessary. People at this maturity level see a reduction of close supervision and an increase in delegation of work by the leader as a positive indication of trust and confidence. Thus, situational leadership focuses on the appropriateness or effectiveness of leadership styles according to the *task-relevant maturity* of the follower. This cycle can be illustrated by a bell-shaped curve superimposed on the four leadership quadrants, as is shown in Figure 3.

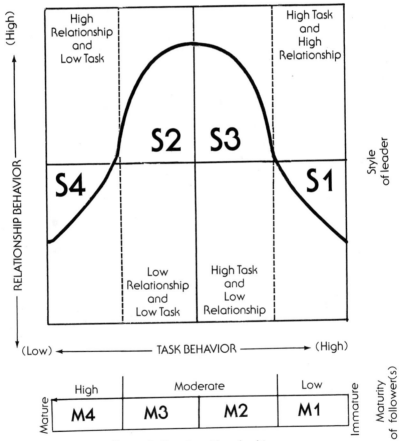

Figure 3. Situational Leadership

Figure 3 relates the maturity level of a subordinate for completing a particular job objective to the "optimum" leadership style of a manager for maximizing the subordinate's job performance. The reader should keep in mind that the figure represents two different phenomena. The appropriate leadership style (*style of leader*) for given levels of follower maturity is portrayed by the curved line running through the four leadership quadrants. The maturity level of the individual being supervised (*maturity level of a follower*) is depicted below the leadership model as a *continuum* ranging from low-level to high-level maturity.

In referring to the leadership styles in the model, we use the following shorthand designations: (a) high task-low relationship will be referred to as leader behavior style S1; (b) high task-high relationship as leader behavior style S2; (c) high relationship-low task as leader style S3; and (d) low relationship-low task as leader style S4.

In terms of follower maturity, it is not simply a question of being mature or immature but a question of degree. As can be seen in Figure 3, some indicators of maturity can be provided for determining an appropriate leadership style by dividing the maturity continuum into four levels of maturity. The maturity level of a person who is (a) unwilling and unable (low on both psychological maturity and job maturity) will be referred to as maturity level M1; (b) willing but not able (high psychological maturity but low job maturity) will be referred to as maturity level M2; (c) able but not willing (high job maturity but low psychological maturity) will be referred to as maturity level M3; and (d) able and willing (high on both psychological maturity and job maturity) will be referred to as maturity level M4.

APPLICATION

The bell-shaped curve in the style-of-leader portion of the model can be used to prescribe the leadership style that is required for a person of a particular maturity level.

Determining Appropriate Style

To determine which leadership style is appropriate to use in a given situation, one must first determine the maturity level of the follower in relation to a specific task that the leader is attempting to accomplish through the follower's efforts. Once this maturity level is identified, the appropriate leadership style can be determined by constructing a right angle (90-degree angle) from the point on the continuum that identifies the maturity level of the follower to a point at which it intersects the curve in the style-of-leader portion of the model. The quadrant in which that intersection takes place determines the appropriate style to be used by the leader in that situation with a follower of that maturity level. Consider the example in Figure 4.

If a manager has determined that a subordinate's maturity level in terms of administrative paper work is low, she would place an "X" on the maturity continuum as shown in Figure 4 (above M1). Once the manager has decided that she wants to influence the subordinate's behavior in this area, she can determine the appropriate initial style to use by constructing a right angle from the X drawn on the maturity continuum to a point at which it intersects the curve (designated in Figure 4 by 0). Because the intersection occurs in the S1 quadrant, it is suggested that when working with this subordinate, who demonstrates M1 maturity on this particular task, the manager should use an S1 style (high task-low relationship behavior). If one follows this technique for determining the appropriate leadership style for all four maturity levels, it will become clear that the four maturity designations (M1, M2, M3, M4) correspond to the four leadership behavior designations (S1, S2, S3, S4); that is, M1 maturity requires an S1 style, M2 maturity requires an S2 style, etc.

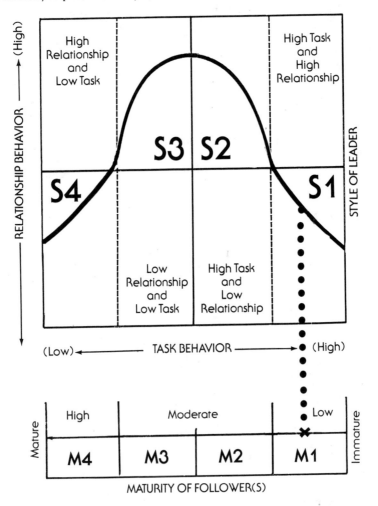

Figure 4. Determining an Appropriate Leadership Style

When we say "low relationship behavior," we do not mean that the manager is not friendly or personable to the subordinate. We merely suggest that the manager, in supervising the subordinate's handling of administrative paper work, should spend more time directing the person in what to do and how, when, and where to do it, than in providing socio-emotional support and reinforcement. Increased relationship behavior should occur when the subordinate begins to demonstrate the ability to handle necessary administrative paper work. At that point, a movement from style 1 to style 2 would be appropriate.

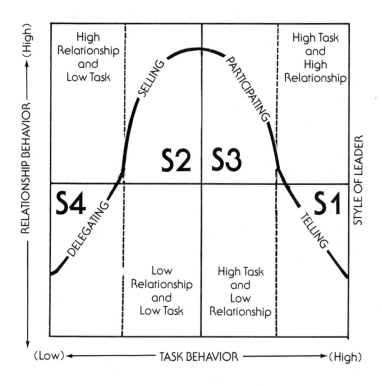

Figure 5. Situational Leadership

Thus, situational leadership contends that in working with people who are low in maturity (M1), a high task/low relationship style (S1) has the highest probability of producing effective results; in dealing with people who are of low to moderate maturity (S2), a moderate structure and socio-emotional style (S2) appears to be most appropriate. In working with people who are of moderate to high maturity (M3), a high relationship/low task style (S3) has the highest probability of producing effective performance. Finally, a low relationship/low task style (S4) is the style most likely to maximize job performance with people of high task-relevant maturity (M4).

Although it is important to keep the definitions of task and relationship behavior in mind, the labeling of the four styles of situational leadership, when they are being used effectively, as in Figure 5, is sometimes useful for quick diagnostic judgments.

High task/low relationship leader behavior (S1) is referred to as "telling" because this style is characterized by one-way communication in which the leader defines the roles of the follower and tells the follower what, how, when, and where to do various tasks.

High task/high relationship leader behavior (S2) is referred to as "selling" because with this style most of the direction is still provided by the leader. He or she also uses two-way communication and socio-emotional support to encourage the follower psychologically to "buy into" decisions that have to be made.

High relationship/low task leader behavior (S3) is called "participating." With this style the leader and follower now share in decision making through two-way communication and much facilitating behavior from the leader, since the follower has the ability and knowledge to do the task.

Low relationship/low task leader behavior (S4) is labeled "delegating" because the style involves letting the follower "run the show." The leader delegates because the follower is high in maturity, being both willing and able to take responsibility for directing his or her own behavior.

It is important to emphasize that *the labels "telling," "selling," "participating," and "delegating" should be used only to describe effective use of styles S1, S2, S3, and S4.* For example, when style S4 is used inappropriately with a person who has low maturity, it would not be called "delegating." It would be more abdication than delegation, and thus would not be given the same label as the effective use of Style 4.

Situational Leadership and MBO

Once a superior and a subordinate have agreed on certain goals for the subordinate and how the accomplishment of those goals can be measured, in most MBO programs it is common for the superior to move to an S4 style (low relationship/ low task) in supervising the subordinate. According to situational leadership, for this movement to an S4 style to be effective, the subordinate involved must be both willing and able (maturity level M4) to direct his or her own behavior in accomplishing each of the agreed-on objectives. Clearly, such a situation does not always occur. Most individuals will be at different maturity levels for different job objectives. That is to say, there are some aspects of their jobs for which they may be either inexperienced and/or unmotivated. As a result, we feel that once goals and objectives are established between a superior and his or her subordinate, the next logical step (but not often the one used) is for both parties involved—superior and subordinate—to negotiate the appropriate leadership style that the superior will use in helping the subordinate accomplish each objective.

If contracting for leadership style does not take place, problems may occur. For example, if the superior leaves the subordinate completely alone, the superior will be unaware until the next interim check period whether this low relationship/low task leadership style (S4) was appropriate ("delegating") or inappropriate ("abdicating"). An S4 style will be effective only for accomplishing objectives in areas in which the subordinate has significant technical skill and willingness to do the job. Conversely, if, after negotiating goals and objectives, a leader continually hovers over and directs the activities of a subordinate, this high task/low relationship style (S1) might alienate subordinates working in areas in which they are competent and capable of working alone.

DEVELOPMENT OF INSTRUMENTS TO MEASURE MATURITY

If a leader and a follower are to agree on an effective leadership style that the leader should use with the follower, both of them must be able to accurately determine the maturity level of the follower on each of his or her job objectives. To help managers and their followers make "valid" judgments about follower maturity—and thereby facilitate their agreement on appropriate leadership styles—we recently have developed two different maturity instruments: the *Manager's Rating Form* and the *Self-Rating Form*. [1]

The Manager's Rating Form

The first maturity instrument we developed was the Manager's Rating Form. In developing this form, one of our first decisions was to consider maturity as a two-dimensional construct. As we discussed earlier, maturity consists of both the *willingness* (motivation) and *ability* (competence) of a person to direct his or her behavior while working on a particular job objective or responsibility. Willingness and ability are referred to, in our work, as *psychological maturity* and *job maturity*, respectively.

[1] These two instruments were developed through a grant from Xerox Corporation. We are grateful to Xerox Corporation not only for providing financial support for the instrument-development project, but for allowing us to involve many of their managers and employees in our development and validation work. In particular, we would like to acknowledge Audian Dunham, Warren Rothman, and Ray Gumpert for their assistance, encouragement, and constructive criticism of our work. The instruments are available through Learning Resources Corporation, 7594 Eads Avenue, La Jolla, CA 92037.

Our next step was to generate a long list of possible rating scales to "tap" each of the two dimensions. For example, with the job-maturity dimension we produced scales such as "past job experience," "job knowledge," and "understanding of job requirements." For the psychological-maturity dimension, scales such as "willingness to take responsibility," "commitment," and "achievement motivation" were written. In total, we produced about thirty scales as potential indicators of each dimension. These scales were later edited and revised by a group of managers and ourselves. The twenty most relevant scales measuring each dimension were selected for further study. We then produced "behavioral indicators" of the end points corresponding to each scale.

For example, with the scale "past job experience," the end points of the scale were chosen to be "has experience relevant to job" and "does not have relevant experience." With the psychological-maturity scale "willingness to take responsibility," the end points of the scale were chosen to be "is very eager" and "is very reluctant" and so on.

As is clear from Figure 6, eight-point rating scales are used in the instrument. Low to high designations correspond to our M1 to M4 maturity benchmarks. Thus, ratings of one or two correspond to maturity level M1, ratings of three or four to maturity level M2, ratings of five or six to maturity level M3, and ratings of seven or eight to maturity level M4.

Next, we conducted four pilot studies using the instrument (Hambleton, Blanchard, & Hersey, 1977a, 1977b). The data collected in each study were analyzed using techniques such as item analysis and factor analysis. In addition, we assessed the reliability of scores derived from the instrument. The results of these pilot studies can be summarized as follows:

1. We were able to select the most appropriate scales (seven in all) from the initial pool of scales to measure each dimension.
2. We determined that leader ratings on as few as five scales measuring each dimension were sufficient to produce acceptable score reliability.
3. We improved the readability and clarity of instrument directions and score interpretations.

In our most recent research on the maturity instrument, we had fifty-one managers each rate one of their employees. Each manager rated the same employee twice, using the same job objectives on each occasion. The time interval between the two occasions varied from a few hours with some managers to about three days for others. In total, the fifty-one managers rated their employees on 224 job objectives. (Typically, a manager rated an employee on four or five job objectives.)

The test-retest reliability of the job-maturity scores (across managers and job objectives) was .84. For the psychological-maturity scores, the test-retest reliability was .88. Clearly, there was substantial consistency in the ratings of employees on particular job objectives across occasions. Of course, the time period between occasions was short; but if the period of time between occasions were lengthened, reliability estimates would be influenced by both inconsistency in manager ratings and real changes in employee maturity levels. The influence of this second source of variation would lead to biased estimates of reliability of the job- and psychological-maturity scores at a particular point in time.

JOB-MATURITY SCALES

This person _____ in performing this objective

Scales	High 8	7 (M4)	6 (M3)	Moderate 5	4 (M2)	3	Low 2 (M1)	1
1. Past Job Experience	Has experience relevant to job 8	7	6	5	4	Does not have relevant experience 3	2	1
2. Job Knowledge	Possesses necessary job knowledge 8	7	6	5	4	Does not have necessary job knowledge 3	2	1
3. Understanding of Job Requirements	Thoroughly understands what needs to be done 8	7	6	5	4	Has little understanding of what needs to be done 3	2	1

PSYCHOLOGICAL-MATURITY SCALES

This person _____ in performing this objective

Scales	High 8	7 (M4)	6 (M3)	Moderate 5	4 (M2)	3	Low 2 (M1)	1
1. Willingness to Take Responsibility	Is very eager 8	7	6	5	4	Is very reluctant 3	2	1
2. Achievement Motivation	Has a high desire to achieve 8	7	6	5	4	Has little desire to achieve 3	2	1
3. Commitment	Is very dedicated 8	7	6	5	4	Is uncaring 3	2	1

Figure 6. A Portion of the Manager's Rating Form of Maturity

Even more interesting than our results on the reliability of job and psychological maturity scores are our results on the percent of agreement across the two occasions in the determination of a leadership style for an employee on a particular job objective. The percent of agreement was over 77 percent. This means that over 77 percent of the time a manager made the same selection of a leadership style across a retest administration (after a short period of time) of the maturity instrument. Since the primary use of the maturity instrument is to facilitate a leader determining the highest probability of successful leadership style in a particular situation at a given time, it is extremely important to know what level of agreement there would be in the determination of a leadership style across two parallel administrations of the instrument. (Incidentally, leaders did not know that they were going to be asked to repeat their ratings of a follower on a second occasion.) A figure of 77 percent agreement is quite high and could be expected to be even higher if managers were to receive some training in completing the instrument. The managers in our study had no prior training or experience with the instrument. Therefore, our reliability results are probably conservative estimates of the results that can be achieved when managers are properly trained to use the instrument.

How the Manager's Rating Form Is Used

A manager, in completing the maturity instrument about a subordinate, is first asked to identify the subordinate's most important job objectives. If the superior and subordinate are involved in an MBO program, the objectives for the subordinate would already have been negotiated between the two. If these objectives really are to useful, tangible, easily measurable indicators of accomplishment also should have been specified for each objective.

Once these objectives have been established, the manager is asked to select the five *most relevant job-maturity scales* (from the seven provided) and the five *most relevant psychological-maturity scales* (from the seven provided) for each of the established objectives and then to "rate" the maturity level of each subordinate separately on each established objective using the scales they have chosen. A manager does not have to choose the same job-maturity and psychological-maturity scales for each of the job objectives being rated. Thus, the manager may decide that the scales appearing to be most relevant to use for one objective are not the same ones that are most relevant to use for a different objective. Managers are given a choice of rating a subordinate on any five of the seven job-maturity scales and any five of the seven psychological-maturity scales, because not all scales will apply equally well to every objective.

A job-maturity score and a psychological-maturity score for each job objective are obtained by adding the total of the five job-maturity ratings and psychological-maturity ratings, respectively. The highest possible score for a subordinate's job maturity or psychological maturity on a particular job objective is forty, and the lowest possible score is five.

Once job-maturity and psychological-maturity scores are calculated, these scores are used wth the interpretation matrix shown in Figure 7 to determine both

DATA MATRIX

	M1	M2	M3	M4
M4	S2 Job 5 to 12 Psy 33 to 40 M2	S2/3 Job 13 to 22 Psy 33 to 40 M2/3	S3/4 Job 23 to 32 Psy 33 to 40 M3/4	S4 Job 33 to 40 Psy 33 to 40 M4
M3	S2 Job 5 to 12 Psy 23 to 32 M2	S2/3 Job 13 to 22 Psy 23 to 32 M2/3	S3 Job 23 to 32 Psy 23 to 32 M3	S3/4 Job 33 to 40 Psy 23 to 32 M3/4
M2	S1/2 Job 5 to 12 Psy 13 to 22 M1/2	S2 Job 13 to 22 Psy 13 to 22 M2	S2/3 Job 23 to 32 Psy 13 to 22 M2/3	S2/3 Job 33 to 40 Psy 13 to 22 M2/3
M1	S1 Job 5 to 12 Psy 5 to 12 M1	S1/2 Job 13 to 22 Psy 5 to 12 M1/2	S2 Job 23 to 32 Psy 5 to 12 M2	S2 Job 33 to 40 Psy 5 to 12 M2

PSY MATURITY (vertical axis) — JOB MATURITY (horizontal axis: M1 M2 M3 M4)

Figure 7. Interpretation Matrix for Job- and Psychological-Maturity Scores

the subordinate's overall maturity level (with respect to a particular job objective) *as perceived by the manager* and the most appropriate leadership style (or combination of styles).[2]

Follower maturity and the most appropriate leadership style for a particular objective are determined by locating the box in the matrix that contains the combination of *job-maturity* and *psychological-maturity* scores for the follower. In the lower left-hand corner of that box is the subordinate's *overall maturity* designation for that objective/responsibility. In the upper right-hand corner of the box is the high probability leadership style the manager should use for that maturity level. (In some of the boxes the maturity level and appropriate leadership style are expressed as being in between two specific designations.)

Suppose a manager judged a subordinate to have a score of twenty-seven in *job maturity* and twenty-four in *psychological maturity* for a particular objective. According to the data matrix in Figure 7, these two scores would fall in the box where the job-maturity and psychological-maturity scores range from twenty-three to thirty-two. As suggested in the box, the *overall maturity* for the subordinate for that objective (as perceived by his or her superior) would be M3, and the

[2]Research on the validity of the interpretation matrix has been under way for some time. Preliminary evidence provides substantial support for entries in the matrix.

most appropriate leadership style to be used with that subordinate would be S3—participating (high relationship/low task).

The determination of a follower's maturity level and the corresponding best leadership style (or combination of leader styles) is repeated for each job objective or responsibility. After some training with the instrument, leaders are able to complete their job-objective ratings of a subordinate in about ten minutes.

Self-Rating Form

Recently, we revised the Manager's Rating Form slightly so that it can also be used for self-ratings by subordinates. The availability of a Self-Rating Form is necessary to initiate a program combining MBO with contracting for leadership style.

CONTRACTING FOR LEADERSHIP STYLE

Before the process of contracting for leadership style can begin, the first four steps of the MBO cycle (see Figure 1) must be completed. Once a superior and subordinate have agreed on and contracted for certain goals and objectives for the subordinate and measures to evaluate goal accomplishment, the next logical step would be a negotiation and agreement about the appropriate leadership style that the superior should use in helping the subordinate accomplish each one of the objectives. It is at this point that the maturity instruments are being used as vehicles to facilitate this process.

Suppose a salesman and his boss (the district sales manager) agree on several objectives for the year in each of his areas of responsibility—sales, service, administration, and team support. After this agreement, if they both were familiar with situational leadership, the next step would be the negotiation of leadership style appropriate for helping the salesman accomplish his goals. Using the two maturity instruments, the process would be as follows:

Independent Assessment

The sales manager would complete the Manager's Rating Form of the maturity instrument about the salesman for each of the agreed-on objectives; the salesman would do the same on the Self-Rating Form. The sales manager and the salesman could then compare their perceptions of the salesman's maturity level and the appropriate leadership style that the sales manager should use with the salesman on each of the agreed-on objectives.

Joint Agreement

The salesman and the sales manager would meet and share their maturity and leadership-style designations. This would be done by discussing, one at a time, each of the objectives agreed on for the salesman.

The first step in this process would be to discuss which of the five scales each of them used in assessing both *job maturity* and *psychological maturity*. Because they each had to choose five out of the seven scales provided for these two dimensions of maturity, it is possible that they may not have chosen the same scales to rate. Because they would be sharing why they chose each of the scales, this discussion would eliminate any concern about either party trying to pick the job-maturity scales or psychological-maturity scales that would make the subordinate look good or bad. This discussion would also give each person some feedback on what the other person thought were the most relevant aspects of *job maturity* and *psychological maturity* for each of the salesman's objectives. This is information that is often not shared between superior and subordinate.

The second step would be to compare their individual overall maturity and leadership-style designations for each of the agreed-on objectives to discover any differences in their perceptions about the ability and motivation of the salesman to accomplish these objectives. With objectives for which they both agreed on the salesman's maturity and the appropriate leadership style, there would not need to be much discussion.

With objectives for which there is disagreement between the salesman and the sales manager about the maturity level of the salesman, a discussion to clarify their different perceptions could take place. This would be an opportune time for the salesman to share with his boss any of his past experience or background as well as insecurities and motivations of which the sales manager may be unaware. At the same time, the sales manager would be able to share with the salesman his good feelings as well as concerns about his work in sales, service, administration, and team support. Through this feedback and disclosure process, they should eventually be able to come to agreement on maturity level and appropriate leadership style. If this agreement is difficult to accomplish, we recommend that the superior (in this case the sales manager) go along with the follower's perception. We feel that this is important, particularly when this contracting for leadership styles is first attempted in a particular superior-subordinate relationship. If the boss "wins" all these early disagreements, the subordinate will soon learn to keep opinions to himself or herself and try to figure out what the superior wants to hear.

The contracting process that occurs between the salesman and the sales manager should result in the sales manager agreeing to use a variety of leadership styles in relation to the agreed-on objectives. Thus, in areas in which the salesman is experienced and has been successful in accomplishing similar objectives over a period of time, such as sales volume, the negotiated leadership contract might be for his boss to leave him on his own (S4). In this case, rather than directing and closely supervising his behavior, the role of the sales manager would be to make sure that the resources necessary for reaching his agreed-on sales volume are available and to coordinate his sales efforts with other salespersons under his supervision. For a goal in an area in which the salesman might have little experience, such as team support (this is a new job requirement for salespersons in this company), they might negotiate significant supervision and support (S2) from the sales manager until the salesman understands his role in terms of team support and is able to function in that area without help from his boss. In another objective area such as service, in which the salesman is competent but lacks self-confidence, the sales manager may agree to give the salesman support and encouragement but little direction (S3). Seldom will a superior and subordinate negotiate an S1 style on a major objective. Although the sales manager may want to begin to prepare the salesman to take some responsibility in an area in which he is unwilling and unable to do so (M1), he would probably not want to set major objectives in this area.

Determining What Each Contracted Style Means

Once the sales manager and his salesman have agreed on the style of supervision to be used with each objective, the next step in the contracting process is to determine what each contracted style means in terms of the sales manager's behavior. Unless what the two have agreed on is translated into specific managerial behavior, the contracting process may end up as only an intellectual exercise. One way to avoid that occurrence is for the salesman and sales manager to sit down with their calendars and set up meetings according to the agreed-on supervision. With job objectives to which an S2 style has been contracted, the sales manager may agree to meet the salesman twice a week for an hour to work on this area with him. In S3 contracted areas, he may make an appointment for lunch with the salesman once every several weeks so that the salesman can show him the progress he is making in those areas and the sales manager can give needed support. And, finally, in S4 areas, the salesman would be responsible for calling the sales manager for a meeting if he needs any help or support.

It is obvious from the way we have been discussing the sheduling of meetings that if the sales manager wanted to develop the salesman in an area in which the salesman was both unwilling and unable to direct his own behavior (M1), he would have to meet with the salesman daily in the beginning to give the salesman the required direction and supervision.

If both persons write down these agreed-on meetings in their calendars, it will insure that there will be follow-through after the initial contracting sessions.

Modifying Levels of Maturity

Once the salesman and the boss have agreed on what each contracted leadership style means in terms of meetings, the sales manager should look for improvements in the salesman's ability and motivation to direct his own behavior so that the frequency and focus of these meetings can be reduced gradually as the salesman begins to mature. (Alternately, if the salesman's performance of a particular job objective deteriorates, it may be necessary for the sales manager to schedule additional meetings.) In the beginning, in areas in which the salesman is low in maturity, the scheduled meetings will be frequent and very structured and directive (S1). As the salesman begins to develop, the meetings gradually will be reduced in frequency and will become more of a "give and take" (S2), then will be less frequent and more supportive and nondirective (S3), and eventually will be called only at the request of the salesman (S4). Note how the sequencing of styles moves forward through the curve depicted in Figure 3. The movement is from "telling" to "selling" to "participating" to "delegating."

In attempting to improve the maturity of a subordinate who has not taken much responsibility in the past, a manager must be careful not to increase socio-emotional support (relationship behavior) too rapidly. If this is done, the subordinate may view the manager as becoming a "soft touch." Thus, the manager must develop a subordinate slowly, using a *little* less task behavior and a *little* more relationship behavior as a subordinate matures. When a subordinate's performance is low, one cannot expect drastic changes overnight. For more desirable behavior to be obtained, a manager must reward as quickly as possible the slightest appropriate behavior exhibited by the individual in the desired direction and continue this process as the individual's behavior comes closer and closer to the manager's expectations of good performance. This is a behavior modification concept called *reinforcing positively successive approximations* (Skinner, 1953, 1961). For example, if the sales manager wanted to improve the maturity level of a salesman so that the salesman would assume significantly more responsibility, the manager's best bet initially would be to *reduce* a little of the direction (task behavior) by giving the salesman an opportunity to assume some increased responsibility. If this responsibility is well handled, the sales manager should reinforce this behavior with increases in relationship behavior. This is a two-step process: first, reduction in direction and, if *adequate performance follows*, second, increase in socio-emotional support as reinforcement. This process should continue until the salesman is assuming significant responsibility and performing as an individual of moderate maturity. This does not mean that the salesman's work will have less direction, but the direction will now be internally imposed by the salesman rather than externally imposed by his boss. This process can be accomplished, as we discussed earlier, by gradually reducing the frequency and focus of meetings between the salesman and sales manager. When this process occurs, subordinates are able not only to provide their own direction for many of the activities in which they engage, but also to provide their own satisfaction for interpersonal and emotional needs.

Managers must learn not only to change their style when a subordinate shows an increase in maturity but also when a subordinate shows a decrease in maturity relative to a particular job objective. Thus, when a subordinate's performance declines, for whatever reason, e.g., crisis at home, change in responsibility, etc., it becomes appropriate and necessary for a manager to adjust his or her behavior backward through the curve in Figure 3 to meet the present maturity level of the follower. For example, suppose a salesman is working well without much supervision and is meeting with his boss only when he calls the sales manager. Then, suddenly, a family crisis begins to affect the salesman's performance. In this situation, it might very well be appropriate for the sales manager to schedule a meeting with the salesman so he can increase *moderately* both direction and support (move back to style 3) until the salesman regains composure. If that does not occur, the sales manager can call more frequent meetings and gradually move back to style 2 or even style 1, if necessary.

Important Things To Remember

Several things should be emphasized in discussing the negotiation of leadership style.

Open Contract. The contract for leadership style should be an "open" contract. Once a style has been negotiated for accomplishing a particular objective, it can be opened for renegotiation by either party. For example, the salesman may find in a particular aspect of his job that working without supervision is not realistic. At this point, he may contact the sales manager and set up a meeting to negotiate for more direction from him. The sales manager, at the same time, may gather some data that suggest that the style being used with the salesman on a particular task is not producing results. The sales manager in this case can ask for a renegotiation of style.

Shared Responsibility. When a manager-subordinate negotiation over leadership style occurs, it implies a shared responsibility if objectives are not met. For example, if the salesman has not accomplished the agreed-on objectives and the sales manager has not provided the contracted leadership style or support, the data then become part of the evaluation of both people. This means that if a manager has contracted for close supervision, he cannot withhold help from a subordinate (even though the manager may be busy on another project) without sharing some of the responsibility for not accomplishing the objective.

Contract Not Always Negotiated. Although we have been discussing joint agreement of objectives and appropriate leadership style throughout this paper, we should emphasize that it is not always appropriate for a manager to engage in this joint process. A process that calls for mutual agreement on anything between superior and subordinate implies a leadership style somewhere between style 2 (telling) and style 3 (participating). Yet, as situational leadership implies, this approach may not always lead to the "best" results, particularly with people who are at either end of the maturity continuum. Involvement and participation in goal setting and contracting for leadership style with people who are "trading time on the job to satisfy needs elsewhere" or who are uncommitted to organizational goals (M1) might lead to less than desirable results. Such people see more responsibility as a punishment rather than as a reward, and, therefore, directive leadership (S1), for which they are told what, when, where, and how to do things, might have a higher probability of success. At the other end of the maturity continuum, with people who are "confused about the difference between work and play" and are very competent, self-motivated, and committed to organizational goals, mutual goal setting and contracting for leadership style might be considered a waste of time. Such people know exactly what needs to be done and how to do it, and goal setting with them might be done best by asking them to send a memo to their boss outlining their job objectives and an evaluation plan. A mutual goal-setting meeting may be unnecessary; a manager merely needs to get out of their way (S4).

EXAMPLE: CONTRACTING FOR LEADERSHIP STYLE

Integrating the negotiation of leadership styles with MBO through the use of our maturity instruments is a new process but is already meeting with some initial success in industrial, educational, and service organizations. An example of some interesting results of this process occurred in a small restaurant chain. In many restaurant chain operations, supervisors are expected to spend a certain number of days each month at each restaurant. This visitation policy is dysfunctional for supervisors who recognize that restaurant managers vary in their experience and competence and therefore have varying needs for supervision. If a restaurant supervisor decides to schedule visitations according to his perception of the competence of the restaurant managers, problems often occur with managers at either end of the maturity continuum. Left alone, a highly experienced restaurant manager may be confused by the lack of contact with the supervisor and may even interpret it as a lack of interest. At the same time, an inexperienced restaurant manager may interpret the frequent visits of the supervisor as a sign of lack of trust and confidence. In both cases, what the supervisor does may be interpreted as negative by the managers.

These problems were eliminated in a small restaurant chain when the supervisors and managers were both exposed to situational leadership; then, using the two forms of the maturity instruments, supervisor-leadership styles were negotiated with each of the restaurant managers on the various aspects of their jobs. It was found that when a delegating style (S4) was generally negotiated between the supervisor and an experienced restaurant manager—because both agreed that this manager was capable of working on his own—infrequent visits from the supervisor were perceived by the manager as a reward rather than a punishment.

The same thing held true at the other end of the maturity continuum. It was found that when negotiation for leadership style took place with an inexperienced restaurant manager who realized that the supervisory system was designed to help managers learn to work on their own, this manager was less reluctant to share anxieties about certain aspects of his job. If the negotiation led to initial close supervision and direction, the manager was able to view this interaction as positive, not punitive, because it was a temporary style and demonstrated the supervisor's interest in helping him to operate on his own.

In summary, establishing objectives and reaching consensus about performance criteria in a traditional MBO program tend to be appropriate for working with subordinates of moderate maturity. If this negotiation procedure is combined with a similar process for negotiating the appropriate leadership style that a manager should use to facilitate goal accomplishment in a specific task area, this additional procedure may help to make the process of MBO more of a developmental process, which can be effective in working with all levels of maturity.

CONTRACTING FOR LEADERSHIP STYLE AND THE OD PRACTITIONER

OD consultants have found the process and instrumentation discussed in this paper to be useful in the initial diagnostic stage of an intervention. When an OD consultant negotiates a contract with managers and their organizations, the first step is determining the human problems or what change efforts the organization would like to work on. Once the change objectives have been determined, the next step is for the OD consultant and the client to assess the ability and the motivation of people in the client system to solve their own problems. If the consultant finds that the organization lacks skills and competencies and is not committed to a change objective, the consultant's starting point would be a directive or structural intervention. If, on the other hand, the participants in the client system seem to be willing, but lack the ability, to solve their own problems, then the consultant must first engage in two-way communication and supportive behavior aimed at providing direction for their change effort. If the organization has the ability to solve its own problems, but for one reason or another is not using those skills, the traditional OD process intervention will have a high probability of success. In the latter case, the consultant does not have to direct the change effort but only has to engage in supportive and facilitating behavior to help the organization provide its own direction. Finally, if the consultant finds that the organization is, in reality, both willing and able to direct and solve its own problems, there is no need for the consultant to make any intervention; the consultant should encourage members of the organization to continue to work on their own problems.

The integration of situational leadership and MBO provides OD consultants with a way of looking at their alternatives and selecting strategies with the highest probability for implementing effective change.

REFERENCES

Batten, J. D. *Beyond management by objectives*. New York: American Management Association, 1966.

Fiedler, F. E. *A theory of leadership effectiveness*. New York: McGraw-Hill, 1967.

Hambleton, R. K., Blanchard, K. H., & Hersey, P. *Development and validation of an instrument to measure maturity*. (Laboratory of Psychometric and Evaluative Research Report No. 59.) Amherst, MA: School of Education, University of Massachusetts, 1977.

Hambleton, R. K., Blanchard, K. H., & Hersey, P. *Validity of situational leadership theory and applications*. (Laboratory of Psychometric and Evaluative Research Report No. 60.) Amherst, MA: School of Education, University of Massachusetts, 1977.

Hemphill, J. K. *Situational factors in leadership*. (Monograph No. 32.) Columbus, OH: Bureau of Educational Research, The Ohio State University, 1949.

Hersey, P., & Blanchard, K. H. Life cycle theory of leadership. *Training and Development Journal*, May 1969.

Hersey, P., & Blanchard, K. H. What's missing in MBO? *Management Review*, October 1974, pp. 25-32.

Hersey, P., & Blanchard, K. H. *Management of organizational behavior* (3rd ed.). Englewood Cliffs, NJ: Prentice-Hall, 1977.

Humble, J. W. *Management by objectives*. London: Industrial Education and Research Foundation, 1967.

Miller, E. C. *Objectives and standards approach to planning and control*. (AMA Research Study '74.) New York: American Management Association, 1966.

Odiorne, G. S. *Management by objectives: A system of managerial leadership*. New York: Pitman Publishing, 1965.

Reddin, W. J. The 3-D management style theory. *Training and Development Journal*, April 1967, pp. 8-17.

Reddin, W. J. *Managerial effectiveness*. New York: McGraw-Hill, 1970.

Reddin, W. J. *Effective management by objectives: The 3-D method of MBO*. New York: McGraw-Hill, 1971.

Skinner, B. F. *Science and human behavior*. New York: Macmillan, 1953.

Skinner, B. F. *Analysis of behavior*. New York: McGraw-Hill, 1961.

Stogdill, R. M., & Coons, A. E. (Eds.). *Leader behavior: Its description and measurement*. (Research Monograph No. 88.) Columbus, OH: Bureau of Business Research, The Ohio State University, 1957.

Section IV:
NEW DOMAINS FOR ORGANIZATION DEVELOPMENT

OVERVIEW

Any domain is a potential area for OD if it involves people in organizations. As OD practitioners move into new domains, they use the accumulated knowledge and skills of the field to address important problems in the organization that need the special kind of attention that OD can provide. There also is reciprocity for OD; as practitioners apply their knowledge and skills in new areas, they can learn from this broader application. The new areas described in this final section are significant ones, and the reciprocal process should have high value for the domains themselves and for OD as a field.

Adams (Chapter 16) is not the first person in the field to be concerned with stress (see Levinson, 1964), but Adams's work is broader; he is concerned with the entire work force, not just with management, and he is more empirical. After describing four major types of stress, he reports on his research in a large, urban hospital. This research showed which organizational events were related most to stress on the part of middle managers in the hospital. Of significance is the finding that dysfunctional norms are the principal sources of daily, on-the-job-stress. Since OD—at least as I define it—is a process of cultural change with particular emphasis on changing dysfunctional norms, stress management is a highly appropriate domain for the field.

Adams also describes a workshop that helps organizational members to identify more effectively stressors that affect them directly and to plan steps that will help to alleviate or at least better manage them.

Perhaps the largest new domain for OD is the quality-of-work-life intervention/project. Nadler (Chapter 17) has been active in this new area as both a consultant and researcher. Nadler's chapter is a blend of old and new: old in that labor-management problems have been with us for decades, and new in the use of a quality-of-work-life intervention to help deal with these problems as well as with broader issues. From an OD standpoint, one of the early reported attempts (Blake, Mouton, & Sloma, 1965) to resolve labor-management conflict was the use of the now standard intergroup-conflict-resolution design (Blake, Shepard, & Mouton, 1964; Burke, 1974). In the sixteen different projects described by Nadler, the difference now is one of goal. With the conflict-resolution approaches the goal is, obviously, to reduce if not resolve the conflict. In the quality-of-work projects the goal is not only to resolve conflict but also to improve both the quality of work life for organizational members and the overall effectiveness of the organization. Interestingly, the quality-of-work-life approach to labor-management differences helps to provide a clearer, and perhaps more operational, superordinate goal. This is precisely what Sherif (1958) had in mind when he did his original research into and theory of resolving intergroup conflict.

Nadler's chapter directs our attention dramatically to the role of the consultant. We know the importance of process consultation in OD work. This facilitative form of consultation remains a critical skill for the kind of work that Nadler describes. But a skill that often is needed as well, and can be just as critical, is direction and energy for action. Groups in conflict, for whatever reasons, refuse at times to take any action or to exercise any power. In these instances, the consultant, working at the boundary (see Margulies, Chapter 5), must infuse the group with energy and provide leadership. Without this, the two groups may never move. Thus, the consultant skill called for is one of "walking the fence" between nondirective facilitation and telling people what to do and knowing when to do what.

The final two chapters are by two of the most experienced persons in the field. Bradford's (Chapter 18) and Schein's (Chapter 19) concerns represent two more new domains for OD, but these chapters also are related in that Bradford calls for OD practitioners to become involved in issues of retirement and Schein, independently, provides a way of responding to the call.

Bradford's chapter is informative, personal, and poignant. Using his own retirement experience as a basis, he explains the need for organizations to pay more attention to (a) the human process of retirement itself (for their benefit as well as for employees in general) and (b) the way in which the organization manages this important action—if at all. Bradford suggests what OD practitioners can do to move into this domain. He also addresses the important and current issue of mandatory retirement and covers both its advantages and disadvantages. With people living longer, with organizational growth in the U.S. more curtailed, and with mandatory retirement extended to age seventy or perhaps eliminated entirely, it is obvious that this domain of organizational life must be considered by OD practitioners.

Schein's chapter is perhaps the most appropriate one to conclude the book since it provides a capstone for much of what has been covered in the preceding chapters. He not only reviews all the elements necessary for a total human-resource-planning-and-development system, but he also shows how all these components should be linked. Schein presents a sound case for tying together the organization's formal planning processes with human-resource planning and for linking development activities to planning events.

The new areas represented by these four chapters provide appropriate arenas in which OD practitioners can practice some risk taking and can, in effect, develop the field of organization development.

REFERENCES

Blake, R. R., Mouton, J. S., & Sloma, R. The union-management intergroup laboratory. *Journal of Applied Behavioral Science*, 1965, *1*, 25-57.

Blake, R. R., Shepard, H. A., & Mouton, J. S. *Managing intergroup conflict in industry*. Houston, TX: Gulf, 1964.

Burke, W. W. Managing conflict between groups. In J. D. Adams (Ed.), *New technologies in organization development: 2*. La Jolla, CA: NTL/Learning Resources Corporation, 1974.

Levinson, H. *Executive stress*. New York: Harper & Row, 1964.

Sherif, M. Superordinate goals in the reduction of intergroup conflict. *American Journal of Sociology*, 1958, *43*, 349-356.

16

Improving Stress Management: An Action-Research-Based OD Intervention

John D. Adams

Concerns for the impact of stress on the health of managers and on their sense of well-being and productivity are very high in most organizations these days. Increasingly, senior managers are becoming aware—both in financial and in human terms—of the costs of their fast-paced, deadline-oriented ways of operating. The pace of change and the daily pressures of life in general serve to compound the pressures of work, often with costly results.

The United States Clearinghouse for Mental Health Information, for example, recently reported that U.S. industry has had a seventeen-billion-dollar annual decrease in its productive capacity over the last few years due to stress-induced mental dysfunctions. Similarly, other studies estimate even greater losses (at least sixty billion) arising from stress-induced physical illnesses. The need for increased competence in stress management is clear. Some more specific examples of the "costs" of stress include:

1. Over twenty million people in the U.S. have hypertension. About the same number are alcoholic. (Each is estimated, conservatively, to afflict one in ten persons.)
2. Nearly 35 percent of all deaths in this country are due to myocardial infarctions (heart attacks). Another 11 percent are due to strokes.
3. Side effects or abuse of drugs is the eleventh leading cause of death in the U.S.
4. Eleven percent of U.S. doctors abuse alcohol and/or drugs.
5. An alcoholic executive (5 to 8 percent) costs his or her organization an average of four thousand dollars per year in lost time, waste, and so on.
6. Hundreds of thousands of persons are killed or badly injured in unnecessary industrial accidents each year.
7. Occupational factors are estimated to be involved in 150,000 cancer deaths per year.

Portions of this paper are adapted from the original action research report by Adams and Margolis, 1977.

8. Estimates of the number of suicides per year in the U.S. vary from 25,000 to 50,000. One attempted suicide in eight is "successful."
9. We spend over 120 billion dollars per year on health care.

One of the basic premises of the approach to stress management described in this paper is reflected in the growing use of the term "behavioral medicine," which emphasizes that the individual, and not his or her physician, must become *responsible* for his or her own health and well-being. The following quotation from a National Institutes of Health conference perhaps sums up the issue of responsibility best:

> Most medical schools, and therefore medical students, (now) place highest value on physical diagnosis (of existing symptoms), secondary value on selecting the appropriate treatment of diagnosed conditions and little or no value on the importance of effective communication with patients in the interests of increasing client understanding of and responsibility for his own health . . . Methods must be developed for teaching health habits that are likely to maintain or improve health, e.g., exercise, nutrition, rest and relaxation, and avoidance of smoking. (Weiss, 1977, pp. 19-20,22)

This approach is the one described in this paper. If "medical" is changed to "OD" and "health" to "organizational," the quotation could become an admonition to organization development professionals. In any event, this approach is highly compatible with organization development and other participative planned-change processes. In many instances, awareness of the consequences of prolonged high levels of stress has caused managers to become committed to organization development programs they previously had resisted as being unrelated to their objectives. Stress awareness helps to bring unity to mind and body and clearly demonstrates the connections between stress level, health, satisfaction and personal growth, and productivity. Stress management requires both effective personal habits and effective (in the OD sense) organizational habits.

This paper describes a stress-based action research intervention carried out over a two-year period in a metropolitan hospital.

WHAT IS STRESS?

Very few specific cause-and-effect statements can be made about either stress-induced illnesses or stress-reducing practices. A large and growing number of population studies give percentages, i.e., numbers of people affected per thousand. These are likely to be accurate predictors on an organization-wide basis, but they cannot tell you, as an individual, that *your* high-pressured life style will lead definitely to a heart attack or that changing your health habits definitely will prevent one. We can say that a person's *chances* of having a heart attack are two-to-three times greater than those of someone whose life style is less stressful and that people who eat a well-balanced diet are likely to have better health than those whose diet is deficient in basic nutrients or is comprised mainly of fats, refined white flour, and sugar.

The stress response is a nonspecific physiological and psychological chain of events triggered by any disruption to one's equilibrium or "homeostasis." It is the same reaction regardless of the stressor; yet each unique individual's outward reaction to stress may be slightly different from another's. The chain of events leading to the re-establishment of equilibrium involves the autonomic nervous system and the endocrine system. These systems combine to speed up cardiovascular functions and slow down gastrointestinal functions, thus equipping a person to "fight or take flight." The triggering of this response frequently over prolonged periods of time causes wear and tear on one's system, increasing the risk of illness or emotional dysfunction. It increases the likelihood that *latent* disease and emotional distress will become manifest. How much stress it takes to trigger this or which illness will occur is different for each person and is based on factors such as heredity, personality, habits, and past accidents and illnesses. We all need some stress in order to be alert and productive, and we each have a unique point at which more stress becomes destructive. Lazarus (Weiss, 1977, p. 51) states that:

> It has become increasingly apparent that stress is important as a factor in illness in general and in chronic illness in particular. Many present day illnesses cannot be explained in terms of a single "cause." Research suggests that a significant portion of the population seeking medical care is suffering from stress based illness.

The manager's personal challenge is to seek *enough* stress, yet to manage his or her stress levels when they go beyond stimulating top performance. As a manager, the challenge is to minimize the amount of unnecessary stress he or she creates for others. For example, changes that are surprising are more stressful than changes that are anticipated and understood. Unilateral announcements about major decisions or policy changes generally are found to be high stressors in departments in which there is low participation and poor communication.

Most approaches to stress management spend little time identifying where the stress is coming from. Understanding the sources of stress is an important prelude to developing a plan for effective stress management. Organizational sources of stress must be identified before processes can be developed for reducing or removing unnecessary stressors. Most stress programs focus only on the individual and his or her ability to withstand stress, e.g., through meditation or "body work"; an OD approach must *also* consider altering stressful organizational norms and management practices. Clients must be helped to identify their primary stressors in four areas, as illustrated in Figure 1.

	On the Job	Away from Work
Recent Events	Type I	Type II
Ongoing Conditions	Type III	Type IV

Figure 1. Sources of Stress

Stress sources I and II are derived principally from the work of Holmes and Rahe (1967) and their colleagues at the University of Washington. They were instrumental in developing the now widely known Social Readjustment Rating Scale, which predicts the growing likelihood of illness following periods of great change in one's life.

Type I stress is recent events on the job, including changes such as: (a) major changes in instructions, policies, or procedures; (b) being required to work more hours than usual per week; (c) a sudden, significant increase in the activity level or pace of work; and (d) a major reorganization. A thirty-one-item list of such events has been developed by Naismith (1975). Each event has a point value that reflects the average amount of readjustment required for one to feel "back to normal" following that change event. In the project described herein, I found the number of readjustment points accumulated by managers during a twelve-month period to correlate significantly with the number of health conditions they experienced.

Type II stress includes recent events away from work, such as: (a) a restriction of social life, (b) marriage, (c) the death of a family member, and (d) a serious illness. Following Holmes and Rahe (1967), a list of change events such as these has been developed by Cochrane and Robertson (1973). Again each change event is assigned a certain number of points that reflect the average amount of readjustment required to "get back to normal." The number of readjustment points accumulated by managers was correlated with the numbers of health conditions they reported.

Results showed that events (both on and off the job) cause disruptions. A chain reaction is triggered in order to restore equilibrium; a certain amount of readjustment is necessary. The more often we trigger the stress response, the more likely it is that we will become ill. Although specific kinds of stress cannot be linked in most cases to specific diseases, with too much stress our latent tendencies to become physically or psychologically ill are more likely to surface.

Stress sources III and IV are derived principally from the work of French and Caplan (1972) and their colleagues at the Institute for Social Research at the University of Michigan. This group of psychologists has worked extensively with the National Aeronautics and Space Administration in the study of day-to-day (or chronic) stress and its effects on health and well-being.

Type III stress includes on-the-job conditions and daily pressures such as: (a) too much work to do in too little time, (b) feedback only when performance is unsatisfactory, (c) conflicts between one's work unit and others with which it must work, and (d) unclear standards and responsibilities. These kinds of stressors are similar to the primary sources of chronic stress identified by French and his colleagues: work overload, role ambiguity or conflict, territoriality, poor-quality relationships, and lack of participation. It is safe to say that most working people today can readily identify with these conditions; few people would be surprised to hear that too much of these stressors can be debilitating. In our project, I found the frequency with which managers were experiencing these kinds of conditions to be correlated with the number of health conditions they reported and to be negatively correlated with their feelings of work effectiveness and satisfaction and growth. This type of stressor is frequently normative in nature. Thus, eliminating negative norms can reduce levels of chronic stress at work.

Type IV stress includes nonwork conditions and pressures such as: (a) pollution, (b) noise, (c) concern over economy and/or personal financial stability, and (d) anxiety about children's activities or choice of friends. Here again, the frequency with which managers experience such conditions as stressful is correlated, though less strongly, with the number of health conditions they report. While this type of stress has had much less attention from researchers than the other three, it is often the one that managers want most to explore.

In summary, daily conditions cause pressures that—even after one becomes accustomed to them—can cause illness and lower satisfaction, growth, and work effectiveness. When on-the-job change *events* occur in large numbers to people already working under highly stressful *conditions*, the incidence of sick leave, accidents, and inattention to work increases rapidly.

PROJECT DESIGN

The format devised to guide our work on stress is portrayed in Figure 2. The mediating variables (context of situation and stress management) may serve either to intensify or to diffuse the impact of the sources of stress (stressors).

The context or "givens" of a situation include: (a) the personal characteristics and background of the individual; (b) situational factors; and (c) quality of support. People inherit strengths and weaknesses and develop them through good or bad personal habits, accidents, illnesses, or abuses. Further, behavioral orientations both predispose us to certain types of stress (e.g., one may need close direction but work in an ambiguous role) and influence how we might break down (e.g., highly motivated, competitive, and achievement-oriented people are more likely to have heart attacks). If one is aware of one's orientations and idiosyncrasies, one is more able to avoid overly stressful situations. The nature of the work organization can either heighten or reduce stress levels for employees. Factors such as the number of deadlines, the way in which crises are faced, and the frequency and nature of client demands all need to be considered for their roles in increasing or decreasing stress. In addition, people who lack social support at work are likely to have more health and emotional problems than people who work in supportive environments. Usually, we cannot change these three context factors (personality, nature of organization, and quality of support) appreciably; but a manager needs to understand how they affect stress levels in order to promote effective stress management.

The second mediating variable is how well an individual manages his or her own stress (see the Appendix). Whereas the context of the situation is often difficult to change, individuals can learn to assess their present behavior patterns and make changes that will buffer the effects of stress relatively easily. Training in this area, first in groups of managers and then in face-to-face work groups, seems to be the most promising approach to managing the high levels of stress in contemporary organizations. Both long-term (preventive) and immediate (responsive) stress-management techniques are needed to protect employees from the effects of too much stress. Although most stress-management training focuses on one basic technique, e.g., progressive relaxation or meditation, it is important to introduce a variety of techniques and to encourage individuals to develop stress-management plans suited to their own situations and preferences.

Depending on whether the context of a situation intensifies or diffuses stress and on how effectively the individual manages stress, high or low levels of *strain* will result. Chronically high levels of strain over a period of time can lead to health changes, lowered satisfaction, and decreased productivity. *Concerns* over prolonged strain responses can themselves become stressors (see dotted line in Figure 2).

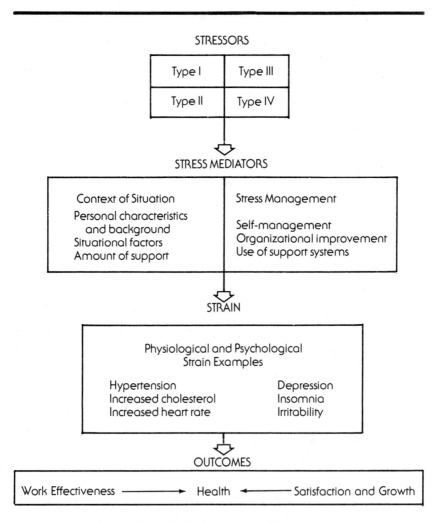

Figure 2. The Experience of Stress

A questionnaire was developed and used to collect data from middle managers responsible for almost every phase of operation in the hospital in which our action-research was conducted. Each section of the questionnaire was designed to yield a total score or rating. These were then ranked to permit comparisons. Following the diagram in Figure 2, the sections of the questionnaire were:

1. Stressors
   (a) Type I stressors: Recent organizational change events
   (b) Type II stressors: Recent life change events
   (c) Type III stressors: Ongoing stressful work conditions
   (d) Type IV stressors: Ongoing stressful conditions away from work
2. Predicted mediators
   (a) Physical exercise
   (b) Nutritional awareness
   (c) Self-awareness (life-style orientations as developed by Friedlander, 1975
   (d) Self-management awareness (self-management, creation and use of support systems, management practices)
   (e) Age, race, and sex
   (f) Amounts of time in present position and at hospital
3. Level of strain experienced (irritability, sleep difficulty, changes in eating and drinking patterns, apathy, depression, disorientation, etc.)
4. Outcome variables
   (a) Felt effectiveness (deadlines, quantity, quality)
   (b) Felt satisfaction and growth (general, learning on the job, sense of accomplishment)
   (c) Health conditions (see the Appendix for a tally of the conditions reported in this project)

For the most part, the data analysis consisted of comparing each variable with the others by calculating the rank-order correlations. Respondents also were asked to name their "top three stressors" in each of the first four sections; this resulted in lists of what the managers felt to have been the most stressful events and conditions in the hospital and away from work. Only on-the-job stressors, however, were addressed in follow-up activities.

FINDINGS

Some of the more general findings are:

1. The hospital managers perceived that they were under a great deal of stress.
2. Most respondents (thirty-two of forty-five) were not able to articulate any significant stress-management repertoire (see the Appendix).
3. The stressors that apparently have the most pervasive impact on respondents are, actually, informal norms (stress type III) rather than specific organizational change events.

4. Stress levels are correlated, at significant levels, with:
   (a) level of strain,
   (b) number of health conditions,
   (c) felt satisfaction and growth, and
   (d) felt effectiveness.
5. Most respondents had poor exercise habits (only 20 percent engaged in regular exercise).
6. A surprising number of respondents had poor dietary habits (40 percent had well-balanced diets, 50 percent had marginally balanced diets, and 10 percent had very poorly balanced diets).
7. Good exercise and dietary habits were associated with low numbers of reported health conditions.

Organizational Change Events (Type I Stress)

The following list of stressors was developed by pooling the respondents' choices of the three most stressful events affecting their work during the previous twelve months. A total of 107 selections was made by the respondents. Of those, seventy-one were included in the following list of eight (of thirty possible) events.

Rank	Organizational Change Event
1.5	Major or frequent changes in instructions, policies, or procedures.
1.5	Required to work more hours per week than normal because of crises, deadlines, etc.
3	Sudden significant increase in the activity level or pace of work.
4	New supervisor.
5.5	New subordinates.
5.5	Major (department-wide) reorganization.
7	Sudden significant change in the nature of work.
8	New co-worker.

Work load and the necessity to adapt to changed policies and new people were experienced as the most stressful events at work. Such changes are bound to occur and often are beneficial in the long run. However, there are ways to implement needed changes so that they do not induce high levels of stress. Changes usually provoke stress in proportion to the degree in which they take people by surprise. Nonstressful introduction of change should be a primary responsibility of every manager and supervisor.

Organizational-change-event scores are correlated positively with the number of health conditions reported ($r=0.33$, $p \leq 0.025$). This finding indicates that those who experience more changes on the job also experience more health conditions. Those who experience fewer changes have fewer health conditions.

People with higher organizational-change-event scores who had lower sociocentric scores reported fewer health conditions ($r=0.49$, $p \leq 0.025$). The people included in this finding comprise the upper 50 percent of the sample of organizational-event scores. Among these people, those with lower sociocentric orientations (Friedlander, 1975) tend also to experience fewer health conditions. A low sociocentric score indicates a relatively low tendency to seek guidance from peers, participation, and consensus management.

People with higher organizational-change-event scores who had higher strain scores reported higher numbers of health conditions ($r=0.62$, $p \leq 0.005$). The people included in this finding also comprised the upper 50 percent of the scores for organizational change events. Those with higher change scores who also reflected high strain scores experienced higher numbers of health conditions. By the same token, those with lower strain scores experienced fewer health conditions.

It appears from the above that an accumulation of significant changes at work requires sufficient adaptive energy to lead to health changes. Comparisons of organizational-change-event scores with felt satisfaction and growth and felt effectiveness did *not* lead to significant correlations. The change events probably happen sporadically enough so as not to affect longer-term feelings of satisfaction and productivity. However, they still trigger the internal stress response and thereby, eventually, exact their toll.

People with high sociocentric scores are oriented toward reaching decisions participatively and prefer to adopt new ways of behaving through consensual procedures. The organizational change events do not lend themselves to these processes since they are usually thrust upon the employee, often taking him or her by surprise. Those with lower sociocentric scores, therefore, seem to be less impacted by change events (as they are presently implemented at the hospital we studied).

Ongoing Working Conditions (Type III Stress)

The following list of stressors was developed by pooling the respondents' choices of the top three daily stressors affecting their work. Respondents noted a total of ninety-four selections. Of those, fifty-eight were for the following list of eight (of twenty-six possible) chronic conditions.

Rank	Ongoing Working Conditions
1	Too much to do with too little time in which to do it.
2.5	Feedback only when my performance is unsatisfactory.
2.5	Lack of confidence in management.
4	Other demands for my time conflict with each other.
5	Unsettled conflicts with the people at work.
6.5	Spending time "fighting fires" rather than working to a plan.
6.5	Conflicts between my unit and others with which it must work.
8	Lack of clarity about what is expected of me.

Ongoing working conditions written in as "other" and selected as most stressful fell into the following categories:

1. Problems with supervisor (department head, head nurse, or assistant administrator);
2. Problems with peers (poor patient care, apathy, covering for others, troublemakers, destructiveness); and
3. Personal work problems (trying to keep everyone satisfied, unable to

obtain needed information, forced to attend low-priority meetings, rumors about self, no time for professional development).

The studies conducted by French and Caplan (1972) found that the primary chronic organizational stressors were role ambiguity and conflict, work load, territoriality, poor relationships, and lack of participation. The list above contains many similarities and conveys a picture of a hectic pace of work and of people who are under a great deal of tension.

Few of the chronic conditions investigated in this study are mandated by policy; rather, they are mostly normative. Norms are unexpressed expectations for behavior or shared habits that strongly influence how work gets done. *Dysfunctional norms are the principal sources of daily on-the-job stress.*

Just as they are not mandated by policy, norms usually cannot be removed by decision making or bureaucratic changes. Changing norms requires intensive efforts on a level-by-level and unit-by-unit basis. The cost-benefit ratio of this much effort must, of course, be assessed. The findings that follow are a first step toward making such an assessment.

Ongoing working-conditions scores are correlated with strain scores (r=0.51, p≤0.005). There is a strong positive correlation between the amount of daily work stress and the amount of strain that a manager experiences. The next two findings suggest that higher strain scores increase one's chances of experiencing a larger number of health conditions.

Strain scores and number of health conditions are correlated (r=0.30, p≤0.025).

Ongoing working conditions are correlated with the number of health conditions reported (r=0.30, r≤0.025). This finding, closely related to the previous two, suggests that higher levels of daily stress lead to larger numbers of health conditions.

Ongoing working-conditions scores are inversely correlated with felt satisfaction and growth (r=−0.37, p≤0.025). In addition to affecting health, this suggests that higher levels of daily stress are likely to reduce feelings of satisfaction and growth on the job. Similarly, the finding below indicates that higher levels of daily stress are likely to lead to lower feelings of work effectiveness.

Ongoing working-conditions scores are inversely correlated with felt effectiveness (r=−0.25, p≤0.10).

Ongoing working-conditions scores are inversely correlated with formalistic scores (r=−0.46, p≤0.005). This finding suggests that people who have low formalistic scores (unlikely to look to the system for guidance and direction) experience relatively higher levels of daily stress. This suggests the bureaucratic nature of the hospital and predicts that those with a preference for working within set procedures and guidelines experience less daily stress. The next finding is related to this one in that those who scored in the upper 50 percent of the daily-stress scores who were also low in their formalistic orientation felt less satisfied with their work.

Those with both higher ongoing working-conditions scores and lower formalistic scores tend also to have lower felt-satisfaction and growth scores (r=0.42, p≤0.05).

Ongoing working-conditions scores are correlated with personalistic scores (r=0.25, p≤0.05). As was the case with *low* formalistic scores, this finding suggests that *high* personalistic-oriented ("do your own thing") people experience relatively more daily stress in the hospital system. Here again, we find that a higher level of stress seems to lead to more reported health changes. In addition, with higher levels of ongoing stress, both felt effectiveness and felt satisfaction and growth decline. Thus, the ongoing working conditions appear to be more pervasive in their impact than the organizational change events. As before, the amount of strain experienced also increases with increasing levels of chronic stress.

People with high formalistic scores tend to look to the authority, the policy, the system, and so on, for direction and guidance. From these data, we can infer that those managers and supervisors who have higher formalistic scores are likely to experience less daily stress; those with lower formalistic scores are more likely to feel less satisfaction and growth on the job. This is probably because most of the jobs in the hospital must fit into a set pattern; therefore, people most willing to work through the system are likely to be less stressed and more satisfied.

People with high personalistic scores prefer to set their own personal standards for performance and to "chart their own courses." These tendencies, at the hospital, seem to lead to higher levels of daily stress. People with less orientation toward behaving in this self-directed manner experience lower levels of daily stress. Once again, we may surmise that people who work through the established system will experience less stress than those in the same setting who have a continuous preference for independent action.

Additional Findings

Major follow-up interventions were derived from two additional findings.

Those who engage in regular, vigorous exercise report fewer health conditions than those who engage in little or no exercise. This finding predicts the importance of *vigorous* regular exercise for maintaining good health. Moderate exercise, in this project, was not significantly better than little or no exercise in maintaining one's health.

Those who regularly eat a well-balanced diet report fewer health conditions than those whose diets are marginally or poorly balanced. As with exercise, those with well-balanced diets appear to be more likely to enjoy relatively good health than those with marginally balanced or poorly balanced diets.

FOLLOW-UP: RECOMMENDATIONS AND ACTIONS

"Stress" has a negative connotation in America. For managers, stress connotes an inability to perform according to standards. When we say of an executive that he really seems to be under stress, we are usually referring to the fact that his performance is slipping.

It is not suggested, however, that a corporate goal should be to eliminate stress from organizational life. A crucial aspect of any manager's job is the intentional creation of stress as a dynamic motivating force in the organization. The point is that this stress should be planned and controlled. It is the uncontrolled effects of organizational stress that may be costly to both the organization and the individual employee.

Since we largely are dealing with norms that are hard to change, one cannot expect that the mere distribution of the above findings will lead to any changes in behavior if no follow-up actions are taken. It is necessary for management to take specific responsibility for implementing educational and change programs concerning stress.

Changes in behavior and in the basic ways in which people approach their work are needed to create normative change. If whatever changes are needed do not take place first at the top levels of the organization, they cannot be expected to take place at any other levels of the organization. To quote Suojanen and Hudson (1977, pp. 7-8):

> The behavior of both the superior and the subordinate can be addictive, and this can repeat itself all the way down from the level of the chief executive officer of the organization to that of the most junior supervisor. If we bear in mind the fact that the behavior of top management dictates the behavior of the other members of the organization and if this behavior is addictive, then the end result often will be an enterprise in which members appear to be "busy" in every respect but which is falling down totally in overall performance. . . . Until the senior manager takes the first step, the other members of top management cannot take it. Organizational behavior change must wait until all members of the top management have begun their individual programs of change.

Although an individual's ability to cope with stress is greatly influenced by his or her personal style, support from the social environment (family, friends, colleagues, mentors), and the person's unique situation (financial status, geographic location, past history), enlightened management can do a great deal to reduce harmful levels of stress at work. The following suggestions are based on the findings of our study and were made to the senior management of the hospital. While many have been implemented, a follow-up study has not yet been conducted to assess the results.

Understand the Origins of Stress

The first step is to identify the sources of stress and whether a stressor is one that can be controlled better. For example, since work load is producing negative consequences, it is recommended that the hospital do an analysis of individual positions in order to determine if some redistribution of work is possible.

If actual work load is not the problem, the chances are that there is a problem with the manager's ability to organize his or her work and time or with the way in which he or she chooses to delegate work. Educational activities can help managers learn these skills; good coaching and performance feedback from executives can support the improvement of these managerial practices. The development of job descriptions and performance standards where they are missing or inadequate also helps to reduce stress. Time management and effective feedback programs can also be developed.

Changes in policy cause stress when (a) the change is unilaterally imposed without consultation and (b) the people affected see no functional justification for the change. What appears to be a logical and simple change in procedure coming from one division can cause a ripple effect of stress elsewhere when the change is unannounced and unexplained.

Unpredictable work flow results in employee dissatisfaction (from having to adjust to rapidly changing work practices). More seriously, it can result in dependence on people with whom there is little face-to-face contact and on environmental conditions over which the employee has no control (e.g., frequent patient transfers, use of contract nurses, heavy reliance on part-time and on-call people). Consequently, in many work units employees have erratic or infrequent work contacts with one another—especially across shifts.

How managers appear to cope with these stressors is quite revealing. The "fire-fighting" climate in the hospital we studied resulted from these stressors and appears to focus on vertical relations at the expense of good lateral and diagonal communications. Under stress, vertical relations tend to become more work related while lateral communications tend to become more superficial and com-plaintive. In addition, managers under stress frequently reduce contacts with various groups in order to concentrate on the problem area. This usually has a negative consequence because it reduces the manager's collegial support at a time when he or she needs it and denies him or her an opportunity to gain a broader and more varied perspective of the problem. In order to support increased lateral and diagonal dialogue among managers, it was recommended that department heads and supervisors in the hospital get together in periodic quasi-social work sessions on a monthly basis. The completed management development program did much to support lateral communications, and a similar new program has now been undertaken.

Sensitivity to the effects of sudden change should be encouraged at all levels of management. The introduction of change in any policy or procedure should be done carefully. The people to be affected by the change should be educated about the what and why of the change before it actually goes into effect, since the amount of stress that accompanies a change seems to be a function of the degree of surprise or unfamiliarity present when one learns about the change.

Reduce Role Ambiguity and the Negative Effects of Role Strain

In examining stressful working conditions (type III stress), there was a high degree of apparent role ambiguity experienced by managers. Role ambiguity is defined as uncertainty regarding what is expected of one in one's job.

In a recent study, Beehr (1976) found that role ambiguity was strongly related to four psychological role strains: job dissatisfaction, life dissatisfaction, low self-esteem, and depressed mood. Further, Beehr found that even with role ambiguity on the job, when there were certain situational characteristics as-sociated with the people in those roles, the role strain was significantly modified. Group cohesiveness, or a *support group*, had a significant lessening effect on role strain. People working in cohesive groups were found to be less likely to internalize the blame for having an ambiguous role; thus, they were less likely to have a lowered sense of self-esteem and/or a depressed mood. People in noncohesive groups were less likely to have the social supports required to "talk out" their problems and tended to blame themselves for the ambiguity. While lowered self-esteem is less likely in a cohesive group, job dissatisfaction is related more strongly to role ambiguity in noncohesive groups as well.

The strongest and most consistent moderator of the relationship between role ambiguity and role strain was the lack of autonomy in the Beehr study. Consequently, it was recommended that a climate supporting the building of peer-support groups and an increase in the degree of managerial autonomy should be reinforced by the hospital management.

The management-by-objectives program already contemplated will help to support increased autonomy because management boundaries will become well defined. Although assistant administrators have been working with department heads on defining job expectations, developing performance standards, and providing ongoing performance feedback, a similar process has *not* been ongoing between division leaders and assistant administrators. It was suggested that the job-clarification process must be started at the top and that doing so will have a high impact on follow-through at lower organizational levels.

Improve Information Flow

This is important so that more people will understand what is happening around them and whether or not developments will affect them. To a large extent, the level of stress is related to the flow of information in the hospital. Information often is not conveyed fully or is distorted as it passes through the manager-supervisor levels. This creates tension as different units or departments begin to interpret a decision or policy in different ways. The organizational change events tend to be more stressful to the extent that they come as surprises. As mentioned previously, if the reasons for policy changes, needs for extra work, reorganizations, and the like are discussed thoroughly, their advent will cause less stress. Too often, managers and supervisors decide that such discussions would be a waste of time or not worth the effort. Likewise, there are few attempts to integrate or ease the transitions involved in introducing new supervisors, subordinates, and peers into a given work setting. These changes would be less surprising to people if there were more sharing of information and advanced planning. To insure improvement in communication problems of these kinds, the top management of the hospital has agreed to meet with the first-line supervisors on a quarterly basis to clear up misunderstandings, misinterpretations, and rumors. Communications are also dealt with in depth in the re-created management-development training programs.

Information flow is again implicated in reviewing ongoing work conditions. As noted previously, many people are unclear about what is expected of them and receive only negative performance feedback. In addition, the "firefighting," conflicts, and work-load stressors are often caused by managers' lack of under-standing of what information they need from their subordinates and what information their subordinates need from them. All of this, then, is probably the main reason why the number-two daily stressor is "lack of confidence in management."

Provide Individual Help to Managers as a Protective/Preventive Measure

The above measures will, if consistently implemented over the long term, reduce the level of episodic and daily stresses in the work environment. Some stress will always be present, however, and occasionally it will be intense enough over a period of time to become destructive. Therefore, people need to learn how to protect themselves. Several protective/preventive measures are being implemented at the hospital.

1. For the detection of physiological and psychological strains from stress, employee health physicals will be required every year. The current physical will be supplemented with more comprehensive blood work and appropriate counseling. Both the manager and his or her boss will be informed if a presumed stress-related condition is found.
2. A counseling and/or referral service to sources of help within or outside the hospital will be developed.
3. Managers will be taught to identify stress problems and symptoms in themselves and in their subordinates through training programs and follow-up work on the job. These programs will be scheduled regularly.
4. Managers will be required to take vacations. A large number of employees, as well as managers, in the hospital take little or no vacation. Some time off will be strongly encouraged.
5. Outlets will be provided through regular vigorous exercise by means of an exercise club and sports activities such as bicycling, running, basketball, and tennis. Yoga classes may be offered on a weekly basis.
6. Educational activities on both nutrition and exercise will be developed and provided. Spouses may be invited. The first such program, combining nutritional awareness with techniques for dealing with tension headaches and backaches, has been very well received. Fresh fruit is now available as an alternative to donuts in all meetings and seminars.
7. Ongoing training in stress management will be continued. This provides an overview of stress and how to deal with it. Self-awareness is considered the first step to improved personal stress management.
8. Stress will be monitored. The stress research will be repeated on a twelve- to eighteen-month basis to evaluate progress.

As the reader familiar with organization development will have noticed, the follow-up activities described here fit nicely into a broader developmental context. The stress-provoking norms in most organizations tend to be both pervasive and persistent. Thus, it is important to the success of any stress-related follow-up program that it be explicitly managed, that it be granted adequate resources that are applied completely and consistently, and that the amount of time required to make complex changes in personal and organizational habits not be underestimated.

APPENDIX

1. The following stress-management techniques are included in the organizational training programs associated with this project. Others are encouraged to add to the list from their own experiences.

   I. Self-management
      A. Vigorous regular exercise
      B. Balanced nutritional habits
      C. Letting-go techniques (relaxation, meditation, etc.)
      D. Awareness of own preferences and idiosyncrasies
      E. Personal planning (time management, life planning, etc.)
  II. Support systems
      A. Diagnosing present sources of support
      B. Identifying needs for improved support
      C. Action planning for improving key relationships
 III. Altering stressful organizational norms and management practices
      A. Diagnosing sources of stress
      B. Developing alternatives for reducing unnecessary stress
      C. Identifying and managing distressed employees

2. Respondents were asked to check which conditions, from a given list, they had experienced during the past year. Chronic conditions, e.g., hypertension, were to receive one check mark and episodic conditions, e.g., influenza, one check mark for each occurrence.

  43 = number of respondents
  20 = number making four or fewer check marks
299 = total number of check marks

69 Tension headache	6 Surgery
52 Diarrhea or constipation	5 Hypertension
49 Common cold	5 Accidents
28 Backache	5 Palpitations
15 Infection	4 Dizziness
14 Allergy	3 Sinusitis
10 Influenza	2 Ulcers
9 Arthritis	2 Anemia
7 Rheumatoid arthritis	2 Severe psychological problem
7 Migraine headache	1 Each: diabetes, laryngitis, benign tumor, kidney stone, tonsillitis

REFERENCES

Adams, J. D., & Margolis, J. *The impact of organizational stressors on hospital managers and supervisors*. Unpublished report to senior management, GSCH. Washington, D.C., 1977.

Beehr, T. A. Perceived situational moderators of the relationship between subjective role ambiguity and role strain. *Journal of Applied Psychology*, 1976, *61*, 1.

Cochrane, R., & Robertson, A. The life events inventory. *Journal of Psychosomatic Research*, 1973, *17*, 135-139.

French, R. P., & Caplan, R. D. Organizational stress and individual strain. In A. J. Marrow (Ed.), *The failure of success*. New York: AMACOM, 1972.

Friedlander, F. Emergent and contemporary life styles: An intergenerational issue. *Human Relations*, 1975, *28*, 329-347.

Holmes, T. H., & Rahe, R. H. The social readjustment rating scale. *Journal of Psychosomatic Research*, 1967, *11*, 213-218.

Naismith, D. *Stress among managers as a function of organizational change*. Unpublished doctoral dissertation, The George Washington University, 1975.

Suojanen, W. W., & Hudson, D. R. Coping with stress and addictive work behavior. *Atlanta Economic Review*, March-April, 1977, pp. 4-9.

Weiss, S. M. (Ed.). *Proceedings of the National Heart, Lung and Blood Institute Working Conference on Health Behavior*. Department of Health, Education and Welfare, National Institutes of Health (77-868), 1977.

17

Consulting with Labor and Management: Some Learnings from Quality-of-Work-Life Projects

David A. Nadler

There has been growing recognition among those who are concerned with organizational behavior that organized labor is an important factor in the work place. This realization is particularly important for the theory and practice of organization development. It introduces another major element into the frameworks that are used to think about organizations and change and implies a need to understand the potential role of labor unions in organizational life. More specifically, there is a need to move beyond the traditional view of organization development as a technology that makes unions unnecessary toward a view of organization development as a process in which unions can play important and constructive roles. If this is to be done, it is critical to learn how to work with labor and management jointly in bringing about planned organizational change.

For some time, organized labor received little attention in the organizational-change literature. With a few exceptions (Lewicki & Alderfer, 1973), labor unions were rarely mentioned in either discussions of change theory or accounts of field work. Recently, work has appeared that reflects attempts to build theory around labor-management interventions (Kochan & Dyer, 1976) as well as efforts to experiment with different approaches to working with labor and management in the field (Drexler & Lawler, 1977; Duckles, Duckles, & Maccoby, 1977; Nadler, 1978). These theoretical works and individual case studies have been useful and should continue. On the other hand, other insights could be obtained if attempts were made to look at a number of labor-management projects and derive implications from the experiences of different organizations, labor unions, and consultants in their attempts to work together in different settings. Such comparative research would be particularly helpful in learning more about the nature of both joint labor-management interventions and consultation with labor and management.

A STRUCTURAL DESIGN FOR JOINT LABOR-MANAGEMENT CHANGE PROJECTS

One way of thinking about the labor-management change project is as an intergroup-conflict problem. Two groups, labor and management, exist within the boundaries of the same organization. The groups may have inconsistent goals, different values, and varying approaches to problem solving. In addition, labor and management typically have developed an adversary relationship over time. Getting these groups to work together to solve problems and bring about change is thus a problem of conflict resolution, and much of the conflict research (Deutsch, 1973; Schmidt & Kochan, 1972; Thomas, 1976) can be utilized. The critical problem is how to develop conflict-resolution mechanisms that are suitable.

A number of models for conflict resolution and management have been developed (Filley, 1975; Likert & Likert, 1976; Thomas, 1976). One approach in particular, however, has been developed from the labor-management context and thus may have particular value for such settings. Walton and McKersie (1965) proposed a framework in which two specific processes for bargaining between labor and management are identified. *Distributive bargaining* is the typical zero-sum conflict situation in which groups work on issues around conflicting goals. *Integrative bargaining* can occur when objectives of the parties are not in fundamental conflict and can be integrated to some degree into problem solutions. Clearly, the development of joint labor-management change projects is an example of an attempt at integrative bargaining.

The design to be discussed here was developed by researchers at the Institute for Social Research at the University of Michigan, along with the staff of the American Center for Quality of Working Life (ACQWL). It is based on the assumption that if joint labor-management change efforts are to succeed, an explicit structure must be created for conducting integrative bargaining on issues of quality of work life and organizational effectiveness. In addition, for such a structure to work effectively, external third-party consultants must be available to aid the process of problem solving within the context of a larger adversary relationship. The structure could take many forms. One approach is to develop a structure for organizational change that is outside of or collateral to the existing hierarchy or set of relationships (Zand, 1974). When intergroup relations are of particular importance, the composition of such collateral groups is particularly important. Alderfer (1977) has proposed a design for doing long-term intergroup interventions; it involves the development of a group that includes representatives from each of the different groups that are in conflict or that might have an interest in the change effort.

Starting in 1973, a series of field projects were initiated to test the usefulness of such a collateral intergroup design as a method for doing integrative bargaining around quality-of-work and organizational-improvement issues. This effort, called the "Quality of Work Program," involved the initiation of labor-management change projects in a number of different settings, with each project having the following basic characteristics:

1. *Quality-of-Work Committees:* At the heart of each project is a joint labor-management committee that serves as the basic forum and structure

for integrative bargaining. These committees, established by representatives from ACQWL, as part of the project start-up activities, include representatives from management, relevant labor unions, and other involved employee groups. The committee in each case is charged with managing problem solving and change efforts in the organization. It is given a mandate to initiate activities aimed at improving both the quality of work life of organizational members and the effectiveness of the organization.

2. *External consultants:* Funding is provided so that each of the labor-management committees can have assistance from a consultant external to the organization—presumably, one with background and skills in the application of the behavioral sciences to problems of organization development. In most cases, these consultants are chosen by the labor-management committee.

3. *External Researchers:* Many organizational-change efforts have been evaluated, researched, and reported by the change agents themselves. While many have argued for the value of combining research and change-agent roles (Argyris, 1970), alternative models have been proposed (Barnes, 1967; Lawler, 1977) that have the advantages of objectivity (Gordon & Morse, 1975) and free the change agent to be primarily concerned with client needs. The design thus includes a separate research team for each site. This team's task is to document and describe the project activities and assess the impact of the project on organizational effectiveness and the quality of work life.

Since 1973, this design has been implemented in a number of different organizations, including a coal mine, a public utility, a medical center, a city government, and several manufacturing organizations with different products and technologies. Over time, several additional aspects of the design have developed:

1. *Multiple-Level Committees:* It is frequently necessary to form more than one labor-management committee to reflect the different interests that exist at different levels of both labor and management. Thus, a labor-management committee might be created at the plant/union local level and then supplemented with a committee at the project work level (a department or work unit) to deal with day-to-day matters or with a committee at the corporate/union international level to deal with major issues of policy. Thus, in some settings, a hierarchy of different committees develops.

2. *Ad Hoc Committees:* In many cases, the labor-management committee at one level would initiate a specific project that would involve a set of workers and managers in one part of the organization. The structure that has emerged in some settings for coordinating these special projects is an ad hoc labor-management committee that reports to one of the permanent committees and that functions as a special task force with a specific charge and a limited lifetime.

The total structure that has developed at many of the project sites is depicted in simplified form in Figure 1. A quality-of-work labor-management committee, with representation from management and organized labor, is formed. The creation of this committee frequently leads to the development of committees at the work-unit level. In addition, ad hoc committees (shown in dotted lines) are created for specific projects. The entire structure is aided by external consultants and observed by external researchers.

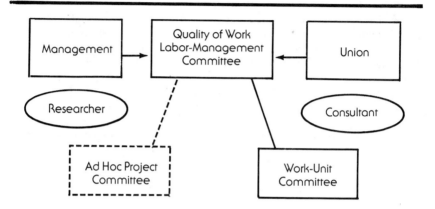

Figure 1. A Structural Design for Labor-Management Quality-of-Work-Life Projects

A PREDICTIVE MODEL OF LABOR-MANAGEMENT-PROJECT SUCCESS

Initial experiences with the quality-of-work project structure have been varied. In some instances, projects have been successful, and significant changes have been made, organizational effectiveness has been improved, and the quality-of-work committee structure has continued to function over a period of years. In other situations, the committees have encountered problems, and in several cases the committee structure has been discontinued. An important question, therefore, is what factors seem to be critical in determining whether a quality-of-work project will be successful or not.

Walton & McKersie (1965), in their discussion of integrative bargaining, propose three major factors that are important to facilitate integrative bargaining: (a) motivation, (b) information, and (c) trust. Building on this approach and drawing from the experiences and case studies to date, a number of specific factors have been hypothesized to be predictors of project success (see Figure 2). One factor that is predicted to be of importance is the degree of *ownership* that labor, management, and the rank-and-file workers feel over the project. The greater the ownership by all parties, the greater is the motivation to make the integrative bargaining process work, and thus, the greater are the chances of success. A second factor, *project goals*, is similarly related to success. To the extent that project goals are clear and agreed on, the rewards for involvement are more certain, and thus motivation should be increased. A third factor is the functioning of the *external consultant*. The consultant appears to play a key role in the project; thus, the consultant's expertise in different areas also should be predictive of the success of the project. At the heart of the structure is the labor-management committee. The integrative-bargaining model implies a need for open communication between the bargaining parties as a necessary element in successful problem solving. Thus, the way in which the *labor-management committee functions* as a group should also be predictive of success. A final factor is that of *organizational context*. A key variable of the integrative bargaining model is trust. It would appear that a predictor of trust in the bargaining process would be the nature of the union-management relationships and the general working relationships within the organization. Thus, factors in the organizational environment of the project also should be predictive of success.

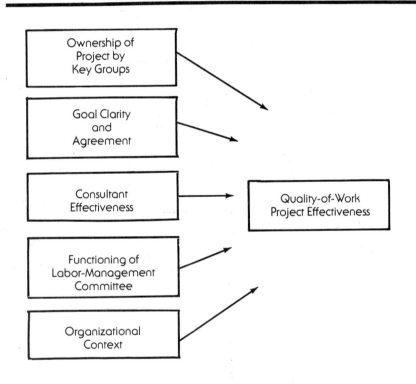

Figure 2. A Predictive Model of Quality-of-Work Project Effectiveness

BACKGROUND OF THE STUDY

In May, 1977, a conference was held for representatives from quality-of-work projects[1]. Invitations were sent to the quality-of-work committees in a number of organizations, and representatives from sixteen projects were able to attend the conference. Of these, nine projects were established as part of the Quality of Work Program and had integrative-bargaining stuctures much like those described in Figure 1. The other seven projects were not officially part of the quality-of-work programs; however, they were similar in project structure and composition. Efforts were made to insure that the delegations from each project were balanced to include representatives from management and labor organizations as well as individuals who saw themselves as representatives of rank-and-file employees involved in the projects. A total of eighty-six individuals attended the conference, of whom approximately 39 percent represented management, 30 percent represented union, and 31 percent represented rank and file (workers who did not see themselves as either management or union representatives).

Questionnaire

A questionnaire was developed to test the predictive model of labor-management-project success. A series of seven-point Likert-type items related to each of the key variables of the model: ownership, project goals, consultant effectiveness, the labor-management committee, and organizational context. Individuals were asked to rate their projects in terms of the effect the project had on quality of work life and organizational functioning. Individuals also were asked to provide a global rating of the total success of the project.

In addition to the structured questionnaire items, a number of open-ended questions were asked in each of the areas. For example, respondents were asked "What do you feel are the major strengths of your consultant?" and "What do you feel are the major weaknesses of your consultant?"

Data Collection

The conference was held at a residential conference center near Washington, D.C. It started on a Friday evening and lasted through midday Sunday. Participants arrived on Friday evening, met informally, and were greeted by staff members from the ACQWL. The following morning, before any of the content sessions, the participants were asked to fill out the survey instrument. They were informed that the survey was voluntary and that both individual and project anonymity would be maintained. Of the seventy-three questionnaires completed,

---

[1]The conference was sponsored by the American Center for the Quality of Working Life (ACQWL). Funding support was provided by Ford Foundation, the National Institute of Mental Health, and the National Center for Productivity and Quality of Work Life.

nine were not usable for analysis—either because the respondents' projects were just being initiated or because they did not understand some of the questions.

Limitations of the Method

It is important to note some of the obvious limitations of the methodology. Although the data enable an empirical test of the hypothesized model, interpretations must be cautious. First, there is a problem of sampling and, thus, of external validity. Respondents were chosen as representatives by the various quality-of-work committees. The selection processes may have reflected a variety of factors, including the availability of members, the interest of individuals, and various political conflicts within the committees. Thus, the sample is not randomly chosen and cannot be assumed to be representative of all project participants.

A second concern is the nature of the criterion variable, project success. Ideally, independent measures of project success (such as changes in measures of quality of work life and organizational performance) would have been obtained. In this case, the success measures are perceptual—the ratings of the individuals who attended the conference.

Given these problems, the survey results must be interpreted carefully. On the other hand, when results are consistent with theoretical predictions and previously identified patterns from case studies, some degree of validity may be attributed to the data. The ultimate test, however, will come through a wider and more representative data collection that includes nonperceptual measures of project performance.

RESULTS

The Predictive Model

Correlations were obtained between a number of the key questionnaire items and the three major measures of project success. The results are presented in Table 1 and provide general support for the model. All the factors are related to project success in the direction predicted, although there are great variations in the strength of the relationships. Consultant effectiveness, the functioning of the labor-management committee, and organizational context all appear to be strongly related to project success; project goals and ownership are less related to measures of project performance.

Consultant Effectiveness Ratings

One section of the questionnaire dealt with issues related to the role of the consultant in the labor-management project. A number of questions were related to success of the project. Respondents were asked to rate how effective their consultant was along a variety of dimensions. The correlations between the ratings of consultant effectiveness and the three measures of project success are shown in Table 2. All the measures of consultant effectiveness are significantly correlated with the global measure of project success. Again, there is variation in the strength of the association. Consultant effectiveness in making things happen, in resolving conflict, in getting people to communicate with each other, and in helping groups to work together more effectively were most strongly related to perceptions of project success.

Table 1. Correlates of Q-O-W Project Success

	Project Has Improved Organizational Functioning	Project Has Improved Quality of Working Life	Project Has Been a Success
Ownership			
Management	.19	.15	.22
Labor Union(s)	.06	.06	.26*
Rank-and-File Employees	.00	.07	.17
Project Goals			
How Clear	.40**	.33**	.39**
How Much Agreement	.28*	.23*	.24*
Consultant Effectiveness			
In General, How Effective	.53**	.46**	.62**
Labor-Management Committee			
Labor-Management Committee Functions Well as a Group	.47**	.37**	.46**
Organizational Context			
Organization is Facing Major Financial Problems	−.35**	−.33*	−.24*
Relations Between Labor and Management are Good	.43**	.46**	.52**
Organization is Open and Receptive to New Ideas	.38**	.51**	.58**

* $p < .05$
**$p < .01$

Consultant Strengths and Weaknesses

The responses to the open-ended question on consultant strengths and weaknesses were content analyzed. First, the research staff reviewed the answers to the questions and developed a category system for coding answers. This category system was then given to two graduate assistants who were unaware of the hypotheses of the study; they used the system to independently code the responses. A third graduate assistant was then given the coding scheme and asked to determine the correct categorization of the remaining answers.

Table 2. Relationship Between Dimensions of Consultant Effectiveness and Perceptions of Project Success

Dimensions of Consultant Effectiveness	Project Has Improved Organizational Functioning	Project Has Improved Quality of Work Life	Project Has Been a Success
Understanding the problems of your organization	.26*	.27*	.22*
Getting people to communicate better with each other	.49**	.45**	.48**
Working with labor-management committees	.37**	.35**	.36**
Getting large numbers of people to feel involved in the project	.26*	.15	.38**
Bringing new ideas and tools to the organization	.40**	.27*	.30*
Involving the rank and file in decision making	.29*	.15	.36**
Resolving conflicts that have come up during the project	.41**	.28*	.48**
Helping groups to work together more effectively	.45**	.35**	.40**
Making things happen	.52**	.44**	.49**
Coming up with specific solutions for organizational problems	.29*	.27*	.29*

* p < .05
**p < .01

Table 3 presents the content analysis of the responses to open-ended questions about the consultants. The categories are arranged in order of the frequency of response.

Table 3. Consultant Strength and Weaknesses

General Category	Percentage of Answers	Illustrations of Category
Active leadership	39.5	Is a strong leader, has personality, is dynamic, makes things happen, provides impetus, has organizing ability, is effective problem solver, maintains L/M interest in project, gets people to participate, sets up meetings.
Technical expertise	18.4	Has team-building skills, has consultant expertise, has experience, shares information, can diagnose problems, has interviewing skills, provides training, provides innovative ideas.
Communication	9.2	Has ability to communicate, is effective speaker, provides good feedback to committee.
High investment	9.2	Works hard, shows genuine interest, displays eagerness, does not get discouraged.
Understanding of organization	7.9	Understands structure of the organization, understands both sides (labor and management), works well with management.
Promotion of trust	6.6	Creates trust, is trusted, gains confidence of employees, is honest.
Facilitating skills	5.2	Gets people to focus on issues, makes people solve their own problems, provides a lever with management, makes management see existing problems.
Understanding of people	3.9	Understands individual motives, understands the people in the organization.
Poor leadership	23.1	Is not forceful enough, does not have enough political impact, observes too much, does not help enough, has difficulty in implementing ideas, sometimes becomes stymied, does not get enough people or rank and file involved.
Lack of understanding of system	23.1	Needs time to understand the system and its political nature, does not understand union-management client relationships or problems, is unfamiliar with actual work activities, is inexperienced with complex, multigroup organizations.
No creation of trust	15.4	Is a game player, cannot be trusted, does not gain trust or confidence, has a divisive effect on groups.
Lack of effective communication	15.4	Is too academic, puts himself on higher level than others, does not communicate well with rank and file, has problems in promoting communication and trust, does not provide clear information.
Low investment	10.3	Does not provide enough time for project, shows lack of interest in project.

DISCUSSION

The Predictive Model

In general, the survey data confirmed the predictive model of project success. All the factors were positively related to the measures of perceived project success. In particular, the effectiveness of the consultant seemed to stand out as the single most important predictor of success. The functioning of the labor-management committee and the larger organizational context were also important factors in project success.

Two of the factors did not appear to be important: ownership and goals. The most disappointing results were in the area of ownership, although this could reflect a measurement problem. In the questionnaire, the concept of ownership was defined as "involvement in and responsibility for" the project activities. Respondents were then asked to rate the degree of perceived ownership by labor, management, and the rank and file. Ownership is a somewhat vague concept, and many may not have understood it. Similarly, it may be difficult to assess the degree of ownership that groups of people feel about a project. In contrast, respondents were asked to rate their own ownership of the project, and this measure was highly correlated ($r = .69$) with the global measure of project success. This would indicate that assessment of group ownership of a project is difficult. The project ownership factor should, therefore, still be considered, and subsequent studies should consider the aggregation of individual ownership ratings to obtain group ratings.

Although questions about project goals were not as strongly related to the success ratings as other items, they still were reasonable, given the model. Because in many situations project goals were seen as relatively unclear ($\bar{x} = 4.1$; SD = 1.58 on a 7-point scale), the potential for agreement on goals was limited and possibly was reflected in the lower correlation for that time.

Consultant Effectiveness

Perhaps the most interesting finding was the strong relationship between perceptions of consultant effectiveness and project success. The major implication of this finding vis-à-vis the model is that the establishment of a quality-of-work structure by itself may not be sufficient to start a project or to assure its success. Clearly, many of the project participants rated the effectiveness of their consultants as a very critical determinant of project functioning.

Some interesting patterns emerge in the responses to both the questionnaire items and the open-ended questions relating to consultants. Two factors in the consultant's performance seem to be critical. One is fairly predictable: *the skill of the consultant as a process facilitator.* Of seven items most related to the measurement of success, four are related to the skills of the consultant in aiding groups and individuals to relate and do work effectively: the effectiveness of the consultant in resolving conflicts, in helping groups to work together, in getting people to communicate with each other, and in working with labor-management commit-tees. Similarly, several of the categories of the open-ended responses fall generally into the class of skills related to process consultation or facilitation.

The second element of consultant effectiveness was somewhat surprising. This factor could best be described as *the extent to which the consultant serves as a source of energy through his or her leadership.* The other three best predictors were based on the consultant's effectiveness in making things happen, involving the rank and file in the project, and getting large numbers of people involved in the project. The pattern is even more pronounced in the open-ended responses; the consultant strength mentioned most and one of the two consultant weaknesses that were mentioned most had to do with the consultant as a leader within the project structure. This finding is interesting because it differs somewhat from the traditional organization-development view of the consultant's role as nondirec-tive and primarily facilitative (rather than active).

A third set of consultant skills related to the content and diagnostic expertise of the consultant. These dimensions included the effectiveness of the consultant in coming up with specific solutions for organization problems, in bringing new ideas and tools to the organization, and in understanding the problems of the organization. In general, these dimensions seemed to be the least important in terms of predicting project success and showed up much less frequently in the responses to the open-ended questions.

A General Interpretation

The patterns that emerge in relation to the consultant's role are interesting and make sense within a general interpretation of some of the dynamics of the quality-of-work project setting. As was mentioned earlier, creating change through work with labor and management is, of necessity, a problem of intergroup relations and is potentially a problem of intergroup conflict. The issue of power—and in particular the relative power of the two parties—is important. Given the general context of an adversary relationship, the exercise of power within a quality-of-work project by one party may be contingent on the exercise of power by the other party. Thus, two patterns can emerge. In the first pattern, traditional conflict, if one party makes an attempt to exercise power in the project, the other party responds with a similar power attempt and conflict results. In this case, the process skills of the consultant—particularly conflict-resolution skills—become very important. The consultant needs to be there to prevent the use of distributive-bargaining tactics and the breakdown of problem solving.

A second pattern is that both parties choose to exercise no power. This can result from a lack of clarity about roles or from a fear that any exercise of power will lead to the conflict situation described above. The basic problem is that there is little precedent for a power-sharing relationship, so frequently both parties wait for the other to act and take a passive stance, and little happens in the project. It is here that the consultant's skills as a source of energy and a source of leadership become particularly important. The consultant is important because, as a third party, it is legitimate for him or her to step into the power vacuum and take initiative. This role is often critical to the survival of the project.

IMPLICATIONS

The model presented here and the data that were analyzed lead to some clear implications for action. The consultant in a new labor-management project needs to consider a number of specific issues that concern both the project in general and the consultant in particular.

Preconditions for Success

The model suggests that certain situations may be inherently more favorable for a labor-management project than others. In particular, the nature of the organizational context of the project is important and should be examined in depth before a project is begun. The data suggest that an organization should have relatively good labor-management relations and a moderately good climate (in terms of openness to ideas and trust) for a labor-management project to succeed. Without these factors, pressures from the environment and a past history of adversary relations may provide more obstacles to integrative bargaining than can be overcome.

  Another element to be considered is financial pressure. The data indicate that the financial condition of the organization is negatively related to project success, although that relationship is not very strong. On the other hand, a number of projects now in existence (but yet to be reported) have experienced great success even though financial pressures on the organizations are extremely great. In these cases, labor and management have collaborated in the face of possible threats to the survival of the organization or possible loss of employee benefits. This response is similar to other instances of labor-management collaboration (Lieseur, 1957). This suggests that a curvilinear relationship exists between financial pressures and success. A project can succeed when financial conditions are good or when the situation is so bad that labor and management need to cooperate for the sake of survival. When financial conditions are poor but not extremely threatening, the project may run into problems. Such a project should be considered very carefully.

The Importance of Entry

Many of the comments of participants concerning problems of the projects related to the early stages of project activities. The degree of ownership of the project by individuals and the clarity of and agreement on project goals seemed to reflect the effectiveness of the entry activities by the consultants and others who were involved in initiating the projects.

  The implication is that the consultant needs to consider carefully the early stages of a project and to plan activities that will make the goals of the project clear and specific. This is consistent with the observations of Kochan and Dyer (1976) and Nadler (1978), who feel that the first steps of the project should be very clear and that payoffs should come in the short run. Goals that are clear and agreed upon can help to create a sense of ownership for the project as well as motivation to make the integrative bargaining process work effectively.

The Need To Be Active

The survey results indicate that important functions of the consultant are to initiate activity, to structure the involvement of individuals in a relatively vague and ambiguous task, and to serve as a source of energy for both individuals and groups. This involves what may be new and different skills for the consultant. In one sense, the charismatic consultant might function better in this situation than the low-key, understated, nondirective-process person. The need to take action is a consequence of the intergroup problem. It also implies the need for a continuing consulting presence. Given the ongoing nature of the pressures stemming from the distributive bargaining relationship between management and labor, the power problems are likely to persist over time. It may be unrealistic to expect a consultant to leave after a period of a year or eighteen months and to expect the integrative-bargaining structure to continue on its own. Indeed, some of the successful projects have, after a period of time, obtained consultants to serve the projects in ongoing roles.

The Importance of Key Process Skills

Although energy is an important aspect of the consultant's role, process skills are most important. When conflict emerges, the role of the consultant is crucial in developing processes for management or resolution of the conflict in ways that will contribute to continued problem solving. Perhaps the most important point of contact between the consultant and the organization is through the various labor-management committees. It is here that the process skills are particularly important. The survey data indicated that how well the labor-management committee functions as a group is an important predictor of project success. Clearly, the consultant plays a major role in determining how that committee will operate. Given the various pressures and the potential intergroup conflict, the consultant cannot pay too much attention to how the process of the labor-management committee develops.

SUMMARY

There is a need to consider labor in models of organizational change. One design for joint labor-management change projects has been used in a number of different settings, and the experience to date—along with a number of theoretical models (such as integrative bargaining)—suggests a predictive model of project success.

The data collected support this model and also provide some important learnings for consultants in such situations. The consultant must consider the organizational context of the project before beginning. Entry is an important determinant of the perception of project goals and of ownership. Finally, the consultant needs to develop and exercise skills as both a leader and a facilitator—in particular, in the context of relations with various labor-management committees. Survey results provide not only some implications to be tested by future research but also some clear directions for practice. [2]

REFERENCES

Alderfer, C. P. Improving organizational communication through long-term intergroup intervention. *Journal of Applied Behavioral Science*, 1977, *13*, 193-210.

Argyris, C. *Intervention theory and method*. Reading, MA: Addison-Wesley, 1970.

Barnes, L. B. Organizational change and field experiment methods. In V. H. Vroom (Ed.), *Methods of organizational research*. Pittsburgh, PA: University of Pittsburgh Press, 1967.

Deutsch, M. *The resolution of conflict: Constructive and destructive processes*. New Haven, CT: Yale University Press, 1973.

Drexler, J. A., Jr., & Lawler, E. E. A union-management cooperative project to improve the quality of work life. *Journal of Applied Behavioral Science*, 1977, *13*, 373-387.

Duckles, M. M., Duckles, R., & Maccoby, M. The process of change at Bolivar. *Journal of Applied Behavioral Science*, 1977, *13*, 387-399.

Filley, A. C. *Interpersonal conflict resolution*. Glenview, IL: Scott Foresman, 1975.

Gordon, B., & Morse, E. U. Evaluation research: A critical review. *The Annual Review of Sociology*, 1975, *1*, 339-361.

Kochan, R. A., & Dyer, L. A model of organizational change in the context of union-management relations. *Journal of Applied Behavioral Science*, 1976, *12*, 59-78.

Lawler, E. E., III. Adaptive experiments: An approach to organizational behavior research. *Academy of Management Review*, 1977, *2*, 576-585.

Lewicki, R. J., & Alderfer, C. P. The tensions between research and intervention in intergroup conflict. *Journal of Applied Behavioral Science*, 1973, *9*, 424-449.

Lieseur, F. *The Scanlon plan*. Cambridge, MA: The M.I.T. Press, 1957.

Likert, R., & Likert, J. G. *New ways of managing conflict*. New York: McGraw-Hill, 1976.

---

[2]The research reported here is part of the Quality of Work Program sponsored by the American Center for Quality of Working Life. Ongoing program support was provided by the Ford Foundation and the Economic Development Administration of the U.S. Department of Commerce. Support for work reported here was also provided by the National Center for Health Services Research of the U.S. Department of Health, Education, and Welfare. The views expressed here are those of the author and do not necessarily reflect the opinions of the American Center for the Quality of Working Life or the other supporting agencies.

Nadler, D. A. Joint labor-management interventions in health care organizations: Implications from a case in progress. *Journal of Applied Behavioral Science*, 1978, *13*, in press.

Schmidt, S., & Kochan, T. Conflict: Toward conceptual clarity. *Administrative Science Quarterly*, 1972, *17*, 359-370.

Thomas, K. Conflict and conflict management. In M. D. Dunnette (Ed.), *Handbook of industrial and organizational psychology*. Chicago: Rand-McNally, 1976.

Walton, R. E., & McKersie, R. B. *A behavioral theory of labor negotiations: An analysis of a social interaction system*. New York: McGraw-Hill, 1965.

Zand, D. E. Collateral organization: A new change strategy. *Journal of Applied Behavioral Science*, 1974, *10*, 63-89.

18

Retirement and Organization Development

Leland P. Bradford

For some time organizations have attempted to meet both human needs and organizational goals. Nonetheless, organizations do create conditions that often make retirement extremely difficult for individuals. Organizational structure provides many vitally important socio-emotional needs: feelings of belonging to a work team and shared companionship; a sense of identity and self-worth; goals; routines; opportunities to achieve and contribute; peer respect; a degree of influence; and a place in the working world.

When an individual retires, suddenly these needs are no longer met. The individual, alone, must discover new ways of finding fulfillment if the vibrancy of living is to be maintained and depression is to be avoided. But two conditions resulting from many years of organizational experience create often insurmountable barriers and inhibit individual initiative in seeking solutions. For too long the individual, probably unconsciously, has been dependent on the organization for the fulfillment of important needs. Now that person is expected to sluff off this dependency and become instantly independent and self-managing. From being outer-directed, the individual is expected to become immediately self-directed. This expectation usually is too much.

The many pressures toward conformity to organizational norms and the need to be innovative about organizational tasks have negatively trained the individual to be innovative about self. Acceptance of the company's values, purposes, and methods can so channel the individual's values, creativity, and innovativeness that the person may lack the ability to seek and find new areas for creativity and usefulness or even to examine the imposed values. Subjection to the management and direction of others or the mores of the organization tends to atrophy the vitally needed will and ability for self-management later.

These conditions, combined with the social expectations that retired persons are less useful, unwanted, and "put out to pasture," cause feelings of futility and uselessness, loneliness and depression, and contribute to the premature aging so common when spirit and purpose in life are lacking.

The theme I will stress in this chapter and in my book (Bradford, in press) is that organizational responsibility for human needs does not end at retirement. Organizations can do much during the working years to help persons become self-managing, self-directive, and reliant on internal resources. But first those concerned with organizational behavior must become acutely aware of the shock and emotional trauma that so many suffer at retirement.

I will describe some of the most difficult emotional upheavals that my wife and I experienced, and finally coped with, when we retired, and I will relate these reactions to organizational analogies. This is written in the first person in order to best reveal the depth of the emotions that we encountered.

I hope by so doing to help others to understand the vivid and powerful emotional traps that lie in wait for the unwary, and thus to help others to discover ways in which organizations can assist their employees throughout the working years to cope with such drastic changes in their lives.

COPING WITH TRANSITION AND CHANGE

Retirement presents this problem dramatically and forcefully. When we retired, we suddenly and surprisingly, even shockingly, discovered that we had become part of a minority group known as "retired people." We felt pushed into a psychological ghetto—we were not supposed to feel a part of the vibrant, dynamic ongoing world. Someone said "people are for living." We agreed. We did not want to be shoved aside.

No matter how much an individual, after long years in a private career or with an organization, may be looking forward to retirement, when the time arrives there may be a sinking feeling that something very important is ending. There may be the sudden awareness that in the future there will be no job to go to, no organization to belong to, no companions with whom to share experiences. One will, in fact, become an outcast.

For us, the suddenness—even though we had planned it—left us feeling lost, no longer needed or wanted, disposable. We abruptly experienced a separation. That hurt deeply. The changes struck deeply at the inner person; feeling un-needed and unwanted were tremendous blows to self-esteem and self-respect. Even more annihilating as we looked ahead was our realization that we were expected to endure quietly the declining years, even though we still felt vigorous and competent. We recognized then that we must find ways to rebuild our lives. We worked together to create a productive and rewarding existence that enabled us to maintain our self-esteem and self-respect.

During this extremely difficult transition, we realized acutely how little our years of organizational experience had prepared us for this situation. In fact, organizational needs had typically taken precedence over human needs.

Organizational Analogies

The following examples illustrate the result when organizational needs take precedence over human needs.[1]

---

[1] These examples are used with permission and have been camouflaged.

Some years ago I consulted with the vice president for personnel of a large company. He told me that the company had just secured the services of fifty badly needed specialists from a company in another part of the country. His company had made every effort, he said, to locate nice homes in desirable neighborhoods and near good schools so that the specialists could go to work immediately. "But we have had all kinds of trouble with them, no matter how hard we tried," he said. "I'm afraid that they will just be troublemakers in the company."

"Were they able to participate in the decision to come or in the selection of their homes?" I asked. "What were their options?"

"They could have quit," the vice president responded. "We just would have been forced to find others."

Around a decade or so ago, one or two reported studies indicated that the majority of acquired profitable companies became unprofitable for about five years after being acquired. How much the neglect of human needs was the cause of this is an unanswered question.

We live now in a "resort village." For over seventy-five years the resort and village had been owned by one family. Then it was sold to a large company just entering the resort business. Shortly after the announcement, I was having lunch with the then president of the resort. He told me that the new company had assured him that little change would take place in the old and famous resort or with its personnel. I predicted that after a year no member of the present personnel, from top to bottom, would be left. I was wrong. After a year the night clerk from one of the hotels and a waitress from another hotel were still employed. All others had departed—fired or left with hurt and angry feelings.

Compare the previous incidents with the following:

The president of a medium-sized industry told me this story. A number of years previously he had participated in one of our training programs exclusively confined to presidents of organizations. One day of the program was devoted to an exercise on acquisitions. A few years later he faced an attractive offer from a larger company to have his company acquired. Having learned and remembered much from the acquisition exercise, he went to his board of directors and secured approval for the following proposal:

1. All workers in the company would be informed immediately of the offer and told that the offer was not yet, and would not be, accepted until the employees had participated in the decision.

2. Each section or grade of employees was to select one person to serve on an investigating team. The investigation would be with similar-level employees in the proposed acquiring company. Members in each section, including the vice-presidential level, participated in suggesting questions that their representative could ask the counterparts.

3. The investigating team was sent at company expense to the proposed acquiring company after its president had been informed of the visit and asked not to encourage his employees to try to "sell" the virtues of their company.

4. Each investigative representative asked such questions of a counterpart as:
   "What do you like about working here?" "What is not so good?"
   "Why have you stayed with this company?"
   "What do you think should be changed?"

5. The investigators reported their findings back to members. The picture was not perfect, but more good than bad was found. The employees voted for the acquisition. It was their decision, and they felt that their needs had been considered.

BELONGING AND COMPANIONSHIP

Feelings of belonging and shared companionship become tremendously important when one is concerned about health, aging, and loneliness. Studies at Duke University, and assuredly in many other research centers, indicate the necessity for socialization for the elderly and the aging to prevent or remedy depression and other emotional problems and mental ills.

Retirement cuts off much of the belonging and sharing that individuals have known previously. Retired peers may move away. Even when together, sharing becomes nostalgic rather than forward looking. For many, retirement means moving to different areas or different homes, new friends need to be gained, new groups to be joined, and new relationships to be built. What now must be shared, if companionship and a feeling of belonging are to be secured, varies extremely from what was shared in the work situation. At work, problems of task and integration of functions mixed with interpersonal feelings or competitive reactions were the essence of what was shared. In retirement, few if any common tasks arise; what is required as the coin of interchange is human warmth and openness to others.

Organizational experience ill prepares persons for this new type of sharing. Competitive concerns—who will get ahead and who will be most rewarded— serve as unspoken inhibitors to truly open companionship. In the organization there are concerns to be shared and the individual does not need to extend himself or herself because belonging is a factor of employment. Hence, most persons have not faced fully the need to extend themselves in order to secure warm relationships with others.

Those with rank, position, title, or influence become accustomed to being approached rather than to approach, and have so confused their titles with themselves that in retirement they wait, usually in vain, to be approached, believing that it is their due. In retirement, previous rank, title, or position has little value. The coin of human exchange now is what the person is really like—stripped of past accomplishments—and how willing the person is to extend himself or herself in true warmth. It is a hard lesson for many to learn.

Organizational Analogies

In a number of one-industry towns with which I have had experience, individuals worked in the factory or mill after completing an elementary or high-school education. After forty or fifty years, they retired. They became outcasts. There was nothing else to do in the towns, and they had no other experience. They stayed home and overburdened their wives. They sat in the local tavern drinking beer and voicing their distress with other retirees. They waited until the quitting whistle and then, as hangers-on, joined workers stopping for a glass before going home. Some moved to Florida, hoping to find a feeling that they had lost.

The Medical Department of the United States Army (1973) during the Second World War discovered that when battle-fatigue cases were placed in a hospital unit close to the front lines, the patients tended to improve rapidly and willingly returned to their units as soon as possible. In other cases sent to hospitals in England, in the United States, or far behind the lines, soldiers seldom returned to their units. The Army study reported that soldiers kept close to their units felt that they still belonged and were wanted back by their comrades, whereas soldiers who felt psychologically removed from their units felt unwanted and discarded and resisted returning. The Medical Department, learning this lesson, revised its procedures and therefore kept more soldiers functioning.

ACHIEVEMENT AND PRIDE

Living on the pride of one's past accomplishments wears thin very quickly at retirement. One rapidly learns that telling others about the past is not effective in establishing new relationships. Others may also have laurels, and even in retirement, one lives in the here and now, not in the past.

I learned somewhat painfully that pride in the past does not maintain self-respect in the present, at least if one is honest with oneself. I learned anew the tremendous importance of continuing achievement—not necessarily in past areas but in any area that seems worthy and is rewarding to self—as a basis of self-respect, self-esteem, and even self-liking. I had long known this intellectually. Now I knew it emotionally.

One of my retired friends has become an accomplished cabinet maker—not for monetary profit, but to please himself and to supply his friends. This area of accomplishment is far distant from his previous profession. He has pride in his accomplishments.

In a venerable building in our village, a very old cobbler has an ancient shop. He is a genius in fixing a shoe, no matter what shape it is in. He fixes your shoe at his convenience. He has dignity, pride, and a sense of self-worth that shines clearly through his quietness.

At work and in a career, achievement is determined both by inner standards and by outer responses. I had not fully realized how dependent one could become on outer reactions in order to feel pride in achievement. I suppose I had never thought deeply about it. But in retirement I found the situation reversed, and this meant an adjustment I had not expected. Now pride in accomplishment had to be based far more on inner satisfaction, because the achievements were largely of value to myself. I was no longer in the competitive world, and there were few others around to react to me. I know a lady, now ninety, who walks a mile a day, even with replaced hips. She does not boast to others. She has quiet pride in her accomplishment and maintains her self-respect and self-esteem.

Through my own search for activities that met my internal standards of achievement to maintain my self-respect, I became more empathically aware of the sad emotional plight of the many individuals in organizations who are prevented from feeling achievement and pride—by hated and unrewarding jobs, by demeaning and destructive supervision, and by subjection to failure by being placed in inadequate positions. What unhappiness, what self-dislike, what anger, rage, hate, and ultimately apathy those individuals must feel.

POWER AND POWERLESSNESS

When I retired, I moved abruptly from a position of some power to one of relative powerlessness. It was a shocking experience. I felt an emptiness that was emotionally acute. Everyone needs to be listened to and respected. Otherwise rejection, depersonalization, even dehumanization occur. The suddenness with which I felt without influence, of being unused and unmissed, hit at my sense of personal significance. Who, now, was I significant to? I complained continuously about this to my wife, Martha.

She, fortunately, withheld no punches. She helped me to see what I was allowing to happen to me. Instead of complaining about my feelings, it was up to me to do something about finding a solution. I saw that if I were not to accept the status of "an old and finished person," I needed to draw on internal resources, to continue to learn and grow, to extend myself to others, to set challenges for myself that I could reasonably meet. Then a new kind of power would be mine: power over myself and much of my future. I could retain the dignity and strength that I wished to maintain for the rest of my life.

The passage I made from a position of power to a state approaching powerlessness and on to a new sense of power gave me a new understanding of the force of power in an organization and the consequences of powerlessness. Obviously power is not, and will not realistically, be equally distributed in organizations. But two conditions should be present for a healthy organization and healthy employees. The acquisition of power and its use must be accountable to many and not merely a few. All persons in an organization need some modicum of power—over a tool, a machine, a skill, or the respect of others.

Power, I realized more fully, helps to provide personal significance and affirmation of unique personhood. Power makes possible avenues for actualizing potentials. Power provides motivation for creativity and effort.

Powerlessness, on the other hand, depresses creativity and wastes potential abilities, to the detriment of the organization. Those who are powerless lack leverage to gain power and so remain victims. Powerlessness creates feelings of worthlessness. It is not that all persons in an organization desire the same amount of power. Some would be overwhelmed by too much. But each individual, often without awareness, has some feeling about the amount and kind of power he or she needs—the boundaries that cannot be transgressed without creating feelings of powerlessness.

The organizational problem is not merely to make employees *feel* that they have power, influence, and opportunities to participate, but to make it so. In the end, most persons recognize manipulative efforts to make them *feel* as opposed to allowing them to *be*.

Organizational Analogies

Two different examples will illustrate diverse aspects of the problem of power.

I consulted with one company over a period of years. The first, and basic, problem I encountered lay with the president himself. Despite medical warnings, he remained highly ambivalent about retirement. His doctor, and his body, told him to retire, but his need to retain power as the chief executive spoke otherwise. The result for the organization was not good. His hints of retirement coupled with no action activated intense rivalry for the top position and almost open manipulation by two of the vice presidents. Their competition, of which the president seemed blandly unaware, naturally disrupted communication and cooperation between the two sections under the respective vice presidents. Throughout the organization, employees were under tension, unsure about which side to join or how to remain neutral and still survive. The cancer caused by the struggle for power and the feeling of need to retain it affected the entire organization.

Experiences I had with two different types of organizations indicate how distrust follows efforts to conceal the use of power. In each organization, as is generally customary, a small cabinet made all major decisions. Then brief statements were sent to all members of the organization describing the decision. Frequently, additional memoranda explaining the reasons for the decisions were also sent out. Both organizations had surveys conducted to determine the morale of members and the effectiveness of communication from the "top." Results were shocking to top management. Data indicated that the more material was sent from the cabinet, the greater was employee distrust. What, employees asked, was being hidden by the small, closed, top group if so much effort was being made to convince them that they were being informed?

GOALS VERSUS THE LACK OF OR CHANGES IN GOALS

I had not thought much about the difficulties and the consequences for me that could result from the transition from the long-range goals I had held so long to the short-range goals needed in retirement. Most of us, during our adult working years, think about and plan for the future—advancement in work responsibility, raising a family, securing sufficient financial assets. At retirement these goals have usually been met. At this stage, "here-and-now" goals are needed for the day, the week, and the month.

The danger in this transition from long- to short-range goals lies in the ease with which one may become goalless. This sneaks up on one unobtrusively. It begins the morning that one awakens with no plans for the day and no good reason to arise. Other such mornings follow. It becomes easier just to sit around the house. It becomes harder to seek new goals. Self-pride soon diminishes. So does self-respect. Rationalizations take their place. Boredom occurs. Energy dwindles. One slows down and feels older. The body cooperates and ages more rapidly.

I teetered on the edge of this condition. One day a friend said, "Do you realize that the purpose of our golf club is to keep useless people alive?" That did it. I vowed that was not going to be my way of life. I sought new goals—some distant from my former life, some closer, but all within my ability to reach. As I sought these goals, I felt a renewed vibrancy.

As I struggled out of the pit of having no goals I reflected often on past organizational experiences. I recalled that after finishing high school I had to work a year to save money for college. I worked for a mail-order company, and my work was to fill orders in one department. It meant traversing countless corridors, going from one bin to another to select the specific garments ordered. The work was monotonous, the days endless. I found that the only relief was to set goals for myself. What short cuts could I discover? How could I, each day and week, set new records for myself? By setting my own goals, I endured that unexciting year. This recollection helped me in retirement.

Then I thought of the many persons in many organizations whose jobs, or the insensitivity or misuse of power of supervisors, cause them to feel goalless. What feelings of worthlessness they must know. What stress on the physical system. What apathy and indifference. I thought, with shame, that I had not always been as sensitive to this human problem for others as I wish I had been. In my former position, I just expected results. I, like so many others trapped in organizational situations, became "hooked" on organizational goals and achievements.

TERRITORY AND IDENTITY

I had long understood the concept of territory. Our dog would cower timorously when away from home at the sight of another dog, but would attack the same dog viciously if it ventured near our home. Our place and the surrounding ground was our dog's turf to defend at all costs. He knew the psychological boundaries of his turf far better than I did.

I also recognized casually that territory had meaning in organizations. I knew that each person must have a work space and that various other aspects of this space have much to do with pride and influence. The few years I spent in government in Washington, D.C., during World War II showed me how important carpets on the floor and a silver water pitcher were as symbols of importance.

It took retirement for me to realize emotionally the tremendous psychological importance of territory, particularly in relation to identity. All my adult life (I suddenly realized) the place where I worked, my responsibilities and duties, even what desk or office space I occupied, was my territory and represented me. Martha almost never came to my office. It would have seemed inappropriate and, yes, an intrusion if she had. Our behavior would have been stiff and unnatural.

She had her own territory. It was the home. Even though I was a part of the home and had certain rights, privileges, and duties in it, she made most of the decisions about it as I did about the office. Essentially the home defined her role and identity. It was her nest, her set of responsibilities, her "turf."

Then I retired. I lost my territory and, with it, much that made up and maintained my identity. I was turfless. I quickly realized that I was intruding in Martha's territory. I suddenly recognized that I was not expected, ever again, to possess anything resembling the turf I had left and its support for my identity. I now understood the desperateness with which animals fight for their territory. I now knew what it was like to feel disposable. It was a terrifying feeling.

At first, when I intruded on Martha's territory, she was very nice about it.

Then, as we bumped into each other, as I got in her way, as her freedom and time for activities were curtailed by my presence, she faced me with it. It became clear to both of us that some marital adjustments were required if we were to continue the satisfying marriage we had known for so many years. Some part of the house and certain new responsibilities were to be mine—a study where I could work, for example. We both needed to be sensitive to the other's needs for territory, space, and privacy. We noticed other couples with whom these adjustments were not made, and strains developed.

All this helped, but it was not enough. I needed, myself, to find other self-worthy activities that were *mine* to restore my dignity and vibrancy. I tried various activities until I discovered which ones were suitable.

We learned the psychological importance of "turf." In couples where no such sensitivity existed, the issue created problems. Some husbands merely confiscated their wives' territory under the assumption that they knew more about efficient organizations. Their wives suffered. Others sat home, listless and apathetic, demanding their wives' constant attendance. The result for the wife was essentially the same. She lost control of her own time.

Retirement taught me how important is possession of something that contributes to a sense of identity and self-worth. Territory, in its broadest sense, means being part of a whole, having significance in society, owning an ability that is self-rewarding. It contributes to uniqueness and personhood.

Organizational Analogy

Those concerned with organizational behavior need to be sensitive to the importance of territory.

In several companies with which I consulted, I encountered one problem of territory and identity that created serious results in the company. The president in each case assumed that he carried the weight of responsibility for the company on his shoulders. His behavior communicated his assumption very clearly to his vice presidents. They, in turn, then felt the responsibility for their department. This made them competitive with the other vice presidents. In one extreme case members of one department would publicly disparage those in another. In these situations one of my tasks as a consultant was to surface the problem and hope, as a consequence, that all the top executives could share psychological ownership and responsibility for the company and spread this feeling to others so that departments could be cooperative rather than competitive.

CHANGES IN THE STRUCTURE OF LIFE SYSTEMS

It is difficult to realize how profound are the changes in life systems needed at retirement. I came face to face with the fact that throughout my life outer forces had provided a structure within which I lived. As a child and youth, parents, teachers, and the expectations of my peers determined much that I did. By learning to fit into social expectations, I was provided a type of security. During my career, certain duties were part of whatever position I held. I was responsible to others. There were certain hours that I was expected to meet which were set by the organization, and these, in turn, determined what hours I arose and when I had meals.

Now, in retirement, these outer forces determining many of my life systems were gone. There was no one, except Martha, who cared what I did with my time. I, myself, had to manage my days. I had to find—we had to find—new life systems to provide a meaningful and workable structure within which we could live meaningful lives. But the shock of suddenly discovering this need, which had been previously supplied, provided deep emotional reactions. It took conscious and collaborative thinking to make the effort necessary to build a new structure.

Organizations and work responsibility provide structure and a certain security within which persons live. There is a job to go to and tasks to be performed. The day, the week, the month is generally predictable. The job and the task may not be enjoyed, but they produce the security of foreknowledge and structure. But when individuals are removed from the organization at retirement, they find that structured jobs are not easily attainable at their age. Where are they to find the initiative, knowledge, and ability to develop the life-system structures that make possible a forward-looking, rewarding life? Again, we need to look at what organizations can do to help individuals create such structures before they are cut off from the organization.

CURIOSITY, CREATIVITY, INNOVATIVENESS, AND THE SEARCH FOR SELF

To remain vibrantly human, individuals must retain an active curiosity about the many aspects of living. Yet many retired persons hold cemented beliefs, attitudes, and stereotypes as a result of past pressures for conformity. Curiosity, the desire to question thoughts or explore new areas, has diminished for many almost to a point of nonexistence. Retirement should not mean closing doors to imagination and seeking. With leisure, freedom, and the removal of organizational pressures, people have the opportunity to view themselves wholly without the masks they have worn. There is now the chance to integrate feelings, stimuli, and experiences from both outer and inner worlds in order to become more self-aware and self-accepting and to reduce the internal conflicts that were created previously by outer impositions. This is a time to discover and express hidden potentials and to develop new abilities to love, enjoy, and grow. Retirement provides the time and opportunity to explore new worlds of experience and knowledge and to expand one's vision.

But if there has been no previous training or experience leading to increased self-awareness, if the individual accepts the social myths that introspection without rationalization and understanding the causes of internal conflicts and prejudices are somehow unhealthy, or, if the individual, suddenly removed from a work career, has no assistance or support in building a new life, the period of retirement can be dull, unhappy, and depressing.

Man is an innovator and an actor in his innovations—a glorious characteristic that is generally peculiar to man. But if innovativeness about self has been allowed to atrophy over the years, energy diminishes with aging, no need is felt to envision new goals, and the barriers to becoming innovative and active in new ways become greater.

In my case, it took will, energy, and, yes, anger about my condition of dependence on the organization I had left to force me to look at myself rather than to blame circumstances, to seek new interests, and to find new areas for innovation.

WHAT CAN AND SHOULD ORGANIZATIONS DO

The idea that organizations should assume more responsibility for the retirement of employees beyond the establishment of pension plans is becoming increasingly significant with the rapidly growing number of persons approaching retirement. The extent to which organizations will accept increased responsibility and the form that such responsibility will take depends on social conditions and pressures and the innovativeness of those concerned.

From my own retirement experience, I would like to suggest important preliminary steps that organizations should take, as well as possible programs to help persons make an effective and forward-looking transition to this new phase in life.

The first step is for those concerned with organizational behavior to become deeply aware of the large number of emotional problems that are faced by many at retirement—of which those described in this article are only a part. Unfortunately, retired individuals tend to suffer their emotional reactions in silence, feeling, somehow, that there is something shameful or demeaning in reacting as they do. Lacking the forewarning and coping support that would help to develop a positive and enriching life plan, too many people accept their apathetic and depressive feelings as conditions of aging. To counteract this dangerous sense of futility (once organizations are aware of the problems), ways can be planned to assist those approaching retirement. This is a necessary, if obvious, step.

A second step is for organizations to review and reassess the psychological environment within which individuals work. Does the environment provide conditions which, on the one hand, fulfill socio-emotional needs of employees, and, on the other hand, encourage self-awareness, self-initiative, and ability to cope with change? Such an environment would contain, among others, the following ingredients:

1. The opportunity to feel a sense of belonging and acceptance, an awareness of contributing, and involvement in the product of a face-to-face working group, even, sometimes, to the completion of a product of a larger organization.
2. An effort to create congruence between organizational values and behavior and the personal values of participation, involvement, fairness of treatment, and respect for the individual's dignity.
3. Provision for each person to experience sufficient psychological space, and encouragement to be innovative and proactive within the boundaries of his or her function.

4. The sensitive use of managerial directions and controls so as not to inhibit creativity in others.
5. An effort to make certain that achievement is recognized not only by those who are higher in authority; an effort to help individuals set and increase internal standards for achievement.
6. Encouragement of growth in the person—in pride of achievement and identity, in actualizing potentials, and in becoming as self-directive as relations with others make possible.

Looking back, I have identified certain experiences that helped me to prepare for retirement, as well as a lack of certain assistance that I wish I had had. Self-awareness, self-understanding, introspection without defensiveness or rationalization, facing up to oneself, self-acceptance—whatever the term—is, I believe, basic to all other characteristics necessary for an effective transition to retirement. Without experience in exploring oneself, blame for new and difficult problems is easily directed outward. Thus the person is absolved from blame for failing to exert efforts to find replacements for losses. Without self-understanding, unused abilities are less likely to be discovered. Inability to know oneself hardens long-held ideas, and the inflexibility of past behavior patterns inhibits inquiry and curiosity and creates reluctance to adventure into new areas of belief and activity.

Yet self-awareness training—in all its present, multiple forms—has been widespread during the past few decades. Organizations have generally found that such training is beneficial; it releases potentials and enriches employees; improves interpersonal, intra- and intergroup relationships; and increases cooperation and productivity. Hence, a continuation of such programs and a repetition of them over the long years of a working career will not only benefit the organization but will help to prepare the individual to be self-managing in retirement. I firmly believe that without my three decades of experience with such training, I would have found my escape from the apathy of retirement more difficult to achieve.

The importance of preretirement planning is obvious, whether it is done alone by the person retiring, jointly by both marital partners, or with the assistance of a counselor or preretirement training program. But such planning needs to be as inclusive as possible of the many aspects and potential problems of this new phase of life. Certainly Martha and I failed to foresee many of the emotionally laden situations that we would encounter later.

Recently we had a leisurely lunch with a couple who were old friends. The husband held a high position in his organization and was an acknowledged expert in certain aspects of the organization's work. He would retire within a year. With our own experience behind us, we were curious. We asked them what planning they had done for retirement. He said that he had arranged their finances—with expert advice—to protect his wife and to establish the best trusts for their children. We persevered and asked what else they had planned. She said that they planned a trip shortly to the part of the country in which they grew up to see if they wished to retire there. We asked what else they had planned. They looked puzzled, so we described some of the problems we had run into. They had not thought about any of those.

Although there is an increase in formal preretirement training programs conducted by organizations for employees, many do not deal with the emotional and relationship problems that are likely to be encountered. From our experience, I would like to suggest some additional ingredients beyond the customary ones of finances, places to live, health, hobbies, etc., that would make preretirement training more effective.

One of the most important adjustments necessary in retirement is a marital review and readjustment. Too infrequently are such adjustments made by careful, joint planning and problem solving. The romantic picture of a couple peacefully and contentedly sharing the golden twilight years may be a beautiful dream but, in our observations, is hardly realistic. Living together all day, day after day, can violate personal privacy and the need for psychological space to an extent that irritations and hostility grow. Personal habits that were endured by the other for years because of the daily hours of escape now become exasperating. Either or both partners can feel overcontrolled and overpossessed. When functions overlap, interference is perceived.

After Martha and I had done considerable sharing through open, nonpunitive discussion, she asked me, one day, what behavior on her part had irritated me over the years, but not sufficiently for me to say anything about it. I thought for a moment and then said that each night, over most of the years of our married life, we had spent a half hour looking for her reading glasses. I then asked her the same question, and the feedback I received led to a profitable discussion.

The type of marital review in which little things that can cause bigger problems are talked through, mutual understanding is gained, and adjustments are made where possible can provide a deeply needed resource for both partners. If the husband and/or wife retires and the couple moves to a different community, both partners have lost important sources of support—the husband his work (and often social) group and the wife her social group, if not also her work group. Although one person does not comprise a group, if marital adjustments have been made, each partner can give sensitive support to the other. Together they can plan how to find new support groups for each of them.

Hence, a crucial part of preretirement training should be the inclusion of *both* spouses. The training program could provide opportunity for groups of husbands and wives to share masculine and feminine—husband and wife—perceptions of what retirement would be like. It is unlikely that there would not be differences in perception. Because such perceptions and anxieties often are not shared by the partners, one's unhappiness as the result of the change to retirement can cause other moves that result in unhappiness for the other. The motivation from a training group could encourage the two partners fully to explore their interests and perceptions by themselves.

A second ingredient of a preretirement training program would be to alert and forewarn participants of the wide range of transitions, radical changes, and emotional losses they might suffer in retirement. Sharing concerns and anxieties about retirement with others about to retire also would legitimatize the admission to oneself that vigorous efforts will be necessary to replace the ways in which important needs are met. Sharing, in small groups, a variety of plans for creating a vibrant, forward-looking life after retirement would do much to remove the feeling that retirement means that one is "finished."

Obviously, support from others is important for any individual who is undergoing a change or transition. Retirement, because of the many emotional losses it involves and because of the aura of finality attached to it, is, for many, one of the most difficult transitions to be faced. Hence, the gaining of new support groups can be critical to prevent loneliness and depression. An effective training program can help persons learn how to seek or create new support groups, realize the need to extend oneself to be accepted, and understand that the price of belonging is human warmth.

Finally, organizations can aid employees to recycle themselves by providing them with opportunities to reduce job loads and work pressure, or to engage in different and less stressful tasks, using new abilities. Such new tasks can renew vigor by offering the individual an opportunity to explore unused potentials.

THE QUESTION OF MANDATORY RETIREMENT

With the tremendous increase in the number of retired persons and those rapidly approaching retirement, pressures are being exerted on legislatures to remove mandatory age limits for retirement. I think that this may be an overly simplistic solution to a very complex problem and that more thought should be given to the consequences of any decision.

There are obviously many advantages to eliminating mandatory age limits for retirement. The emotional losses discussed in this paper would be delayed until they were less severe because of aging. Many scientists in fields concerned with aging believe that average longevity will shortly approach one hundred years. If so, with present mandatory limits, people will live a third of their lives in retirement, with little opportunity for productivity and achievement, self-respect, and self-esteem. Society will lose the resources of millions.

On the other hand, certain problems—both social and personal—could emerge with the removal of all mandatory limits. As I understand the potential situation, either the individual or the organization would make the decision about the time for retirement. The individual left with the decision—unless obvious health problems, deep dissatisfaction with work conditions, or rejection of the work ethic (Barfield & Morgan, 1979) make early retirement desirable—may feel ego needs to continue working in spite of flagging energy or body signals indicating the approach of a serious health problem. If the organization is to select those who will continue working from those who will be retired, pressures will increase on the individual to please those in authority and to become an "organization man" in order to be allowed to continue working. Consider the serious effect on a person's self-image of being selected "out." A mandatory age limit allows no comparison of competence. From the social point of view, the removal of mandatory age limits serves to block the upward mobility of younger workers, perhaps decreasing their motivations for outstanding performance.

Other alternative solutions to this problem should be explored. One such alternative might be the concept of the "new career." Five years, more or less, before expected retirement, organizational programs could aid employees who wished to continue to be productive to investigate and prepare for new and less demanding work careers that could continue beyond the present mandatory age limits. Organizations could either find it economically feasible to provide such new jobs or could cooperate with other organizations and agencies in locating appropriate work opportunities. The new career would help to maintain self-esteem and the satisfaction that comes from achievement, as well as social and financial rewards, but in a situation containing less competitive stress. Legitimization of the new-career concept could help to identify many new functions that serve social needs.

Whatever the answer to this problem, it is clear to me, having experienced both the depressive aspects of retirement and the renewed vigor and self-respect that resulted from developing my own new career, that some such alternative as this is vitally needed to help elderly persons to maintain good physical and emotional health. Productivity, achievement, and growth, which bring self-esteem and self-acceptance, are critical to the maintenance of health and vigor. Belonging to supportive groups meets important human needs.

SUMMARY

My purpose in this paper has been to indicate that organization development efforts should be directed not only toward creating conditions for human achievement and satisfaction at work, but also toward helping employees grow in their ability to be self-managing, creative, innovative, vibrant, and aware of their inner identities so that they can make retirement a forward-looking and self-rewarding phase in life. Those concerned with organizational behavior need to become keenly aware of the many social and emotional deprivations that are likely to occur at retirement, and of the need for persons at that time to find new and different ways of replacing these losses.

This paper stresses the proposition that organizations should accept the responsibility to aid persons in learning how to cope with the emotional reactions to retirement and in learning how to develop a richly productive and healthful life during that phase of existence. The ways in which such a responsibility best can be met will require much thought and study.

REFERENCES

Barfield, R. C., & Morgan, J. N. *Early retirement: A second look*. Ann Arbor, MI: Institute for Social Research, 1970.

Bradford, L. P., & Bradford, M. J. *Coping with emotional upheavals at retirement*. Chicago: Nelson-Hall, in press.

Neuropsychiatry in World War II (Vol. 2, Overseas Theaters). Washington, DC: Medical Department, United States Army, 1973.

19

Human-Resource Planning and Development: A Total System

Edgar H. Schein

INTRODUCTION

Human-resource planning and development is increasingly recognized as a critical process in organizations. This chapter will analyze the process from the perspective of the manager of the organization. All too many analyses have focused exclusively on individual career planning and growth, leaving the manager confused about how to manage a total system that will meet the needs of both the individual and the organization.

The process of human-resource planning and development, when viewed from the managerial perspective, is highly complex for several reasons:

1. Human resources are not the only resources that have to be managed in the total process of creating an effective organization. They have to be meshed with other resources such as money, technology, space, information, and so on.

2. Human resources are not passive or stable. People react to how they are managed, and they change over time. What may work for a young subordinate may not work for that same person in midlife.

3. Human resources are critical resources that can make the difference between organizational failure or success. If the organization has the wrong people for the job, or if people work below their potential or fail to learn new skills as organizational needs change, the organization is less likely to be effective in achieving its goals.

4. In most organizations the complexity of the task requires a wide variety of people to get the job done. This means that no one approach to human-resource management can be applied to everyone. People's needs vary, requiring managers to develop more flexible approaches to the development and management of their various categories of subordinates.

This paper draws on material from Edgar H. Schein, *Career Dynamics: Matching Individual and Organizational Needs*. Reading, MA: Addison-Wesley, 1978.

We will deal with this complexity by showing how a total human-resource planning and development (HRPD) system should be conceived as a set of components that interact with each other and, therefore, must be linked explicitly.

THE COMPONENTS OF AN HRPD SYSTEM

The components of an HRPD system and their sequential interrelationships are shown diagrammatically in Figure 1. Organizational activities are shown on the left side; individual activities are shown on the right side; and the various matching processes are shown in the middle column. The various components will be discussed sequentially, but it must be recognized that the system has many feedback loops and typically is engaged in all the activities simultaneously.

Organizational and Human-Resource Planning (Boxes A and B)

An effective HRPD system must explicitly link its organizational planning to its human-resource planning (boxes A and B in Figure 1). The long-run strategic direction in which the organization is headed has tremendous implications for the kind of work that might have to be performed in the future and it is not safe to assume that somehow or other the human resources will then be available to do that work. As work becomes more complex and as certain kinds of specialists become more scarce, it becomes more essential for all organizations to think in long-range terms about what kinds of skills they will need.

The short-run tactical or operational plans of the organization provide the most immediate input to the human-resource plan in specifying what kind of *jobs* need to be filled and in what *numbers*. It should be noted that such input cannot be a one-way link. Rather, both the long- and short-range organizational plans should be checked provisionally against human-resource plans to determine how realistic they are in terms of (a) the immediate availability of people, (b) the changes in developing the talent that may be needed, and (c) the possibility of recruiting such talent if it is not available. In many planning processes that I have observed it was the constraint on human resources that, in the end, determined critical decisions such as growth rate, acquisitions policy, decentralization, etc. The question that must guide the planning process is whether we have the people to manage and run the kind of organization we envision in the next one to five years, and, if not, how we get them. If this question cannot be answered explicitly, the strategic decision needs to be re-evaluated.

Strategic planners often argue that human-resource planning is too difficult or vague to be taken seriously as a consideration in the total planning process. One reason for this argument is that organizations have not developed some of the other components that Figure 1 shows and that would make the process less vague and less difficult. In other words, effective human-resource planning implies the presence of an effective performance-appraisal system that feeds relevant and useful information into an inventory (on the basis of which more informed planning decisions can be made).

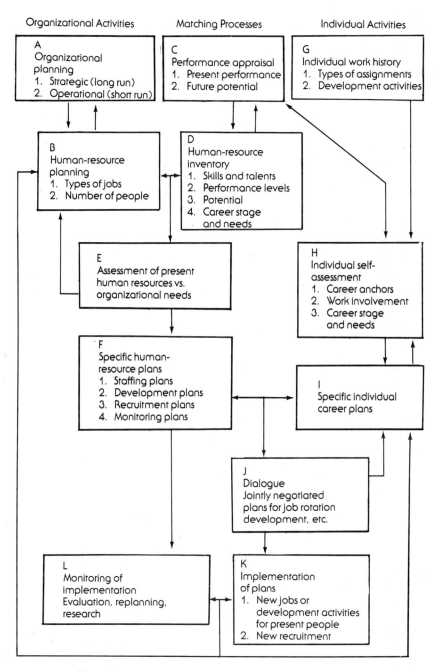

Figure 1. The Components of A Human-Resource Planning and Development System

Performance Appraisal and the Human-Resource Inventory (Boxes C and D)

In order to plan effectively, one must have valid and useful information on the present state of the human-resources organization. Any HRPD system, therefore, needs to develop a way of collecting information about present levels of skill and talent, present levels of performance, potential for growth—both in technical-functional areas and in various categories of management, and the career stages of present employees (and, by implication, their career-related needs and motives). Such information usually is collected as a by-product of the performance-appraisal system or through a portion of that system that is specifically designed to provide organizationally relevant information.

One of the real dilemmas in this area is determining initially what information should be collected and then developing a method of collecting it that will produce valid information without creating undesirable side effects. For example, from the organizational point of view it may be highly desirable to rate or rank each person in terms of his or her long-range potential for higher-level managerial jobs. But two problems arise: (a) how to make such estimates of the future reasonably valid, especially when the rating or ranking may be made by supervisors who themselves do not know what the future requirements for a manager may be; and (b) how to make such ratings or rankings without revealing to the people rated that they have been classified in this manner. If the ratings are treated as "open" and to be shared with the employee, there is evidence that they will be less valid, because supervisors will not be willing to make negative • judgments that might in some way harm the career of an immediate subordinate. On the other hand, keeping the ratings completely secret creates tension in the • system because everyone knows that the ratings exist and wonders where he or she falls. A further complication may be the new privacy laws, which will make it difficult for the organization to keep any information of a personal nature secret from any employee who requests such information.

Furthermore, the other basic purpose of performance appraisal—to stimulate open communication between a boss and a subordinate for purposes of improving performance—is undermined to varying degrees by global ratings that are designed to go into centralized files and inventories. One solution is to separate the two processes in time and to use different procedures and forms for each. For performance *improvement*, the process should emphasize detailed behavioral descriptions and incidents that facilitate a dialogue on a day-to-day basis and that maximize feedback from which the subordinate can learn. For purposes of building the human-resource *inventory* the process should emphasize more careful review of the various skill areas in which the employee has had experience, more details of the work history, more information about the employee's own career aspirations, and more global estimates of potential by the supervisor. Such estimates of potential should be reviewed by the next-level supervisor to insure that they are based on more than stereotypes or vague impressions; only if there is agreement by two or three people should such information be treated as "valid" and entered into the system.

When and how such information is fed back to the subordinate is a complex issue. At a later stage in the dialogue on development planning (box J in Figure 1), it is often necessary to give some feedback, but it can be global and general rather than specific and detailed. Organizations vary in the kinds of cultural norms that grow up around "openness," and individual supervisors vary in the degree to which they feel comfortable in giving generalized feedback. However, whether or not feedback occurs and how it occurs does not influence the "needs" of the HRPD system for some kind of valid information on human resources that can be stored for planning purposes. Such information then serves as essential input to the human-resource-planning process (box B), which in turn serves as input to basic organizational planning (box A).

Assessment of Resources Versus Needs (Box E)

Once the planning process has specified a set of organizational "needs" and the human-resource inventory has specified what is available, some assessment can be made based on a comparison of the plan with the inventory. Such an assessment either will identify critical constraints that will force a more fundamental replanning of strategic or operational goals, or will lead forward to more specific human-resource plans. The issue here is one of organizational linkage: who is to be involved in making these assessments and by what process should they be made? The question is whether it is sufficient to have an inventory on paper for planners to use, or whether it is necessary to have a dialogue between those primarily concerned with planning and those primarily concerned with inventory. Since both the planning process and the process of "measuring" people are relatively imprecise, it is probably essential to bring the people involved into explicit dialogue. Though it may be more time consuming, it seems essential to have this dialogue in order to check assumptions, perspectives, and points of view before drawing conclusions about what is or is not possible with a given set of people who represent the organization's "human resources."

Specific Human-Resource Plans (Box F)

Specific human-resource plans involve the actual jobs and actual people of the organization, in contrast to the generalized planning that must be done for job families and categories of people in box B. If the general plans hold up after the assessment activity (box E), specific plans must be made to fill certain jobs, to create development programs for certain people, to launch recruiting activities in areas where new skills are involved or where it would take too long to develop people inside the organization, and to create monitoring systems to insure that the above activities are producing the desired results.

Several comments have to be made about the linkage of this activity to others in the total system. First of all, it needs to be noted that in many organizations this specific planning activity is the *only* piece of the system that the organization has in operation. As jobs open up or as people need to be promoted or moved, representatives from personnel meet with line managers on an ad hoc basis and decide how to juggle the pieces of the puzzle. Some organizations have committees that may be called "management-development committees." These worry about position planning (how future openings will be filled) and people planning (how high-potential people will be moved in an optimal fashion). The information that is used comes directly from individual supervisors, often in an ad hoc, unsystematic fashion. The process may or may not use any input from the individual and is often a political process reflecting the relative power of different managers. Whether or not longer-range organizational plans are taken into account is a function of whether the managers who are working on a particular move are themselves oriented toward those long-range plans. Positions are filled and people are moved, but little monitoring is done to determine whether the moves are of benefit to either the individual or the organization.

If the organization needs no more than such a process of position and people planning because it is in a fairly stable environment, there is no reason to worry about all the other components. But it is dangerous to assume that such a process is a complete system and that it could meet organizational needs in a more dynamic environment. It is certain that such a process will *not* produce optimal development of the human resources involved because it will be insufficiently linked to individual issues such as career stages, career anchors, work/family conflicts, dual careers, and the like.

A second general point about the activities in box F is that they can come into conflict *with each other*. For example, a common problem that I have encountered is a conflict between staffing plans and development plans. In order to fill a position, it is proposed that a given person should be moved into it. However, that move may not be—from a developmental point of view—the best move for that person. What then is more important in the long run: to fill the position or to create a developmental opportunity for a person who may represent an important *future* resource? If the decision is made to keep the person on a developmental plan and to recruit elsewhere for the open position, this decision may create another conflict in that the recruiting budget may be overrun. Without a more centralized human-resource policy or plan (at the level of box B), it is difficult for the organization to determine what its recruiting and development budget should be. The danger is that decisions are made in terms of *short-run* costs and benefits without assessment of long-range costs and benefits. This policy usually favors staffing policies that move people simply because the organization needs them there in the short run. This undermines both development and recruitment activities in the long run.

If specific human-resource plans are to remain responsive both to changing organizational needs and to changing individual needs, it is essential that they remain linked both to the more general organizational planning activities and to the needs of the individual. Those individual needs can be represented partly through the human-resource inventory, but a better matching system would insure that some dialogue actually takes place between the individual and the manager who is making a specific plan for that individual, before the plan is implemented. If such a dialogue is to occur, the individual also must be prepared for it. This brings us to the next portion of the total system: the "individual activities."

Individual Work History, Self-Assessment, and Career Planning (Boxes G, H, and I)

It has been the experience of many managers that they sit down with a subordinate to discuss that subordinate's "future career with the company" only to find that the subordinate becomes virtually nonverbal or utters platitudes about wanting to "get ahead" or receive a "couple of promotions." If a dialogue is to occur between a manager and a subordinate, both parties must be prepared, must have thought about career issues, and must have some information about themselves and the organization. Therefore, a total HRPD system must include some means of support by which each and every employee can become more career conscious and it must provide guidelines, workshops, training materials, or whatever else seems suitable to aid this process. By "every employee" is meant everyone—up to the top management of the organization—because only a boss who has thought about his or her own career can have a useful dialogue about career matters with a subordinate.

Organizations have various means to stimulate individuals to think through their work histories; to attempt to gain insight into their own career anchors; and to think through their work, family, and self-development needs. Such means include company-sponsored career-development workshops, inside or outside testing and counseling, the use of assessment centers to help individuals gain better self-assessment, the use of self-administering work books or training manuals to help the person perform self-assessment, and encouragement of the use of the performance-appraisal feedback session as a career-exploration device. Externally stimulated activities such as the posting of job openings also serve a critical function in helping individuals to think about what they want to do next and to provide feedback opportunities during the internal job-application interviews.

Probably the most important activity in this regard is supervisory encouragement. If the organization signals to all of its people a concern for career-development issues and backs this concern up with self-assessment opportunities, people will find ways to obtain better insight into their own needs. What managers in the organization must come to realize is that such a positive climate for career development right through to the top of the organization is not merely of value to the individual, but is a crucial component of the total HRPD system because it facilitates optimal, long-range human-resource development.

Dialogue Between Managers and Career Occupants (Box J)

The dialogue between manager and career occupant is, in a sense, the critical juncture in the total HRPD system. It is in this dialogue that individual and organizational needs meet and that some kind of ultimate matching must take place. If the organization has done its homework in the form of adequate planning and inventorying, and if the individual has done his or her homework in the sense of getting some self-insight into needs, goals, and aspirations, a real dialogue can occur. Such a dialogue is not necessarily a single meeting between a boss and a subordinate. It may be a process that occurs over a period of weeks or months, in which both individual and organizational needs are explored. A management-development committee trying to fill some important positions may talk to many applicants, their supervisors, personnel representatives, and even outsiders to see what the recruiting possibilities are, but the conversations take place with a mutual exchange of information as the goal.

The trigger for such a dialogue usually is when a position opens up and some movement of people has to be made, or when a person is clearly ready for a promotion or a rotational assignment. What is important at this point is to avoid the process becoming a "monologue" in which managers or personnel specialists make up their own minds about what would be best for everyone and then simply sell the decision to the individual and to various other managers who may be involved. Any job rotation, major change in assignment, movement from techni-cal to supervisory work, or special development activity such as attending a university or in-house training program requires a balanced discussion in which the individual has a chance to express his or her needs and in which there is an opportunity to determine whether or not the projected move will be mutually beneficial to both the organization and the individual. Out of such dialogue there should come a *jointly negotiated plan* for future career moves that meets the needs of the organization and the needs of the individual.

To provide a clear example, one need only look at the growing tendency of multinational companies to involve not only the manager who is being considered for an overseas assignment but his or her family as well in a totally negotiated decision to insure that the new assignment will be compatible with personal and family needs. What is currently done for such major moves should, in principle, be done for any move across any organizational boundary. The growth of *dual-career families* will make it even more important to have a real dialogue and to build HRPD components that will prepare both the manager and the subordinate for such dialogue.

Implementation of Plans (Box K)

Once a decision has been made to move an individual, to send someone to a development program, or to launch a recruiting drive to fill a job, some system must exist to implement the plan. This point may seem trivial, but many personnel-development systems stop with a jointly negotiated decision that is written down on an appraisal form and sent to the personnel department, only to die there. For example, a supervisor and a subordinate may agree that a move from one function such as engineering to another function such as marketing may be in the best interests of both the individual and the organization. But this agreement alone will not make that happen unless some mechanism exists in the HRPD system to pick up such information and launch an implementation plan. Similar-ly, the decision may be made that a person should attend a university manage-ment-development program, but no mechanism or budget may exist to implement that plan, nor may there be any provision for replacing the person while he or she is attending the university.

There is no one best way to organize the implementation function, but it should probably combine some segment of the personnel or development activity in which information is centralized and can be analyzed in terms of total organizational implications and some line-management committee that has the power to allocate funds and to initiate moves. Many organizations use personnel-development committees consisting of senior line managers and staff from personnel development to review development plans, recruitment plans, and other staffing activities, and to decide how to integrate and implement these various plans. If such a group includes, or has the backing of top management, it insures better implementation and also validates the entire HRPD function, thereby increasing the quality of all of its components.

Monitoring, Evaluating, and Replanning (Box L)

The total HRPD cycle ends with activities that systematically monitor whatever has been done, evaluate the outcomes of these activities against the goals set for them, and feed back this evaluation into the basic planning process. For example, if a person was moved from engineering to marketing, or if a person attended a university development program, someone in the organization (often that person's supervisor) should assess how the move or the program worked and feed that information back into the system. Not only the organization but also the individual will evaluate any given activity, so the feedback information will go back into the individual's self-assessment as well.

The best way to organize the monitoring and evaluation activities probably is to have a centralized monitoring system in the personnel-development organization that identifies what needs to be monitored, who should do the evaluation, and who should get the results of the evaluation. But the actual work of evaluation is obviously the job of the individual supervisors and possibly members of the personnel-development committee. The development of *procedures* for evaluation, the schedule, and the monitoring is the job of a centralized staff organization. The work, the assessment of implications, and the replanning must be returned to the line organization. Ultimately, the information must end up as input into the planning process (box B), to the human-resource inventory (box D), and to the individual (box G).

If this total process is working well, it should not only improve human-resource planning, but it should also provide information on how to improve development activities themselves. From the evaluation of present activities, the organization can learn something about optimal career paths, the kinds of rotational moves that work well and the kinds that do not, the sorts of development programs that are beneficial to whom and the way they should be timed, the optimum lengths of time for assignments, and so on. Most organizations have much information about their own career-development system ready for analysis, but someone must see the value of such analysis, must pull the information together, and must begin to make inferences from it. All too often, every individual manager has his or her own theory about development, and these theories never are checked against facts that might be readily available within the organization. As part of the monitoring and evaluation activity, one might consider a small personnel-research unit that focuses specifically on human-resource development in order that the organization can learn better from its own experience.

SUMMARY AND IMPLICATIONS FOR ORGANIZATION DEVELOPMENT

This chapter has described the necessary components of an HRPD system and the linkages that should ideally exist between them. The actual organization of such a system will vary from organization to organization. Such variation is entirely appropriate since different organizations need different things. What is important is to view the components described as a minimum check list of activities that must be present in some form or another, and to insure that the organizational and individual activities remain in balance with each other. As organizations become more vulnerable to environmental turbulence and as they become more vulnerable to the vicissitudes of their people, it becomes more important to maintain a healthy balance in the system between activities that serve the needs of the organization and those that serve the needs of individuals.

The organization development function, whether represented by an individual or by a group, has a special role to play with respect to such a system. It has been my observation that OD people are most likely to see the human-resource problem from a total system perspective and to have the sensitivity to realize the importance of linking the various components to each other. All too often too much emphasis is given to individual needs and individual career planning. It becomes crucial for the OD specialist to create a system that will produce a real linkage between such individual activities and the more formal business-planning and performance-appraisal systems that may be in operation. If the OD specialist is really concerned about total organizational health, real attention must be given to creating an HRPD system that will meet organizational needs as well as individual needs.